The trees were so thick there was
Nowhere to Look But Up!
Early Settlers of
Morton and Mineral
Washington

by LaVonne M. Sparkman

To Mr. Jerry Radio Ekberg
with best wishes,
LaVonne M. Sparkman

— A Maverick Publication —

ISBN 0-89288-177-1

FOREWORD

The author has tried to tell the stories of pioneer families who arrived in the Morton, Mineral, Kosmos, and Glenoma areas before 1910. Certainly only a limited number have been included since it has depended on the opportunity to contact descendants of those families. Since all the early settlers faced the same challenges and problems there are necessarily similar experiences.

It is with much gratitude that I thank all the people who have granted me interviews and shared photographs. This has truly been a labor of love coming from an urgency to preserve some of the stories of the pioneers before they were lost to all time.

Special thanks go to Katherine and the late Harry Cooper who encouraged and helped me from the very beginning of this project that has extended over a number of years.

I am indebted also to my editor Georgina Winsberg, and to Mae Cornwell for typing the final manuscript, to Dick and Leslie Dunlap for Mineral photographs, and to Marion Camp for generously loaning me his camera to copy old pictures.

LaVonne M. Sparkman

Table of Contents

INTRODUCTION

Morton, a small town of 1300 people, is located in the Cascade foothills within the shadow of Mt. Rainier. A central location — one hour south of Tacoma, two hours south of Seattle, two hours west of Yakima, and two hours north of Portland — combines the quiet life style associated with a small town and the convenience of being near large centers of trade. Logging, sawmilling, and other forestry related occupations are the economic base of the community as well as supportive businesses and industries.

One pioneer made the observation that "the trees grow so thick, the only way to see is to look straight up!" Indeed, trees have been Morton's main reason for existence from earliest times when settlers floated shingle bolts down the rivers to Kelso and Longview shingle mills to the present day with three sawmills and many logging operations in the area.

Although early trappers and explorers passed through the Morton area, the existence of four trails converging at the present location of Morton was, in later years, to focus the stream of early travelers in the wilderness toward the crossroads at Morton. The trails were the Bear Canyon Trail from the west via the Tilton River and Bremer; the Harmony Trail from the southwest via Mossyrock and Harmony crossing the Cowlitz River, over Riffe Gap, Highland Creek and into Morton; the Big Bottom Trail (part of the old Cowlitz Indian Trail) from the east via Randle, Rainey Creek Valley, Fern Gap and Davis Lake; and the last from the north running from Elbe over the Divide between Mineral and Morton then following the Tilton River into Morton.

The time from 1880 to 1910 can be labeled the era of economic isolation. The settlers, lacking easy access to markets, raised most of what they needed themselves and made occasional trips to market in Chehalis or Tacoma. This era is a colorful display of the pioneer's individualism and fellowship, exemplified by barn raisings and livestock drives.

Alternate sections of land had been granted to the Northern Pacific Railroad by the Land Grant Act of 1864 and more was reserved under the Forest Reserve Act of 1891, land which was made available to settlers for $1.25 an acre. Besides that there remained thousands of acres open for settlement in the Cascade valleys under the provisions of the Homestead Act of 1862. Settlement of Morton began in the late 1870's and early 1880's with the arrival of A. H. Boomhauer, Albert M. Greene, and H. M. McCune who settled in the Davis Lake bottom lands, about two miles east of present day Morton. Although Davis Lake was not a part of the town of Morton in the 1890's, it is considered to be within the legal jurisdiction of Morton today. Since Davis Lake and Morton lie in the same valley (commonly referred to as the Morton-Davis Lake Valley), the influence of early settlers in that area can not be ignored. More settlers—some of the more prominent and the first few into the valley—went by the names of Hopgood, Cottler, Knittle, Temple, Reed, Perigo, Herselman, Bergen, Crumb, Clevinger, Edlund, Stout, and Conley.

From 1880 to roughly 1910 homesteading opportunities in the Cascade valley bottoms drew several thousand settlers, and Morton received a fair number of them. The American immigrants from the Great Lakes Cutover counties, the Southern Appalachians, the Ozark uplands, and the Great Plains were accustomed to arduous life and were willing to accept the hard conditions in the Cascades.

In Morton there was and still is a large percentage of people from the areas of Kentucky, West Virginia, and Tennessee. Names such as Blankenship, Clevinger, Riffe, Coleman, Davis, Hatfield, Stiltner, Green, and countless others abound. Prior to 1900 the Appalachian section of the country experienced a "go west" movement.

Since many of the young men were employed in the waning lumber industry there, they were attracted by the free land and better wages in Washington. Once a few of them moved, they wrote home to tell all the "kinfolk" about their new life; consequently, a large scale migration occurred between Washington State and the Appalachians. One still hears of sections of country in and near Morton referred to as "Little Kentucky" and "Little Tennessee." Nevertheless, the bulk of Appalachian emigrants, along with European immigrants from Scandinavia, Germany, and Switzerland with limited capital and a hunger for land moved into the Morton-Davis Lake Valley and others similar to it throughout the Cascades.

As the population of Morton increased the need for schooling became a pressing problem. The first school in Morton was opened in April, 1894. This was a three month term and the building was the Burnap home, about two miles west of Morton. It was a two room log and split shake cabin. The living room was heated by a fireplace and was used as the school room. The school board consisted of H. C. Temple, John Monk, and Mr. Burnap. Gus Temple was the school clerk. There were thirteen pupils: Anna, Fred, and Ida Mienars, Ella and Anne Bergen, Grace and Gold Temple, Vannie Monk, Clarence Ross, and four Nicols boys. Miss Jennie Kory was the first teacher. With the assistance of the mail carrier, Lewis Inman, and Bert Murray of Bremer, she made the trip from Napavine to Morton on horseback in two days. She boarded with Mr. Reed, the postmaster, and later with H. C. Temple.

During the summer of 1894 lumber was hauled from Cinebar to build a dance hall. School was held in this dance hall the second year. In 1896 a log schoolhouse was built by H. C. Temple, Ed Knittle, Pius Cottler, Thomas Hopgood, and John Monk. In 1910 another room was added, but two years later the log schoolhouse was outgrown and the first two-story frame grade school was erected. In 1912 the ninth and tenth grades were added to the curriculum. From 1894 to 1913 the school district was known as District 91.

In 1913, by vote of the school patrons, the Consolidated School District Number 214 was formed, merging the districts of Morton, Bergen, Bremer, Mineral, Pleasant Valley, Flynn, River-side, Randle, Lewis (Packwood), Cora, Vance, Tower Rock, Mountain View, Lindberg, Highland Valley, and Davis Lake, a total of 16 school districts.

With the establishment of an economic base and the beginnings of a school system, the need for the development of a business district within Morton was necessary. In 1909 Robert Herselman and Thomas Hopgood plotted the town of East Morton. The streets were fifty feet wide and lots were fifty feet wide, one hundred-fifty feet long, and the price was $100 per lot. There were no zoning rules or building codes to restrict the wooden buildings from being built back to back, easily destroyed during the fire of 1924.

George Hopgood owned and operated the first store in Morton in 1890. He dealt with groceries and general merchandise in his store in old town.

The first settlers in the Morton area had to travel about 23 miles to the nearest post office of Tilden, on the Bear Canyon road, which was nothing more than a trail through the timber. The party making the trip to the post office would pick up the mail for others living in this section, and leave it where it could be called for.

As more settlers came to the Morton area, the need for better mail service was felt. In 1889, the year Washington became a state, an application was made to the post office department for a post office in the Morton area. Although the settlement as yet had no name, Mrs. Boomhauer was in hopes of having the village named after her because she was the first white woman in the valley. Instead the name of McKinley was sent to Washington D. C. asking for the establishment of a post office by that name. In searching the files of the post office it was found that Washington State had one post office already named McKinley, so the name of the vice-president of the United States, Levi P. Morton, was used instead as the official name of this new community.

When the Tacoma Eastern Railroad reached Morton in 1910, the economic picture changed dramatically. Businessmen such as Larson Phelps, Charles Winsberg, Fred Broadbent, Gustaf Lindberg, and Billy Fairhart were to build the modern economic base of Morton. The train also initiated the logging and forestry industries on a large scale; the railroad made it economically feasible for logging to take place in the virgin forests surrounding Morton. Prior to that time logging was very limited and the lumber produced was used locally only. Mining also became important, especially in the area of coal and mercury.

Once the railroad penetrated the wilderness into Morton, production and exportation of rough lumber and ties was a profitable business. It was during this time (1915 and lasting until 1950) that Morton earned the name "tie capital of the world," boasting the longest and largest tie docks to be found anywhere in the world.

Fred Broadbent and George Francis founded the Lake Creek Lumber and Shingle Company in 1911; the West Fork Logging Company and Lytle-Inch Lumber Company were founded before 1925. The Lytle-Inch Lumber Company employed 100 men and had a daily output of 60,000 board feet of rough cut lumber. Perhaps the largest mill of the district was that of the Taylor Logging and Lumber, founded by Gustaf

Lindberg in 1918. When the train reached the area that bears his name today, he began to invest in logging and coal mining operations. The brick houses he built for his mill workers are still in use today.

Today Morton is a logging town, dependent upon logging, sawmilling, and other forestry related occupations as its major means of existence. With the completion of the White Pass Highway (U.S. Highway 12), Morton is linked to the north, west and east by a modern highway.

The spirit of the people is just as alive today as it was during the 1880's and 1890's. The Morton Loggers' Jubilee is an outward manifestation of the pioneer spirit to "work hard, be independent, and play hard, too."

From a thesis by
Everett George "Pat" Winsberg
Used with his permission

THE TOWN OF MORTON IN 1913 is viewed from the hill on the east looking down Main Street to the west. The town was incorporated the same year.

Chapter 1

THE COOPER-STUDHALTER STORY, BREMER PIONEERS

For many years, Harry Cooper was consulted whenever there was a question about the history of Morton and most particularly about Bremer, a farm area located on or near the Butts Road, nine miles west of Morton on Highway 508. Harry's family was among the pioneers in Bremer, and his wife Katherine was from the Studhalter family, early settlers on a nearby homestead.

Harry was the only child of Ed and Emma Pearl (Casto) Cooper. His father Robert Edgar "Ed" Cooper was born October 25, 1872, in Harrisonville, Missouri. When he was about four years old, his mother died, leaving five sons and two daughters. There was not much education available in those days, but Ed was able to finish the fourth reader, the approximate equivalent of the fourth grade today.

When Ed was 13 years old, he went to work in a meat packing house where the work day was from dawn to dark, and the pay was 50 cents per day. At first he could hardly stand it that when the noon whistle blew the men sat down on any convenient carcass to eat their lunch, but before long it seemed commonplace to him, too.

When he was 20 years old, Ed Cooper and his four brothers came west in 1892 with their father James A. Cooper on an immigrant train to Chehalis. James homesteaded first in the Harmony district north of Mossyrock. Shortly after that Ed came over the mountain to Bremer with a packhorse. He followed one of the two Indian trails from Harmony to the Tilton River, then had to cut a trail for the horse from the river to his previously chosen land.

Ed bought 40 acres of land from the Northern Pacific Railroad which had been granted all odd sections of land in a 40 mile strip along its tracks across the country. Ed built a house, part of which is still standing as the kitchen of an existing home; the property lies beside Highway 508 a short distance east of the Butts Road.

JAMES A. COOPER, born in 1831, came from Kentucky in 1892. Ed, one of his five sons, settled in Bremer, where Ed's son Harry was born and raised. The picture was taken in 1908.

Harry's mother Emma Pearl Casto came to Oregon in a covered wagon with her parents, the Enoch Castos, and her brother Ed and sister Mary in 1885. The Castos came from Missouri, stopped for a while in Oklahoma, then in Kansas, finally crossing the mountains to Oregon. Another daughter Viola (called Vida) was born in Oregon; she was three years old when the family moved to Washington in 1896. They came by covered wagon, ferried the Columbia River between Vancouver and Portland, and arrived in Harmony just at the end of hop season. (Hops are used in beer production.)

Pearl's brother Ed Casto and his wife had preceded the rest of the family and were already settled in Bremer Valley. While the wives and families waited in Harmony, the Casto men crossed the trail over the mountains taking four days to find Ed's place and return.

There were three married couples and four bachelors besides Ed Casto and his wife living in Bremer when the rest of the family arrived there. The couples were: the Bert Murray's, the George Bremer's, and the Robert Picken's. The bachelors were: Anthony Leurquins, Billy Stockings, Ed Holden, and Sam Conger. There were also some Indian families living near the Tilton River.

Pearl's father Enoch Casto bought land for $1.25 an acre in Bremer Valley. He built a house of split cedar boards, planed by hand. As soon as possible he started a garden and orchard. (Ed Casto's place already had an orchard that had been planted by a Frenchman named Hagan.) Enoch traded his rifle for a milk cow and two heifers. He received a pension as a Civil War veteran of $30 a month which was enough to buy groceries and cattle feed. After the wagon road was built, the trip to Chehalis for supplies took most of four days (about 42 miles one way). Every few months Castos or their neighbors made the trip which involved fording Bear Canyon Creek near where the present bridge stands.

Enoch S. Casto's background begins with his birth in West Virginia on July 17, 1846. When he was two years old, his parents moved to Missouri where they filed on government land. Enoch lived with his parents until the outbreak of the Civil War. Being too young to enlist in the regular Army, he joined the state militia and served until he was old enough to join the regulars where he served as a soldier in the Federal Army until the end of the war. On August 28, 1870, he married Barbara Helen Ryerson, who was born in Indiana on June 13, 1852. Their children, Ed, Mary, and Pearl were born in Missouri before they started their trek west. When they settled in Bremer about 1896, Morton consisted of one store (Hopgood's) and a handful of families.

The Coopers and Castos were neighbors, and when Ed Cooper was a strikingly handsome young man of 25, he wooed and won pretty almost-16-year-old Pearl Casto for his bride. They asked William T. Crumb, a Justice of the Peace, to come from Chehalis to perform the marriage ceremony on December 23, 1897. Mr. Crumb walked to Bremer, performed the ceremony, and walked back home for the fine sum of $5.00.

To earn enough cash for basic supplies, Ed Cooper trapped, cut cascara bark and shingle bolts. The cascara bark was stripped from the trees, dried, then sold in Chehalis for use in drugs, especially laxatives. These cash products provided enough money for winter supplies. One winter there was not sufficient money to buy enough coffee to last the season; they had to substitute dried peas that had been parched and ground.

The shingle bolts were a very important source of income for all the early settlers. The bolts were sections of cedar logs about four and a half feet long, enough length to cut three shingles 18 inches long. The men cut the bolts during the fall and winter and stored them in ponds formed by damming small creeks. During high water in the spring, there was enough water to provide a large "head" of water to float the bolts to a larger stream, the Tilton River in this case, then crews would follow the cedar bolts to shingle mills in Kelso. Coopers had a dam on the little creek that flowed by their place.

The shingle bolt drives required a crew of ten to 15 men and a team of horses to assist in the trip down the river. The horses were used to haul the bolts off gravel bars and out of log jams. One or two men were hired as cooks and set up a tent on the river bank, so that the cold, wet men could have hot meals. Ed Cooper was one of the cooks on the drive of 1907. He had two pairs of wool socks that an Indian woman, Louis Castema's wife Mary, had knit with wool yarn she had made, spinning some of her long hair into the yarn for added strength. The socks were such good ones that the other men tried unsuccessfully to buy them from Ed.

In later years, Ed worked on the county road and had a threshing machine used for a month or six weeks each harvest season. He threshed oats, wheat, and barley for neighbors from Cinebar, Bremer, Highland Valley, and the areas north and east of Morton. One team of horses pulled a wagon with the gasoline engine for power, another pulled the thresher and separator, while

ED AND PEARL COOPER often went hiking. When their son Harry was an infant in 1899, Ed made a backpack to carry him. Pearl made their waterproof hats from cedar bark.

a third team pulled the "trap" wagon with supplies such as bedding and gasoline barrels. Four men were required for the crew; three who worked at different times were George Stout, Charlie Thompson, and John Parnel.

On March 4, 1899, Ed and Pearl Cooper's only child was born, a son Harry William. Indian Louie's wife Big Mary took care of the household tasks until Pearl could be up and around again. Ed paid her for her work with a cast iron stove, which she loaded on her horse and took home by herself.

Ed made a horn with a wooden thread spool for a mouthpiece out of a cow's horn. Pearl used it to call him in from the fields; neighbors reported the horn could be heard on the top of the hills above Bremer Valley at least two miles from the homestead.

Pearl was an outdoor person, quite a tomboy, really. She loved to fish as much as Ed did; they spent much of their spare time fishing throughout their lives. In the early days, rivers and creeks were full of fish with salmon running up every tiny stream.

When Harry was an infant, Ed made a packsack to carry his son on fishing trips. The packsack was made of deerskin with the hair on the outside, fashioned to hold the baby lying down. Pearl wove hats for them of thin strips of cedar bark that were not only good looking, but were waterproof. Harry prized a snapshot of his father carrying him in the pack while wearing the cedar hat with his mother proudly looking on.

When Harry was a small child, his father built him a little wagon which afforded him many hours of fun, that could be hitched to his dog. His parents bought him a tricycle that he rode for "miles" around the house in a figure eight pattern that must have almost worn a track in the floor. Later he had a bicycle, probably the only one in the area, which he learned to ride by coasting down the slope in the pasture.

Harry started to school in the first Bremer School, a small log house located on the old Bremer Road, now the Butts Road. At that time, each student had to furnish his own bench, but Harry's Aunt Vida (Viola Casto) was already attending school there, therefore he was allowed to share her bench. After three months in the log house, a new building was completed about 1906 near the Bremer Bridge where the school was moved. By the time Harry was in the upper grades, all eight grades usually numbering close to three dozen children were taught there. A school term lasted only five months during the summer at first, later it was extended to six months.

Grandpa James Cooper lived with Ed and Pearl for some time when Harry was a boy. Grandpa was always cold and sat close to the wood heater, insisting on a roaring fire with the stove dampers wide open. Because the rest of the family were uncomfortable, Harry would slip up behind the heater to try to turn off the chimney damper before Grandpa would notice. Sometimes he succeeded, but more often Grandpa was quick enough with his cane to give Harry a whack before he could scoot out of reach.

While still in grade school, Harry earned money selling cascara bark, sometimes making as much as $2.50 for one day's work collecting the bark. He also raised white ducks for sale. He picked feathers every year from the live ducks, then after they were killed he picked the down for pillows and quilts. When Harry was 14 years old, he earned enough money peeling cascara and cutting shingle bolts to buy his first deer rifle for $14.80.

Several times Harry was sent to Morton to get the doctor for neighbors. He had a horse, Prince, which was a good night traveler that could be depended on to make good time no matter how dark the night.

Harry remembered one time Pearl was extremely ill when he was too young to be sent to Morton for Dr. Feagles who came by horse and buggy down the old wagon road. At one point he had to ford the river, where the water was so high it ran across the floor boards of the buggy causing him to lift his feet to keep them dry. Dr. Feagles found Pearl so ill that he didn't think she could stand a buggy ride; consequently several men carried her on a stretcher the long miles from Bremer to Morton and from there several miles further on to Glenovan where the railroad ended at that time. There she was placed on the train to be taken to Tacoma General Hospital, where she recovered.

THE STUDHALTERS

Harry's wife, Katherine Studhalter, moved to Bremer from Tacoma with her family, the Louis

Studhalters, in 1912. Her father was born in Lucerne, Switzerland, on Dec. 9, 1860. After serving his compulsory military training, he migrated to Tacoma where he worked in a brewery for 25 years. He was a hard worker who had been advanced to a position of responsibility.

Katherine's mother Louise Kunz came from Birkenfeld, Germany, when she was an 18-year-old girl. She was born April 10, 1872. Her father died when she was six years old, and her mother died when she was 14. She lived with a sister for a while, then worked for three years for a minister and his family. Her brother Ed Kunz who migrated to Orting, Washington, wrote to Louise urging her to join him. Louise braved the journey across an ocean and a continent with a girl friend of about the same age. She found employment with a wealthy banker in Tacoma helping care for his large and elaborately furnished home.

After Louise had worked for the banker for three years, she and her fiance Louis Studhalter were married in August 1893 in Tacoma. Louise wore a lovely lace-trimmed gown for their large wedding at which they received many beautiful gifts. They built a large house on Portland Avenue on property that included six lots.

By 1912 the family had grown to nine children, including two sets of twins. (Harry was born later in Bremer.) Louis wanted to leave his job in a brewery which led to the decision to leave their city home and move to the pioneer area of Bremer Valley where they bought the farm from Louise's brother Ed Kunz. The trip from Tacoma to Bremer was a memorable event as well as a miserable experience. Father and mother and nine children came by train to Morton, then by wagon to the farm. (For the story see a separate chapter.)

One of the three cows that the Studhalters brought with them had twin calves before they moved. The children made pets of the calves training them to be ridden and to be hitched to logs or other things they wanted to pull.

Louis made a living on the farm selling cream and supplementing his income by occasional work on the county roads. The children earned money digging Oregon grape roots and picking foxglove leaves, selling both to be used for medicines.

As time passed, the Studhalter children and Cooper's son Harry grew into young people. Harry began courting Katherine Studhalter. The handsome young man with the attractive young lady made a good looking couple as they rode around in Harry's two-wheel buggy which was built like a racing cart painted a bright yellow, thus the nickname "Yellow Jacket". The main entertainment then was the regular dances held in halls at Bremer and Morton. Everyone in the community, young and old, came to the affairs, spending all night dancing folk and square dances (quadrilles) and playing group games. Harry, Katherine, and Yellow Jacket were soon at many of the dances where Harry learned to call the quadrilles.

THE SHINGLE BOLT CREW were driving cedar bolts down the Cowlitz River to the mill in Kelso. The men spent most of the day in the cold river.

A CREW OF MEN on a shingle bolt drive in 1907 are shown by the cook tent. Ed Cooper was one of the cooks, who served hot meals to the men.

They laughed about the time that Harry was taking Katherine to a dance in a horse-drawn sled on a winter evening. Just after crossing a creek, they went up a steep bank that tilted the sled causing them to come within a hair's breath of taking a dip in the icy water.

Katherine and Harry were married on June 1, 1920. They drove to Chehalis which then took several hours in a Model T Ford. After they got their marriage license, they were married by Rev. McKenzie in the Methodist Church that stood where the County Courthouse is now. Returning to Morton, they set up housekeeping in an apartment over the garage on the corner of First and Main.

After three months they bought the house on First and Division where they lived from then on. The house was built by the pioneer Pius Cottler who rented to Dr. Feagles for a while before the Coopers acquired it. Their small house sat right in the corner of the property; later they had it moved back and the living room added.

Ed and Harry Cooper's interest in automobiles began early for Ed had the first car in Bremer Valley, a 1916 Model T Ford touring car that was a couple of years old when he bought it from Ed Finby, a ranger at Mineral. In 1918, Ed purchased the garage and gas station business from Pucket and McLain on the corner of First and Main in Morton. The large building had been converted from a livery stable to a garage

with an apartment upstairs in what had been the hayloft where Harry and Katherine lived.

Harry and Ed built an addition to the building for a repair garage along with the service station. In addition, they rented the converted livery stable for automobile storage. Quite a few loggers stored their cars there while they were up in the woods in logging camps. Ed and Harry had two "for hire" cars they called "jitneys", four-cylinder Overlands. They used the jitneys for taxi service, picking up the loggers when they came out of camp and transporting them to Morton for 50 cents a mile; sometimes they were paid to take someone to Tacoma.

They continued to run the garage, service station, and taxi service together for 14 years. During this time the old wooden building burned, but soon they replaced it with a modern brick service station built with bricks that Harry hauled from Glenoma. The bricks were left over from the construction of the Glenoma Grade School in 1932.

In 1934, the Coopers were raising two sons, George born September 17, 1921, and Harold born April 28, 1927. This country was in the midst of the Depression and steady income for a growing family was hard to maintain when Harry went to work for the county driving a truck. He was paid $2.75 a day; however, sometimes he had to stay in Randle where he had to pay a dollar a day for board. Ed continued to

ED AND HARRY COOPER'S garage was in a former livery stable on the corner of First and Main streets. They added the service station on the left side of the building.

FATHER AND SON ED AND HARRY COOPER were inside their garage that they bought in 1918 and ran as a partnership until 1932. The wooden garage burned and was replaced with the existing brick building.

run the service station until his retirement in 1938.

In 1936, Harry decided to launch out into the trucking business on his own. He bought his first dump truck over Katherine's protests because going into debt at that time was a serious matter which worried her about the outcome. However, Harry's wages jumped from $2.75 a day to $1.75 per hour for himself and the truck which was hired mostly for road work. The wisdom of his business venture was proved when three years later he traded the old truck for a new one and paid cash for the difference.

Harry's first tie truck was a 1941 Chevrolet truck which was the beginning of another enterprise. At that time Morton was called the "tie capital of the world" with about 50 mills in the vicinity making railroad ties. When Harry was hauling ties and slabs from the hills, he bought an army truck with four-wheel-drive to negotiate the occasional 25 percent grades.

His next job was hauling short logs for several logging operations from 1946 until 1952. Then he and Jack Winslow went into partnership in a logging operation; this continued until the fall of 1959 when they sold out to the Forrest Brothers. Harry retired while Jack cut meat in Winslow's Shopping Center for several years.

One of Harry's greatest pleasures in retirement was to have plenty of time to fish. His mother and father instilled that love of fishing in their

FISHING FOR ED COOPER continued in retirement as his life-long enjoyment. Sometimes he used a canoe where he sat on one end with Harry in the bow out in the Cowlitz River.

son at an early age; the parents never lost their enjoyment of the pastime, either. Ed and Pearl enjoyed many, many enjoyable and successful fishing trips together with their homemade poles that had self-designed brakes on the reels. The poles were made of serviceberry shrub, a native bush that has strong, flexible stems.

The Coopers' salmon fishing was done with the aid of wooden "sleds" they floated into the middle of the river to hold the line in exactly the position they desired. The sled was held in position with a line fastened kitestring fashion that ran overhead, then it was secured to a tree or rock. Many large salmon were landed by this method. Another system they used was to fish from long "outrigger" poles set up in the end of a canoe that extended into the river with the other end firmly secured to the bank. It was not unusual for Harry, Ed, or Pearl to land 25 or 30 pound salmon; Ed's largest fish caught in 1931 weighed 40 pounds 2 ounces. And those were fishermen who had the photographs to back up their fish stories!

Chapter 2

"THE GOOD OLD DAYS" FOR THE STUDHALTERS

Can you imagine a large, up-to-date home big enough for nine children in Tacoma being traded for a split-cedar shack in the pioneer settlement of Bremer? The Studhalter family did just that in the early days of this century!

The story begins with the wedding of Louis Studhalter, a Swiss immigrant, and Louise Kunz, an immigrant from Germany. They met in Tacoma where he worked in a brewery, and she worked for a wealthy banker; they were married in August, 1893.

They lived briefly on K Street, then they built a house on Portland Avenue on six lots, which gave them room for an orchard, a garden, milk cows, some chickens, and pigeons. The house was modern for the turn of the century; furnished with fine furniture, running water, electricity, a full bathroom, but no telephone. The family was accustomed to the convenience of street cars for transportation and hired women to help with the heavy housework. This was soon to be traded for the rigors of pioneer life with none of the conveniences, except a telephone on a "farmers' line."

By 1912, the family had grown to nine children, including two sets of twins: Ed, Louis, Otto and Bill (twins), Katherine, Carl and Caroline (twins), Louise, and Elsie. (Harry was born later in Bremer.)

Studhalter was weary from working long, hard hours in the brewery where he had advanced to a stressful position of responsibility, but his health was suffering and he was advised that country living would be much better for him. Louise's brother, Ed Kunz, was already homesteading in Bremer, the Tilton River Valley that extends from the Bergen Bridge (the second bridge west of Morton on Highway 508) west to Bear Canyon.

Finding that Kunz wanted to sell out, the Studhalters bought the farm that lies just east of the Butts Road turnoff and they prepared to

LOUIS AND LOUISE (KUNZ) STUDHALTER were married August 2, 1893 in Tacoma where they met. He was Swiss and she was German.

EDWARD AND JOSEPHINE (VAN OY) KUNZ were pioneers in Bremer near the Butts Road. They sold their property to Louis and Louise Studhalter; Louise was Ed's sister.

STUDHALTERS LARGE HOME IN TACOMA was exchanged for a cedar shack in Bremer. In front are: Louis, Edward, twins Bill and Otto in the buggy, and mother Louise holding Katherine. Four more children were added before they moved in 1912 and one was born after that.

move from the city to the country.

It was the first day of March 1912 when the father and mother and the nine children boarded the train at Tacoma's Union Station for what turned out to be a most miserable trip; not only was it a long ride in one day, but the children all suffered from motion sickness! They rented a boxcar for their possessions and livestock, including three cows and twin calves (which the children later taught to be ridden and to pull light loads), pigs, chickens, pigeons, and a dog. Clothing, bedding, and furniture for 11 people required a lot of space.

The parents were relieved when the train finally pulled into the Morton Depot where they found many of their neighbors-to-be had met the train. The new friends unloaded the boxcar into their wagons before starting the next leg of the trip which proved to be another ordeal for the weary family.

The road west from Morton in those days went along the side of Little Mountain (north of the present Highway 508). It was nothing but a muddy track that had been graded and laid with split logs (puncheon) in the swampiest places where as the wagons crossed the mud squirted up between the logs; other places the wagon wheels sank into the mud. In addition, some of the hills were so steep the horses could barely pull the loaded wagons up the grades.

It was a cold, rainy day with winter still in full force when the trip got off to a bad start with the necessity of fording the North Fork of the Tilton River because the bridge had washed out in a winter flood. The river was so high that water came into the wagon beds wetting some of the family possessions.

The next-to-oldest boy Louie drove the cattle, and instead of following the round-about road, he cut down through the shorter valley route, closer to where the highway is now. Knowing the river was so high and Louie had to swim across it twice, the family was almost frantic with worry before he and the cattle arrived at the homestead.

The bedraggled family finally arrived at their new home in Bremer thoroughly soaked, chilled and hungry; the parents and children were exhausted. Their house was clean, but cold and damp with no place ready to eat or sleep. The neighbors on the place next to theirs, the Ed Coopers, generously took the family in, feeding all 11 of them and making sleeping arrangements for all of them. The Coopers' only son, Harry, eventually married Katherine, one of the Studhalters' girls.

After breaking up housekeeping in the large two-story Tacoma house, there was too much furniture to fit into the little split-cedar home. There were only two bedrooms while in the living room there was barely enough space for a table that the family could gather around for meals. There were two steps down to the kitchen which held a huge "Majestic" wood range with a pantry in a small lean-to off the kitchen. The walls were papered with newspaper, but later were wallpapered.

Several of the boys were quartered in a small cedar out-building that had a wood stove for winter heat. The ceiling was made of sawed cedar boards that were so warped they dipped down over the beds. The boys remember a lot of pillow fights went on in the little building.

Of course, there was no electricity or bathroom in the house. The only running water was in the nearby creek. The children hauled the water, stepping out on a plank over the creek, dipping two buckets full and carrying one in each hand for balance. The creek was handy, too, for there was a deep hole where they could always catch a batch of fish.

After seven years in the shack, the family were together under one roof when they moved to a

LOUISE STUDHALTER WITH HER SONS celebrated her 82nd. birthday in April 1954. The sons were: Louis, Harry, Carl, Otto, Bill, and Ed. Also included was Katherine, one of her daughters.

large house on the Dodge Road.

The family milked cows, separated the cream to sell it in five or ten gallon milk cans. They took the cream to the Morton Depot where it was weighed on a spring scale on a moveable arm which swung out from the side of the wagon. Then the cream had to be stirred with a special utensil before it was tested for butterfat content to determine the price they received. They sold sacks of potatoes and carrots in Morton and also to the East Fork logging camp in Lindberg where they got a better price.

The Studhalter children earned some money peeling cascara bark, digging Oregon grape roots, picking foxglove leaves and selling all of it for medicines.

Mrs. Studhalter's only reluctance in leaving Tacoma was her concern about the children's education. The older children did get a few months of schooling by walking a mile and a half to the Bremer school near the Bremer bridge. Each of the girls had one school dress that often had to be washed after school, dried and ironed to be ready for the next day. The heavy iron "sad" irons had to be heated on the stove and exchanged for hot ones as they cooled.

Despite the hardships of pioneer life, Mrs. Studhalter came to love the mountains with no desire to live any other place. One of the Studhalter sons said, "There were not very rich people here," in Bremer in those days, but for a family that raised ten children to responsible, respected adulthood, their wealth was not the tangible kind.

Chapter 3

W. T. CRUMB
FIRST SETTLER IN HIGHLAND VALLEY

WILLIAM T. AND ANNA MARIE (ROCKWOOD) CRUMB were married December 3, 1889 and they made their first home in a little alder and cedar hut. He was 26 years old and she was 18.

THE CRUMB FARM in Highland Valley consisted of 160 acres taken over from homesteader Hyland in the 1880's. The huge barn was a landmark in the valley near Morton. The George Engle farm is in the background.

William Thomas Crumb, known as W. T., was the first settler who put down roots in Highland Valley west of Morton. A man by the name of Hyland came first to the valley that carries his name (with incorrect spelling). However, he was here only briefly before selling out to Crumb, whose story was told by his grandson Eugene Bingaman, who knew his grandparents well.

W. T. was born April 30, 1863, in Milton, Pennsylvania, to a mother who died shortly after his birth, and a father who died from being shot in the lungs in the Civil War. When he reached 18 years of age, as an orphan he received $2500. Coming west to Nebraska, he acquired a substantial amount of property which he sold before taking the train to San Francisco. From there he traveled north to Portland where he bought a horse and then continued north to Woodland. He heard about the Big Bottom country which sounded like a place to investigate. From Woodland, he followed the old Indian trail up to Elk Pass on the east side of Mt. St. Helens down into the Big Bottom, but it didn't appeal to him.

Later W. T. was in Chehalis where he met Hyland in a tavern, who told him about the 160 acres in a fertile valley where he lived. When he offered to sell out for $10, W. T. took him up on the deal that included an alder and split cedar shed, a grubhoe, broad axe, cross-cut saw, and some cooking utensils. Hyland's directions to the place which is now on the Crumb Road were to follow the Tilton River, passing so many good sized creeks until he came to Highland Creek (so named later), then following the blazed trees to the property.

In the early days there was a trail through Highland Valley that went on over the hills to the swinging bridge and ferry over the Cowlitz River. This was a main trail that came from Carbonado and Wilkeson over to the Busywild, down into Ashford, following the Nisqually River downstream, then up over the Divide. This was a well-established Indian trail that divided in the Morton area with one branch going down Bear Canyon and the other going through Highland Valley to Riffe. Indians followed the trail to Puyallup dragging their poles with their belongings on their way to pick hops. Also coming through were bands of gypsies "with all their tassels" as Eugene noted. As a boy he would run up through the hayfield and sneak up behind a tree to watch them, "Beautiful dark-skinned people" he said, but storekeepers including Bill Fairhart dreaded their arrival.

W. T. lived on his land and cleared more of it including a garden spot, but didn't improve the little lean-to. The first year or so he was here, he and pioneer Ed Knittle went to Puyallup to pick hops for "some cash money." W. T. made regular trips to Chehalis, stopping at the Rockwoods in Shoestring Valley. The Rockwood family included Anna Marie in her late teens; she was born September 15, 1871, in Kansas. Anna Marie's father told her, "He's a big strapping man on a big, strapping horse and you ought to latch on to him." She did, and they were married on December 3, 1889.

Anna Marie remembered her family's trip from Kansas to Oregon City by covered wagon pulled by seven big mules. She was nine years old at the time and could vividly recall that the Indians "pestered them to death to borrow sugar, flour and bacon." Her job was to gather "buffalo chips" for the supper fire. She told about following the Oregon Trail where it was such a "chore" to get across the rivers, but the mules were very little trouble. After arriving in Oregon City, her father sold the mules and wagon for $2500; then they later came to homestead in Shoestring Valley.

The day after their wedding, W. T. and Anna Marie set up housekeeping in the little alder and cedar hut that had a spot in the back corner for a fire and a hole in the roof for the smoke. Starting with raw, timbered land and almost nothing else, they cleared land with Anna Marie grubbing stumps right alongside her husband. As soon as they could, they built a nice house where they lived until it burned in May, 1946; then it was replaced by the two-story house still standing on Crumb Road. According to Lewis County records, W. T. Crumb got a deed from Northern Pacific Railroad on July 2, 1890, for almost 120 acres in Section 3 of Township 12.

W. T. and Anna Marie's first child Annis Jane was born April 11, 1891, followed by Isaac on Sept. 12, 1892, and Frances on Dec. 22, 1893. Frances married Frank Bingaman; they are Eugene's parents. Three boys came next: Thomas July 7, 1895, Joseph August 3, 1896, and William Sept. 27, 1898. Then they had two more girls: Ruth on June 5, 1901, and Anna on May 12, 1903, and finally Gilbert on Feb. 18, 1908. In a diary Anna Marie wrote, "The children were all born in the old house on this homestead in Highland Valley, except Gilbert, who was born in Chehalis due to a serious break in my health. I had to be placed in a hospital. Gilbert weighed at birth without any clothes 14 and a half pounds, a lovely baby. I could scarcely believe it."

W. T. was a Justice of the Peace for many years; in that office he performed many marriage ceremonies. Many times he held court where the Coast to Coast store is now. He wrote, as Eugene said, "a beautiful hand, the sweeping old Palmer method" in his distinctive habit of straddling the pen with his fingers. Although W. T. had only three or four years of formal education, he was a great reader with an excellent memory; he could tell what he read six months later.

Anna Marie was "a fiery little Frenchwoman" according to Eugene, "She had a temper and lots of ambition." In the days when women wore skirts to their ankles, she had a habit of gathering her skirt up between her legs, pinning it in front, and going to work. She told about the times she and W. T. went down to Davis Lake where she would take off her shoes and stockings to pick wild cranberries. This reminded Eugene that W. T. brought the first Evergreen blackberries for their fruit into the area. He gave some vines to a fellow in Mossyrock, who some years later wanted to know how to get rid of them.

One source of income all the early settlers shared was cutting shingle bolts. There were three dams on Highland Creek where the bolts were stored until flushed down a flume to the river. Sometimes they did not get paid for their cedar until a year-and-a-half to two years later, all depending on when their branded bolts went through the mill. When Eugene replaced the boards on the spillway, a splash dam on the creek created a good swimming hole in the summer.

When the Crumbs bought a cook stove, W. T., who was a very strong man, carried it in pieces on his back from Shoestring Valley from about where the old school house is located. Eugene remembers his grandmother cooking on the old Acorn stove many years later.

After Jane, the first girl, was born, the Crumbs wanted her to learn to play the piano as soon as she was old enough. W. T. went to Chehalis, bought a piano, "hired it hauled as far up as they could get, then took an axe and nails and made a sled behind his horse, brought it up here and it is in the Masonic Hall today," Eugene said. Jane became an accomplished musician on what was the first piano up here.

Anna Marie was determined that her sons would have a good education; she and W. T. made arrangements for the boys to stay with people and work for their keep while they went to Stadium High School in Tacoma. Morton High School was not accredited then; therefore, they took their last two years at Stadium. Two of the boys, Joe and Tom, went on to college; Joe graduated from the University of California. When it came Gilbert's turn, "times were pretty tough"; W. T. stayed home on the farm. Anna Marie went to Seattle to work for a woman there while Gilbert went to Broadway High School. Eugene emphasized, "She saw to it they got an education" even though "she was just an old time pioneer, lived as everybody lived."

In the field across the highway from where Eugene's sister Joan Morris lives just west of the Roadhouse Inn, there is a fenced off place that was an old Hudson Bay Company camp where trappers stayed while they trapped Davis Lake Valley. They believed that if beaver smell wood smoke they will not come out; for that reason they camped by Highland Creek while trapping in the lower valley. Eugene related, "When I was a little boy, there was a kind of cedar shed there and some old square nails and a couple of old iron pots and the pots had written on them 'Hudson Bay Fur Company'.

Right across from Morris's there was a croquet ground on land furnished by W. T. where people came by horse and buggy from Morton, Riffe, and Nesika to play the game. There was a fancy picket fence around the playing field with space to park the buggies.

One time when Eugene was about six years old, he went with his grandfather W. T. to get a horse from near the old Cora School, just across the Cora Bridge. "We rode a horse up there, him in the saddle and me on a gunny sack on a big work horse. My poor little legs just stuck right straight out." They rode all the way to Cora and stayed overnight at Kitchen Rock; the next day they picked up the new horse. Eugene rode the same one to Morton — "Just about killed me!" They took a gunny sack with groceries, including some boiled corn beef. W. T. was "a great man

for corned beef;" he would corn quite a few barrels of it, enough to last all winter. It was too salty to eat until it was parboiled, after which they lived on it before refrigeration.

Crumbs were fortunate during World War I when Eugene said, "There was a lot of cascara on the place and cascara went sky-high and they took from $8,000 to $9,000 off that place and that was a lot of money in those days."

As far as Eugene knows, the Crumbs donated the land that was the start of the Morton cemetery district. The property was the corner of a homestead that belonged to Anna Marie as wives were allowed to homestead on their own; her 40 acres were later sold, except for the cemetery.

In 1923, the Crumbs bought a Model T Ford; W. T. never learned to drive, but Anna Marie did. The car dealer George Chesser delivered the car, parked it with the motor running and left it for her to figure out how to drive it. Before she accomplished it, she tore down two cherry trees and one pear tree. Eugene laughingly said, "It was a sight in those days, everybody learned to drive that way, you got in a big field and you just went around and around until you mastered it." But it was funny, her brother Jim Rockwood did the same thing, he tore down his wife's parents woodshed learning to drive. Eugene pointed out that they didn't dare go out on the highway until they were able to drive well.

There was a plank road to Glenoma with turnouts; when the driver heard or saw a car coming, whoever was closest to a turnout had to back up to it; sometimes there were big arguments over that. If the car got off the planks, they were stuck, and there were no wreckers to help.

"I practically grew up on my grandad's farm," Eugene stated. "He and my grandmother treated me real good. I lived there with them when I got big enough to work and milked cows and helped in the hay; grandsons generally did that in those days. You got your room and board and a little spending money. There wasn't much spending money. I remember those milk checks coming in from Borden Milk Company in Chehalis — $8 to $10 a month and they lived on that. But everybody did, the whole valley up there, the Woods, the Comptons, Engles, and all. Everybody had 15 to 20 milk cows. That's where they made their living, where they got their hard cash and they raised the rest of the stuff."

During the Depression, to pay his poll tax, W. T. hired out with his team on the county roads. Gilbert drove the horses that pulled a slip-scraper on the Tilton River to haul rock to a rock crusher. George Stout and nine or ten other teams hauled rock to make gravel. "The men got $4.50 a day for themselves and their horses, but by the time they drove the team back to Highland Valley in the evening and fed them, they didn't make much money by the time they bought the oats," Eugene remarked.

W. T. lived to 71 years of age, passing away on Oct. 14, 1934. Anna Marie lived on until July 4, 1952, when she was 80 years old. "Not to work out and raise all that family and educate them, W. T. must have had something on the ball," Eugene commented, "He'd give practically every cent he had if he thought you needed it worse than he did." Of such were the pioneers built.

Chapter 4

FRANK BINGAMAN, MILL BUILDER

Frank Bingaman, who spent much of his life building sawmills in widely separated places, came to Morton in 1911 to build a mill with his father Ephriam M. Bingaman. They built a steam-powered sawmill where the Standard Oil plant was located for many years, northeast of the corner of Main and First Streets. The timber industry was the source of Frank's livelihood all his life.

Ephriam Bingaman was Pennsylvania Dutch while his wife was English from Ohio. Her parents, the Lovells, had the post office in Cinebar for several years. The elder Bingamans, attracted here by lumbering arrived in Lewis County in 1884. When they arrived in the area, they already had their first child.

Frank was born in Evaline, near Napavine, on January 9, 1891. He spent his early childhood in Vader, then when he was nine or ten, his parents moved to Cinebar 12 miles west of Morton.

In 1908, at the age of 17, Frank went to work in the Palmer Lumber Company in Chehalis doing a variety of jobs which included the main one of making porch pillars in vogue then. For local bowlers he also repaired wooden bowling balls which had splintered around the finger holes. His work there came to an end when he became extremely ill with typhoid fever blamed on polluted drinking water from the Newaukum River.

Frank's father had a sawmill on the Cinebar homestead which he used to cut lumber to build their home and other settlers' houses. In 1911, he helped his father move the mill to Morton where there was thick second growth timber which followed a long ago fire. There were only two mills here which belonged to Charlie Thompson and Mel Winheart. At first the Bingamans cut three-by-12-inch planks for bridges; later they made railroad ties which contributed to Morton's reputation as the "Tie Capital of the World."

He and his father had three teams of horses with hired men to do the logging. They raised feed for the horses on the farm on Mienars Road where Al Coburn now lives (formerly the Cooper place, but known then as Van Monk's farm). Coming by the farm was the road from Chehalis which was impassable in the winter in those days, since it was just a dirt trail; most of it was without either puncheon or gravel.

Frank's father moved those of the family of nine children who were still at home to Morton the same year that he moved his mill. Frank continued in sawmilling until his father died; then he went to sawing.

When he came to Morton, there was just a cluster of houses in Old Town. The railroad had recently arrived, and businesses were being constructed at the Main and Second Street intersection. Frank was one of the 60 signers of the petition to incorporate the city in 1913; many years later he was the last survivor of the group.

Frank built a house up the hill from the warehouse currently used by B and C Recycling. He finished it before he was married. He met his wife Frances Naomi Crumb when she was working in Winsberg's store in the Lindley Building. During a hot spell of weather, he went in to buy a straw hat. They didn't have one to fit him, but Frances took a shoelace and threaded it around the hat to make it fit. Frank was impressed with Frances who he found was two years younger than himself, having been born December 22, 1893.

The next time he saw Frances was at a "basket social" held in the Hotel Hilts. A "basket social" was a money-making event where girls prepared a lunch; then young men bid on it for the privilege of eating with the girl. Frances's sister tipped him off which basket was Frances's, but to avoid looking too obvious, he bought two baskets even though hers was bid up to $6.50. After the social, he walked her home one-and-a-half miles up in Highland Valley. It was a clear evening and the moon was shining. "We sat on a rock for a time. I don't know if she was tired or what,"

Frank recalled, "I couldn't read a woman's mind, I guess I was too young." Some of their courting took place when he walked to her home to accompany her to Tom Hopgood's movie theater, afterward walking her home. After Frank and Frances were married in 1913 in Tacoma, they made their home in the house Frank had built.

The Bingamans had four children: Eugene born Jan. 16, 1915, who married Vivian Clevinger and lives in Morton; Margurite born Jan. 18, 1917, and died in 1965; Phillip born June 6, 1920, now living in Missouri; and Barbara Joan born April 3, 1927, married Don Morris, now living in Morton.

The date of the first Masonic Temple dedication in Morton was vivid in Frank's memory, because he had to "fetch" Dr. Feagles, one of the first doctors in town, from the temple during the ceremony to deliver his first child Eugene.

Frances and Frank enjoyed hunting and fishing together. "She always caught more fish than I did," Frank said with a laugh. One time they went fishing at Westport on a very rough day and she got sick, for that reason she never went out on the ocean again.

In 1928, he built the house he lived in the rest of his life. It was the first house on Division Street in Cottler's Second Addition to the city of Morton. At that time, Division Street divided the town from the outskirts.

Bingaman called himself a mill builder because in addition to his own mill, he built a big mill with his brother on Lake Union; then he built one in Everett for Weyerhaeuser, another in Ketchikan, Alaska. The next one was at Saltchuck, which was an ore mill for the Alaska Plating Company located on the coast of Alaska. While he spent about three years in Alaska, he moved his family there with him.

He started working at the M. R. Smith Shingle Company in Mineral in 1933; he was employed there for seven years. From there he went to Lake Pleasant on the Olympic Peninsula where he spent nine months building a mill with ten machines. He did the drafting as well as building the mill that was still running in the 1970's. That area had dense forests of huge cedar, some making logs 11 feet in diameter, so large that they had to be split to run through the mill.

After World War II, Bingaman built a mill on the Falls Road between Kosmos and Randle where he figured he cut 22 million feet of timber.

He made good money then and as he said "salted it away" to live on in his retirement years. He bought timber from Milwaukee Railroad, cut ties, then hauled them to the tie docks along the tracks on the east edge of Morton. The price of hauling ties went up in 1948 from $6 to $12 a thousand feet, then jumped to $32 which eventually eliminated the tie mill business that was the main industry around Morton then. There was an estimated 80 to 100 mills in Eastern Lewis County at one time.

After the tie business "fizzled" out about 1950, Frank and his son Eugene started a "gypo" (contract) logging outfit. St. Regis and Kosmos Timber in the meantime had moved in and boosted the price of stumpage so high that the small operator couldn't buy it or make wages logging it, but Frank said, "I had sense enough to quit at the right time and didn't lose money." When Frank retired within a few years, Eugene went to work for St. Regis.

Always active in community affairs, Frank was a lifetime member of the Masonic Lodge and Eastern Star. He received his 50 year certificate as a Mason for which he was master in 1933. He served as Worthy Patron for Eastern Star eight different times, and he and Frances started the Morton Chapter of Rainbow Girls in 1935.

He was very involved with the Loggers Jubilee for many years, especially in the days when it was held in the grade school grounds. He said, "That's where I came in, securing the poles in the ground eight or nine feet deep." In addition, four falling trees had to be set up for each performance with Frank down in the holes securing the poles. Referring to the doubt about which year the Loggers Jubilee started (1937 or 1938), Bingaman told how the first contests between loggers began with climbing competition on a limbed tree growing in what is now the Collar-Wood Addition. The next year, the climbing tree was located on the banks of the Tilton River where "If you wanted to see a climber you had to hike up there to do it," he said. Other contests were held in town, such as bucking with the "misery whip" (cross-cut saw). As more contests were added, the name of the celebration came about and the Loggers Jubilee became a community event. One exciting event was based on the tie industry when a contest required men using a pickaroon and lots of muscle to transfer a load of ties from one flatbed truck to another.

FRANK AND FRANCES (CRUMB) BINGAMAN are shown with their first children: Margurite, Phillip, and Eugene. Bingamans were married in 1913.

After his retirement, Frank skillfully fashioned curly maple lamps, candle holders, goblets, and bowls on his lathe. He continued to garden and can a variety of fruits and vegetables after Frances passed away on August 29, 1966. Although it was difficult to cook for one, he took pride in his good meals.

Throughout his life, Bingaman thoroughly enjoyed hunting; in his home his prowess was displayed in trophy elk and mule deer heads. For over 15 years, he was camp cook with the same bunch of hunters for annual hunting camps in Eastern Washington. Well into his 80's he continued to hunt and cook. He said, "I suspect some of the fellows came as much to eat as to hunt."

Known as a man well liked by everyone, Bingaman, the mill builder, was highly respected. When he passed away on November 31, 1979, his 88 years had spanned the growth of Morton from a cluster of houses to a city which he helped to prosper.

Chapter 5

THE EDLUND BROTHERS
PIONEERS IN DAVIS LAKE VALLEY

After John Fredolph "Fred" Edlund arrived in Seattle in 1889, he wrote back to Sweden to his brothers Erik Edward "Ed" and Anton Olaf urging them to join him in "the land of opportunity, where everyone was rich." The story of these very early settlers in Davis Lake Valley was told by Ed's children Victor and Alma.

When Ed and Anton arrived in May 1890, Seattle was rebuilding after the 1889 fire that destroyed much of the city; therefore, there was plenty of work for the men. However, the brothers did not like Seattle; they went to Sedro Wooley where they worked briefly in a logging camp, moving on to another logging outfit in Clifton (now Belfair) located at the southern tip of Hood's Canal.

At this time, the Edlund brothers heard of the fertile Davis Lake Valley and the Big Bottom Country. In the spring of 1891, all three of them moved to Eastern Lewis County and took up homesteads. Ed settled on the hill above Davis Lake, Fred on Kosmos Hill, and Anton above Rainey Valley (now called Meade Hill). Later their parents came from Sweden to join them.

When the brothers arrived, there were a few homes on the south side of the Tilton River, which is now "Old Town" west of Seventh Street. Lewis F. Reed had a little store with the Morton Post Office across the Tilton River.

The first business building of much importance to the early settlers was built on the southeast corner of Seventh and Main Streets by George Hopgood, a Civil War veteran. It was a two-story building with a general merchandise store on the ground floor and a hotel above. At the grand opening in 1894, Ed and Fred played their violins at a dance that lasted all night. When a collection was taken to pay the musicians, it yielded $1.90 plus a few buttons, as the story goes.

After the Saturday night dance, without rest, the brothers set out on foot for Cosmopolis where there was supposed to be work in a mill. Jobs were scarce due to the 1894 panic and depression. They carried their fiddles and a ten pound lard pail containing some eggs, salt-pork, baking powder bread, and coffee, along with a few belongings. They followed the Bear Canyon trail through Alpha to Centralia and on to Cosmopolis. By walking all day, they covered the 70 miles to be ready to report for work Monday morning. However, every morning there was a line of men trying to get on at the lumber mill. "The first work that they got was to dig a grave for a Finlander who had just died. For this they received the tidy sum of $4.00 which helped pay expenses until they got a job at the mill," Victor wrote.

THE EDLUND BROTHERS: Ed, Fred, and Antone were Swedish immigrants who were among the first settlers in Davis Lake Valley.

They worked at the mill until they had to return to their homesteads to do the work necessary to "prove up" on their land which involved doing a certain amount of work each year before the U. S. Government would grant a patent (deed). Ed received his patent in 1907 over the signature of President William McKinley.

In 1899, Ed married a widow, a Mrs. Mienars, who had several children. Before the marriage failed, Edward W. "Eddie" was born in 1900; Ed received custody of the child.

The Edlund brothers were noted for their strength, especially Ed, about whom it was said that he could lift a man on each arm. He and one of his brothers carried a cookstove with a pole through it resting on their shoulders from Tacoma through LaGrande.

From 1900 to 1904, the Edlund brothers had a contract to carry the U. S. Mail on horseback from Mossyrock to Verndale (later called Glenoma), a distance of 24 miles each way. There was no bridge across the Cowlitz River which could be forded during low water, but during high water stages the mail was carried by Indian canoe with the horse swimming behind. During one of several narrow escapes from drowning, the canoe capsized, and Ed had to grab the horse's tail to be pulled across the dangerous river. Whenever the horse had to swim the icy river, they would make it gallop to warm it up.

About this time a market opened for cedar shingle bolts providing work and income for many of the pioneers. This, the first industry in the region, allowed Ed to hire men to cut the abundant cedar on his 320 acres, skidding the bolts into Davis Lake, then down Lake Creek to the Tilton and Cowlitz Rivers, finally to Kelso shingle mills. Later Fred M. Broadbent had a mill at the mouth of Lake Creek, eliminating the difficult river drive to Kelso.

Alma wrote, "Working for my father and hailing from Alleghany, New York, were two Randle homesteaders, John and Chris Bucher of the Bucher oil family, the great-great-grandsons of President Sutter of Switzerland." The family had pioneered in opening oil fields in Pennsylvania. The brothers wrote to their sister Catherine to come west to cook and keep house for them; she arrived in 1905. Soon Ed was courting Catherine, which led to their marriage in 1906 in St. Leo's Church in Tacoma. Her family were unhappy with her choice since they were sure she

had married "a fortune hunter." As Ed prospered in later years and visited the Buchers, they changed their minds about him.

In 1907, coal was discovered on Ed's homestead; the next year he sold the property with the mineral rights for $15,000 to Slayden and Fletcher from Tacoma, who sold stock in the mine. At one time known as the "Hi-Carbon Coal Mine," the property was sold and resold a number of times. About 1925, a railroad spur was constructed, but the mine never produced a profitable amount of coal.

Having sold their homestead, Ed and Catherine bought out Henry Clay Temple's homestead also in Davis Lake Valley in 1908. Known now as the Clifford Butts place, it lies about two-and-a-half miles east of Morton. Temple's place was one of the first homesteads in the valley. All of the Edlunds' children were born in this home, except Marie and Geneva. They were Victor, Leonard, Evelyn, Oscar, and Alma.

The State Bank of Morton was chartered in 1911 with Ed Edlund listed as one of the original subscribers; later he was also one of the directors. Active in civic and community affairs, Ed served as a school director for the Davis Lake and Morton schools, and later after he moved to Glenoma, he was a director there giving him a total of 16 years on all the boards.

Ed often loaned money to other early settlers with a handshake sealing the deal and nothing in writing or signed. For instance, he loaned $500 to Homer Johnson to start in the logging business. He never lost any money on those transactions. "In those days, your word was your bond," Victor said.

Victor's birth in 1909 was attended by a

ED AND CATHERINE (BUCHER) EDLUND were married in 1906. Their wedding attendants were her brother Chris and a friend Anna Lindblom.

midwife, since Dr. Feagles had not yet arrived in Morton; Mrs. Short and Mrs. Batson were the midwives for many births. When he was three years old, he remembers a trip to New York to stay with an aunt while his parents went to Sweden.

Victor started to school in the Davis Lake School, then after three years he went to Morton. Mrs. Maude Anderson was his first teacher; her husband Rev. O. R. Anderson was the minister when the first Methodist Church was built in Morton in 1909. She was a large, powerful woman. "She could grab the big Johnson boys and shake them thoroughly and crack their heads together; eighth grade boys probably 15 years old," Victor remembers with awe. Mrs. Anderson rode a pretty, sorrel horse each day to the school that was located where the Morton Gun Club is now. She put the horse in a shed next to the school, unsaddling and saddling it each day by herself. One time she challenged the students to a snowball fight as an incentive to get their lessons perfectly, an idea that backfired as can be imagined.

Fred, Ed's brother, had a shoe shop in Morton in 1913-1914 located on Main Street before he went to Alaska where he homesteaded in the Matanuska Valley. There was no town yet at Anchorage, just docks to unload supplies to be ferried to the Russian town of Knik up Cooke's Inlet. He had to build five miles of road in 1915 to bring his family, his team, horses, wagon, cattle, and farm implements to the homestead. He fathered 12 children and reared 11.

Alma wrote about Catherine, "Mother had a busy life raising eight children and assigned each of us specific duties daily. Clothes were washed by hand over the 'board', bread was homebaked,

and fruits, vegetables, and meats were home canned, about 1,000 quarts a year. Being an excellent seamstress, Mother made each child three outfits to start the school year; another if we 'made' the Christmas program and a special one for May Community Day, if, as honor students, our work was on display."

Alma tells about how her mother used really clever psychology on the children. For instance, she would say one of them could scrub a floor like no one else; naturally they each worked harder for that kind of praise. With her talent for sewing that had been developed under an expert seamstress, she clothed all the children with attractive outfits. Catherine often bought remnants of fabrics or those on sale; she would accumulate drawers full, so that when it was time to sew for the girls they could choose the yardgoods they liked best for their dresses.

Sons Eddie, Victor, and Leonard inherited their father's talent as musicians and for many years they played violin, banjo, and drums in their dance band, the "Melody Kings."

The Ed Edlunds moved to the top of Kosmos Hill, then about 1927 to Glenoma on the present Anderson Road, where Earl and Norma Boren now live. After high school, three of the girls, Evelyn, Geneva, and Alma, graduated from Moler Beauty College in Tacoma. They operated beauty salons in Enumclaw and Tacoma between 1937 and 1946.

Catherine died at their Glenoma home in 1942, and Ed passed away in 1944 at age 82. Victor wrote in tribute to his father, "Although he was a farmer, most of his income was derived from dealing in land and timber. He was always kind, generous, and honest with his fellow man. He helped many of the early settlers to get a start."

Chapter 6

EDWIN KNITTLE
One of the First SETTLERS In MORTON

EDWIN AND NELLIE (WARNKE) KNITTLE were married February 28, 1901. He had "batched" for 16 years on his Morton homestead before he married at 46 years of age — she was 14.

When Edwin Knittle came to what is now the town of Morton, the Temple family were among the few settlers in Davis Lake Valley according to his son, Otis Knittle. In Highland Valley, William T. Crumb settled there about the same time Knittle did. In the year 1885 there was not even a good trail to follow east of Cinebar when Ed Knittle walked from there with a pack on his back.

For 16 years the bachelor Knittle worked his homestead by himself. His solitary life ended when he met and courted Nellie Warnke; they were married February 28, 1901. As a young girl, Nellie had made three trips across country on foot from Michigan following rodeos and fairs. There was a wide difference in their ages — Edwin was 46 and Nellie was only 14 on their wedding day.

Knittle was from Pottsville, Pennsylvania, where he was born in 1855 on his parents' farm. He struck out on his own when he was 13 years old. He was 30 years old and working for 50 cents a day when he heard about the homestead property available here. When he had chosen his land, he surveyed it with a compass so accurately that his property lines did not have to be changed later when a certified surveyor worked here.

He homesteaded 160 acres on what is now the eastern edge of Morton, which became the Collar-Wood Addition, the Morton Junior-Senior High School site and additional school property of about 100 acres, the Jubilee Field, the Jubilee Park, and the airport.

On a prominent knoll in the northeast corner of the homestead, Knittle built a cabin of split cedar planks and shakes which measured 5" by 16". The cabin size was about 14 ft. by 18 ft. with a rock fireplace and a dirt floor.

Huge cedar trees that grew on what is now school property supplied the material for the cabin; cedar with the addition of fir posts was also used for the barn he built about 1886-87. Otis told of the custom in the early days of "barn raisings". When someone would decide to erect the heavy framing for another building, all the neighbors would get together to help. The person who was having the barn built would give a big dinner, making it a social event, too.

The cedar was also a major source of income when he cut shingle bolts, branded them, and floated them down the rivers to the shingle mills in Kelso. Edwin also picked hops in the Mary's Corner-Ethel area for his winter grubstake. Even so, there was one winter when he ran out of everything but potatoes which he had to eat without salt.

By about 1910, the family had outgrown the small cabin, and the family lived in a log cabin across the road before Knittle raised the roof of the original cabin to make another floor and added a large two-story addition to the east end. He put siding over the cedar walls of the cabin and sealed it inside to form the kitchen of the new home, leaving intact the original building.

Material for the house that was not available in Morton had to be hauled from Chehalis by team and wagon. Otis related that on the load that included windows, "The team ran away coming down Bear Canyon and upset the wagon. When he picked the load up he found to his surprise, not even one window had been broken." To eliminate the chore of cooking over the fireplace, Knittle brought in a cookstove from Chehalis by dragging it behind his horse on poles like the travois used by the Indians.

It wasn't long after settling here that Knittle cleared enough land on the knoll by the house to set out an orchard. Without another source of fertilizer, he took advantage of the large fall salmon runs in Lake Creek by taking his horse and a sled to the creek bank where he could use a pitchfork to throw the fish out of the creek, then haul them up to his young trees. In later years a dam across the Tilton River put an end to the salmon runs in Lake Creek.

The Knittle home was a convenient stopping place for those traveling from the Big Bottom country especially. The men slept in the barn with meals furnished for them and feed for their horses.

In the 1880's and 1890's, there were quite a few Indians in the area who were friendly with the settlers. One time the Indians had killed a bear that they prepared for a feast. They dug a pit, put the bear carcass in it, and heated rocks to place around and on the meat. When it was done, they invited Knittle to share the roast bear, but he had seen the bear hanging after it was skinned. It looked so much like a human being, he was repulsed by it and could not eat a bite. When Otis bought the homestead in 1948, the rocks the Indians used were still there on a ridge that ran across the valley.

By 1911, the Knittle family consisted of Ervin born in March 1902, Lillie in May 1903, Otis in January 1906, and Alice in April 1911.

About 1912, Nellie contracted tuberculosis, and on the doctor's advice she went to the drier climate of College Place in eastern Washington where she stayed for two years. Otis remembered

starting to school there adding, "I had a walnut tree started from a nut I brought here from College Place." His mother did recover and lived to be 70 years old.

Otis wrote, "About the turn of the century the need for a cemetery arose. Dad (Edwin) cleared the first half acre of what is the older part of the cemetery. As part payment he received the Knittle family block of eight graves. While clearing, he found a tiny fir seedling and planted it by his lot saying that it would make shade for his grave later. This is the large fir seen in the cemetery by the Knittle block."

Some years later Nellie and several other Morton residents became concerned with the plots in the cemetery that were not being taken care of. Most of them were tended by family members, but some were neglected. After quite a bit of work, they were able to turn the cemetery care over to the city which has taken good care of it ever since.

Morton was still just a small settlement when the first school house and social hall was built on the Hopgood property that is Backstrom Park now. Knittle played a violin that he made out of local maple wood for the dances that were held there, mostly square dances. The whole family came in the evening after farm chores were done; when the children got sleepy, they were put to bed on the stage or benches. Dancing continued throughout the night, breaking up when daylight arrived so that they could see their way home to

THE KNITTLE'S LOG HOUSE was their home for several years before they built the large frame house of later years. In front are: Edwin, Otis (seated), Ervin, Lillie, and Nellie.

THE KNITTLE'S TWO-STORY HOUSE was built on a knoll just east of Morton on the Davis Lake Road. The original log house became the kitchen. In the foreground is the Tacoma Eastern Railroad.

do the morning farm chores.

In his memoirs Otis related, "My Dad founded the Elkmount Dairy which furnished bottled milk in Morton for a good many years. The name was derived from the fact he found a large set of elk horns when he was clearing the knoll for a building site. Thinking he would find others, he threw them in the fire. No others were found, however, much to his later disappointment."

Margaret Perrigo, who became Otis' wife, was born in North Dakota, lived in Wisconsin and Canada before her family came to Morton in 1923 when she was 13 years old. She married Fred Adams in 1926 when she was 16, but after her son George was born, they parted and her parents adopted George and reared him. Otis and Margaret were married in December 1930.

Their children are: Alfred, Dorothy, Irene, and Melvin. Otis liked to say he and Margaret were never apart overnight until after they had been married 24 years.

Edwin Knittle passed away in 1930, long before his homestead became part of the City of Morton. In 1948, Nellie sold 20 acres to the Wood brothers (Ben and Al) and Harvey Collar, which was annexed to the city as the Collar-Wood Addition. Before she died in 1957, Nellie had sold the remainder of the property to Otis, who in turn sold to the Chamber of Commerce and the Morton School District No. 214. Nellie saw the property which once held the family home become the home sites of many young families along the street named Knittle's Way.

Chapter 7

PIUS COTTLER, MORTON HOMESTEADER

Pius Cottler is believed to be the second settler who homesteaded property that now lies within the city limits of Morton. Cottler arrived in New York in 1884 from the town of Baden in the district of Baden in Germany. He arrived in the Morton area in 1887 to stake out a homestead on property now known as Cottler's Addition — the area south of Division Street.

According to records in the Lewis County Courthouse, Cottler received the patent to his land on July 6, 1893, for 160 acres in the SW 1/4 of Section 2, Township 12, Range 4E. The only pioneer who received title to his property in the present townsite before Cottler was Fred D. Reed, who homesteaded in the same section for which he received his patent in 1892.

Cottler spent his first year in this country in New York after arriving on a boat in steerage passage, working for his fare by helping with the cattle aboard ship. In New York he worked on a dairy farm where a woman taught him English in the evenings. He had thought of going to Switzerland when he left Germany, but at the last moment decided to make his new life in the United States. He left without telling his mother goodbye which always grieved him. Before the outbreak of World War I, he had a ticket to visit his homeland, but because of the war he didn't get to go and he never did return.

Cottler lived at Sedro Woolley first when he came to Washington, then he moved to Puyallup where he bought a pack horse and bedroll and set out to prospect. He and Robert McNee did find gold on a claim on Niggerhead Mountain in later years, but he was not able to keep it due to his wife's illness. He also found a cinnabar vein some place in this area, but it is not known if it was the same area that was later mined near Morton.

While homesteading in Morton, he lived in Puyallup where he worked nine months of each year, spending the summer months working on

PIUS AND MATTIE (STOUT) COTTLER were married in 1909 when he was 40 years old and she was in her teens. They had seven children.

his property. He worked for Ezra Meeker when the Extension Station was being established.

In 1888, Cottler blazed a trail to Harmony and helped build the trail that gave access to the road to Chehalis from other homesteads. He was one of the most active workers in building the first log schoolhouse in Morton and also worked on the second school building. He served several years on the school board of directors and was clerk of the district at the time of consolidation in 1913.

In 1901, Cottler married Mattie Clara Stout, daughter of Andrew and Clara Stout, who were also pioneers in Morton. They came by covered wagon in the year 1886 from Denton County, Texas, when Mattie was five years old.

Pius and Mattie had seven children, three sons: Herbert, Walter, and Clifford, and four daughters: Edna, Ruby, Hazel, and Irene.

Cottler built their original home across Lake Creek on a knoll just below the outcropping known as "Cottler's Rock." Later he built a new house in town on the corner of Division and First

THE COTTLER'S FIRST HOME was located on a knoll at the foot of Peterman Hill across Lake Creek. Until the 1930's, the hill was called Cottler's Rock. Later the house burned.

Streets. Later fire destroyed the old home. He and his family lived in the new house until they moved to Tacoma in April, 1918. He sold his homestead to Glen Fisher, who lived there while raising his family and for many years after that.

A building known as "Cottler's Hall" was erected by the pioneer on the corner of Division and Third Streets which was used for several things including a skating rink, and later it was a movie house. Even later it was used as a school gymnasium. Another name in the movie business was the fellow pioneer Thomas Hopgood who had a theater on Main Street.

In the very early days, Cottler ordered a stove from Sears, Roebuck that he had to pack in from Tacoma. Later they bought an organ and they had to pack it in, also. After the wagon road to Harmony was built, they could make the shorter trip to Chehalis for goods.

Mattie was always on call to help neighbors; one day she left after starting a batch of bread, leaving the girls instructions to work it down, let it rise again, then make it into loaves. Edna and Ruby were working with the bread when they started throwing a piece back and forth and they dropped it, then made it into rolls. The next day they had company for dinner. When the girls started giggling at the table, their mother made them confess.

Another time while the older girls were left in charge of the younger ones, they used good sheets and blankets to make a tepee, and they decorated their faces with chalk and charcoal. When their mother returned, one of the girls said, "It was no more Indians!"

Mattie used to tell the children that the first time they had a feather tick over fresh hay it was the "nearest thing to heaven." She was noted for her sense of humor and always played with her children.

The children adored their father, too, and thought he could do anything. He was a handy man who could, among other things, mend their shoes and make clothes for the boys. He was strict with them, sometimes using a little strap for spanking, but Mattie was softhearted and hated to punish them.

Both the Cottlers were devout religious people and very faithful to church. Cottler was a Catholic when he came to this country, but when Ruby was a tiny baby, a friend called Mattie to invite her to a revival meeting in Old Town. Because she hated to go without Pius, she invited him to go, too. When he decided it wouldn't do him any harm, they walked to the meeting with Herbert, Ruby, and Edna. After the service, they asked the minister to have dinner with them. While Mattie cooked, the minister began using the Bible to show Pius the way to salvation. The conversation went on all night. Finally at 5 a.m., Pius said he was convinced; he repented and joined the church. In later years the family attended the First Christian Church where they never missed a service except for illness. They always asked the blessing at meals, and they had family prayers every night.

Cottler was such a patriotic American that Germany became so remote to him and English so much his language that one time when he received a letter from his sister he couldn't read it. One of the reasons he left Germany was because there was compulsory service, and the military was extremely strict. His daughter said, "He was too gentle a man for that."

Cottler was so easy with people and so trusting that sometimes people took advantage of him. He simply couldn't say "No" to anyone; therefore, he had a hard time making a living on the farm. After moving to Tacoma, he worked at Fort Lewis and later in a shipyard.

One of the family has what was thought to be a diary in German kept by Cottler during his homestead days, but when it was translated it was found to be poetry inspired by his love for this part of the country.

Once when he was clearing land by slashing brush, he accidentally cut his upper lip, from

TENT REVIVAL MEETINGS were held in Morton in the early days. Pius Cottler attended with his wife and children; he became a Christian through the guidance of the preacher.

then on he always wore a mustache to cover the scar. Another time when he was clearing land, in his haste to get the burning started in a circle of stumps and brush, he found himself in the middle of a ring of fire where he was almost trapped.

Cottler was very active in the Odd Fellows Lodge and attended all their meetings. He even attended an assembly in Chehalis when he had to walk the distance, his children recalled.

The family remembers incidents in their childhood, such as the time Herbert was milking while reciting "Old Ironsides." Suddenly a dog came into the barn, startling the cow who kicked over the milk bucket, ending his recitation.

Before moving to Tacoma, Edna remembers working with Herbert to get in the hay; they had to shock it; then they carried it into the barn on pitch forks. One year there was such a poor hay crop that Pius had to buy baled hay and store it in the barn that was located at First and Adams Streets. The children were given strict orders not to crawl between the bales, but they couldn't resist, and they were caught and punished.

They remember the highlights of the school year were the picnics at the river and Easter Egg hunts in the woods.

While they still were in the old house, Edna recalls two accidents. When Ruby was three years old and Edna was five, they were climbing over a rotten log with Edna carrying an axe. Just as Ruby put her hand on the log, Edna brought the axe down and cut off the end of Ruby's finger. Dr. Feagles grafted it back on, and when it healed even the fingernail was all right.

Another incident occurred when Edna was chopping with a sharp double bitted axe on a stump just outside the house, when somehow Herbert moved into the way and was cut on the nose. Their father packed the wound with flour and it healed nicely.

The last winter they lived in Morton, Herbert and Edna were at their grandmother's house when there was a big snowstorm that snowed them in. Finally they were able to get home by taking a shortcut by the cemetery, through the trees and across Lake Creek. It was quite a trip for two small children.

Cottler passed away at the age of 74 in 1930 from cancer. Mattie lived until 1958 when she died in Tacoma at the home of one of her daughters. Up until his last illness Cottler looked much younger than his actual age. He was 40 years old when he married, but looked at least 15 years younger.

The Cottlers were good friends of the Knittles who came to Morton a short time after them. They were all community-minded people and active in their town.

The Cottlers were "of the stuff" pioneers were made and they made their contribution to the founding of the City of Morton.

Chapter 8

THE STOUT-WASTE FAMILIES
of MORTON

In 1886 the Andrew Stout family left Texas by covered wagon, taking two seasons to reach Wallowa, Oregon. Their daughter Ella was about eleven years old then, old enough to vividly remember the many times she and the other children had to stand on the side of the wagon to keep it from tipping over in the deeply rutted Oregon Trail. Ella told about reaching the present Oregon State border where the scouts for the wagon train tried to persuade them to take a southern route that was a shortcut to California instead of continuing north in the Oregon Territory. Part of the wagon train followed the scouts' advice; later it was said that all of that party were massacred by Indians.

The patriarch of the Stout family Andrew Jackson Stout was born April 25, 1843, in Boonville, Kentucky. He and his wife Clara were married October 14, 1862, in Versailes, Missouri, migrating first to Denton County, Texas.

Although the Stouts' son George was only 16 years old when they left Texas, he was already an accomplished horseman, well experienced in breaking horses to ride. While the family lived in Oregon, he worked on the Union Pacific Railroad in Oregon and Utah. George had five sisters: Ella, Janie, Nora, Lena, and Mattie.

After a year or two in Oregon, the Stout family went north into eastern Washington where they lost most of their cattle on the dry grass. Next they moved to Lake Washington where 16 year old Ella met her husband-to-be quite romantically. Charles Edward Waste and another young man were riding by the Stouts' place one day when they spotted an attractive girl in the yard. The men decided to toss a coin to see who would get the first chance to make friends with her. Charlie won the toss, courted Ella, and soon they were married at Bryn Mayr, Washington, on July 19, 1891.

About this time Andrew Stout was receiving letters from Barney Blankenship, who had served in the Civil War with him. Barney encouraged them to move to Randle because the "Big Bottom" country was wonderful for cattle raising. Attracted by his descriptions of the country, Andrew took up a homestead about a mile above Packwood. He built a log cabin and barn on the place that stood for many years.

By now because George was old enough to establish his own homestead, he located near the present White Pass school location. Also settling in the area was a cousin, Billy Job. He had come west with the Stouts on the wagon trip from Texas, riding a bull calf. Later he was killed by the same animal at Randle, on the Ward place by the old hop house that stood near Cora Bridge.

The Stouts moved next to Hopkins Creek where they lived a short time. Ella and Charlie Waste also moved to the area, settling in Rainey Valley. There a son James Andrew Waste was born, the first of a large family. Before long they decided there were better opportunities in Charlie's home state of Wisconsin. During the years they lived at Fairchild, Wisconsin, three children were added to their family: Milton, Katie, and Gladys.

About 1895, George Stout married Leila A. Young, a daughter of Randle pioneers. They lived on the homestead a while where their first daughter Winnie was born. Later they moved to Morton and lived for about a year with George's sister Mattie and her husband, Pius Cottler, a German immigrant, who was one of the earliest Morton homesteaders, first coming to the area about 1887. While living with the Cottlers, George and Leila's daughter Gladys was born. After this they bought some property and moved there where their son Ivan was born.

Andrew Stout sold his place in Randle and homesteaded another place just west of Morton in Highland Valley. In 1912, "Grandpa" Andrew

THE STOUT-WASTE FAMILIES with patriarch Andrew Stout include in front: Mattie (Stout) Cottler, Gladys Waste, Kate Waste, Ella Waste holding Eunace, mother Clara Stout with Clara McNee, little Esther McNee, Nora (Stout) NcNee, Bob McNee, Leila (Young) Stout holding Ivan, Winnie and Gladys Stout. In back are: Pius Cottler holding Herbert, James Waste, Milton Waste, Charles Waste, Helen Stout, father Andrew Stout, Robert McNee holding Wade, and George Stout.

Stout had just taken a man to see a dappled stallion put through his paces when on the return trip to the house he dropped dead. George and his family took over the homestead. He built a house in 1914 and he lived there until he moved to Centralia twenty-seven years later. The lumber for the house that is being lived in now was cut at a mill located nearby.

At one time George Stout had the job of carrying the mail on horseback along a wagon road. He went west about twenty-five miles to Alpha, back to the Bremer post office about eight miles west of Morton where he would lay over, then the next day go on to Lewis (now named Packwood). One time when he was coming from Alpha, he saw something move just ahead; as his horse reared, he saw that a cougar was lying there with his tail across the trail.

Because George had been a bronco buster since he was a boy, he thought his son Ivan should follow in his footsteps. Ivan's mother did not like the idea at all, and one morning she witnessed a frightening incident. Ivan was only about six years old when he mounted the horse with the reins still tied. When the horse bucked, his feet became entangled in the reins causing his mother to scream for fear he would be killed. After this she insisted that George get rid of that horse; later he traded it for a sixteen-gauge shotgun that Ivan had all his life.

George owned and drove one of the first school busses in the area. In 1918, he had two Model T Ford trucks with benches along the sides and canvas side panels that could be unrolled during bad weather. George picked up children from the upper end of Highland Valley to Morton, and Ivan went north to West Fork for a load.

Now to continue with Ella and Charlie Waste's

THE FIRST SCHOOL BUSES in Morton were two owned by George Stout in 1918. His route was Highland Valley and his son Ivan went to West Fork.

THE GEORGE STOUT HOUSE built in 1914 in Highland Valley was where he lived until 1941. After remodeling in the 1950's, it is being lived in.

story. After their stay in Wisconsin, they returned to Washington in 1900. On the railway trip west Gladys, a six-month-old baby, was extremely ill with measles.

The next several years the family lived on a ranch near Davis Lake, just east of Morton on property that is now known as the old Johnson place. While living there, Hobart, Eunice, and Nuna were born. Hobart was named for Grandmother Katherine Waste's brother, Garret Hobart, who was Vice-President of the United States under William McKinley. Mr. Hobart died about two years before McKinley was assassinated, thereby missing his chance for a more prominent place in history.

About 1907 Charlie moved his family to Elbe where he worked in a mill and logged. Chester was born there in 1908. Their house near Davis Lake was rented to a Music family when it burned down; that incident prompted Charlie to return to the ranch and build a shack for his family.

While living on the Davis Lake property, four of the children decided one day to go for a walk; soon they were playing in a logging pond that belonged to their neighbors, the Coonhausans. The children: Milton, Katie, Gladys, and Nuna, had strict instructions not to play around that pond, but the temptation was too great. Evening came and reluctant to go home, they accepted the neighbors' invitation to stay for supper. Gladys pleaded with her brother and sisters to go home before dark, but they wouldn't pay any attention to her.

When their father Charlie came home from work, he started out with a lantern to find them.

HOTEL TINDALL on Main Street was operated for some years by Charles Waste and his wife. The wooden sidewalk raised pedestrians above the muddy street.

As soon as he had the children home, he began to give each of them a sound whipping. Katie wanted to skip her turn, ran out the door, across the yard and through the front gate with her father right behind her. As he ran by the gate, his overalls caught and a big hole was ripped in them. He gave up the chase, stomped back into the house, and announced that he was through; their mother would have to punish them from then on.

An unfortunate incident happened one time after Charlie had been working outside. When he came in, he leaned his handsaw up against the old pump organ which sat in the living room right at the foot of the stairs that led up to the attic room where the children slept. Hobart got up, and as he sleepily descended the stairs, he missed the bottom step and fell heavily on the saw, cutting a severe wound clear across his hand. Fortunately, his mother was an experienced practical nurse. In fact, Ella was one of the neighborhood women who helped Dr. Feagles, the doctor in Morton, before he had a regular nurse. She was a midwife for her neighbors, too.

Hobart was a sickly child; often he was seriously ill. Ella had to take him to Chehalis for medical care more than once before the first doctor came to Morton. It was a very hard journey to transport a sick child on horseback. One time Ella dreamed that she was starting to take Hobart to Chehalis when a man with a horse and wagon offered them a ride which she gratefully accepted. Not long after that the dream came true.

In 1911, Charlie and Ella bought the Tindall Hotel in Morton next to Fairhart's first store which was just a small store with groceries on one side and dry goods on the other side. Ella ran the hotel while Charlie ran a sawmill up in Highland Valley. Because some of the sawmill crew roomed and boarded at the hotel, the family used to joke about Papa paying the men and Mama taking it away from them.

Charlie's sawmill was located above the old Crumb place in Highland Valley. The timber was cut on the hills then dragged to the log chute where they slid into the mill pond. Because the chute was extremely steep, the logs gathered so much momentum that they hit with enough force to dig the pond deeper and deeper at the end of the chute where some logs stuck in the bottom of the pond. The logs were cut in the sawmill into 2 by 4's, ties, and other sizes of lumber, then sent down a flume that stretched from the mill almost to the cemetery. Constructed of sawed planks, the flume was fed with water from Highland Creek. There was a walkway beside the flume that allowed someone to watch for jams and break them up quickly, a job the Waste children helped with sometimes. Chester remembered that they could catch salmon in the flume with a pickaroon.

There was a separate flume to carry the sawdust to the pile down near the Tilton River. The Waste children also helped watch that flume to see that the sawdust did not go into the river because the state game department had strict regulations to prevent killing the fish. One day Gladys was watching the sawdust flume when it got out of control. Because she couldn't think of anything else to do, she sat in the end of the flume and just let the sawdust pile up behind her.

At the end of the main flume, the lumber was loaded onto wagons to be hauled to the railroad dock that was located about where the tie docks were later built on the east edge of Morton. Bill Wood had charge of the men and teams that hauled the lumber.

Later Charlie had financial difficulties beyond his control which caused him to lose the mill. Because he went to work for other people to pay back wages he owed his sawmill crew, he earned the nickname of "Honest Charlie" from former employee Q. L. "Les" Chapman.

Chester was just enough younger than Hobart to be a nuisance to his big brother. Being about five years younger, Chester wanted to do everything that Hobart and his friends did, but he couldn't keep up with them. He soon earned the name of "cry-baby boy" from Hobart. One time Hobart had given in to Chester's pleas to take him fishing. When they started home, the trip took longer than Hobart had anticipated, because the river was flooded and spread out in little streams that had to be waded with five-year-old Chester, carrying the string of fish and the fishing pole, on his back. Chester was crying every step of the way, and when it grew dark, he cried over and over, "I want my mama." Finally their father met them with a lantern to guide them safely home.

Hobart was so tired of his crybaby brother that when another child was born during the years they lived in the Tindall Hotel, he was convinced that it would be another cry-baby brother. The day Lou Ethel was born, Hobart came home from school for lunch, and when he was told that the baby had arrived, he turned and stalked out of the house without asking about the baby or taking time to eat. One of the girls had to run after him to tell him that the baby was a girl!

There was an ice house behind the hotel where ice cut on Davis Lake with a cross-cut saw and hauled to the ice house was stored. Davis Lake was also used for ice skating as were the mill ponds. The winters were much colder then with deep snow every winter. Small children often had to flounder through waist-deep snow to reach the school. Everyone, children and adults, went sledding on the hills around town.

Main Street in Morton was planked, but many of the planks were broken which allowed mud to splash anyone crossing the street. The children always thought it was funny to see a nicely dressed lady picking her way across the planks, only to step on a broken one and have her boots and long skirts splattered with mud. The sidewalks along Main Street were built of planks raised far enough off the ground to provide crawling space for children who took advantage of this with frequent success to hunt for lost coins under the sidewalk. Between Third Street and the school house there was a gully that was crossed by a wooden bridge, just sidewalk width. In those days the gully was partly filled in where Main Street crossed it.

Later the Waste's sold the Tindall Hotel and moved to Inland, a logging camp above West Fork and Nineteen Creek where Charlie worked in the woods. One time when Hobart and Gladys were picking blackberries near their home, they thought they heard someone calling them. They answered several times while starting to work their way toward the voice. Finally when one of them looked up and saw a large cougar watching them, they ran home as fast as their legs could carry them without spilling a berry. Later a cougar that measured nine feet from nose to tail was shot near there.

In 1916, Milton and James along with Herb Sadie and Tom Scalf enlisted in the army to help in the trouble in Mexico where Pancho Villa was harassing the United States across the border near Calexico. Most of the town turned out to see the boys leave on the train.

Milton went on to serve in France during World War I. After the war he worked his way around the country on jobs ranging from the wheat fields in Montana to an ostrich farm in California. He served as the respected and well-liked postmaster of Morton from 1936 until 1958.

The Waste family with the children who were still at home in 1924 moved into a house near the end of the Tilton River bridge. The house was one of the oldest in Morton. When it was torn down in recent years, Lou Ethel's husband found square nails used in the construction and papers in the walls dating back to 1890.

The Stout and Waste families each contributed much to the settlement of this area, including a number of hard-working, reputable citizens. Many of the family members are gone now, and their descendants have scattered around the country, but their share in the history of our town will not be forgotten.

Chapter 9

THE CLEVENGERS
CLEVINGERS and STILTNERS

From *Clevenger, Clevinger and Stiltner Families of Washington State*
By Woodrow R. Clevinger, Burton G. Stiltner and Donna Stiltner Wildman

Shortly after 1900, a large number of Clevengers, Clevingers and their close relatives by marriage, the Stiltners, moved in strength to new land in Eastern Lewis County, according to two booklets published in 1970 and 1971. The following is compiled from that research.

In Woodrow R. Clevinger's booklet entitled "Cascade Mountain Clan, the Clevengers and Stiltners" he wrote, "This clan, now numbering in the hundreds, became related in the Cumberland Mountains of Virginia, West Virginia and Kentucky in the period 1800-1900. After 1900, many families of this kinship moved northwestward across the United States to become prominent pioneers in Lewis County of southwestern Washington."

"The ancestral leaders of this migration were five blood-related men of Southern Appalachian Mountain stock. Discontented with the poverty in the Virginia and Kentucky hills, they with strong faith and courage, moved their entire families to the Cascade Mountain foothill country of Eastern Lewis County. These West Virginians and Kentuckians who led this migration were Milburn Jackson Stiltner (1847-1919), Joseph C. Clevinger (1857-1937), Charles Clevenger (1869-1954) all pioneers of the Rainey Valley and Nelson Clevinger (1858-1935) and Franklin Pierce Stiltner (1856-1934) who were pioneers at Morton."

During early American history, the families developed into the Clevengers and some into the Clevingers (with the "i") as appeared in many legal records.

About 1816, John Clevinger married Polly Stiltner in Buchanan County, Virginia. This marriage formed the blood relation of a very large number of persons, many of whom became Washingtonians. John and Polly reared a family of eleven sons and one daughter. Grandsons of John, the children of Levi and Lewis migrated here even sooner. Lewis died in 1910 just as most of his sons and daughters were planning to move with the Stiltners to Lewis county. His widow and several of her children reached Glenoma between 1910 and 1917.

Levi, a mountain farmer and woodsman, lived in Pike County, Kentucky. One of his sons, Nelson, emigrated from that poverty stricken area to this state.

Nelson Clevinger (1858-1935) was the patriarch of a large group who left Pike County, Kentucky, after 1900 and by 1910 settled in Morton and Randle. He married Mary Childers in 1880. Nelson was a logger and log driver on the Big Sandy River who was attracted by higher wages to the Ozarks in southern Missouri in 1903, then with a number of other Kentuckians came to log in Grays Harbor, then found out about land in Lewis County.

Nelson's main goal was to settle on good land which was fulfilled by taking up a homestead in the Big Bottom Country. There were so many of his relatives and neighbors from his home state that some called that part of Lewis County "Little Kentucky."

The Nelson Clevinger family contributed much to the development of the Randle and Morton communities. He and his son William developed an 80 acre livestock farm out of the Davis Lake swamp, cleared and built several houses on their acreage in the Cottler Addition to Morton, were part owners with their brother-in-law Lorenzo D. Childers, in one of the first

IN 1912, WILLIAM K. CLEVINGER, having migrated from Pike County, Kentucky, was riding the Big Bottom trail at Fern Gap.

general stores in Morton and were trustees of the Methodist Churches in Randle and Morton.

The womenfolk of the family, Mary Childers Clevinger, Priscilla Adams Clevinger, and Daisy Clevinger Spears were noted for their hard work in church and school functions and their folk arts and customs brought from Kentucky. They practiced home spinning, homemade soap making, quilting, drying green beans ("leather britches"), and cooking in the tradition of their mountain culture.

Nelson and Mary (Childers) had a large family born in Kentucky, but matured in Washington and are scattered about the state. Their children are Cora, William Keenus, Daisy, Millard, Orville, Charles Bradshaw, Landon, Ernest, and Josephine.

John and Polly (Stiltner) Clevinger's youngest son, Joseph C. (1857-1937) was a well-known pioneer in the Glenoma area and was the only son from that large family to move west. Joseph and his wife Virginia Perdew moved their entire family of 12 adults and children by train about 1911, because logging in West Virginia had fallen on hard times. He and his older sons settled in Rainey Valley and worked in the logging camps and mills around Morton. With his sons-in-law, Grant Stiltner, Patrick Dodrill, and Charles Riffe, this was probably the largest related families ever to move from the hills of West Virginia to Washington.

Joseph was the head of the large families in Eastern Lewis County and was widely known as "Uncle Joe" because he had so many nieces and nephews living in the area. At Joseph's death in 1937, he was survived by nine children, 37 grandchildren, and 22 great-grandchildren.

Lewis Clevinger, an older brother of Joseph, died in West Virginia about 1905, and his widow, Polly Jane (Colly) and their sons, Thomas, Elias, Elijah, Charles P. "Snide", and daughter Diadama accompanied or followed their Uncle Joseph in the move to Washington. They settled in Morton and Rainey Valley. Thomas changed the spelling of his name to "Clevenger" and raised a family in Morton; Charles P. "Snide" married Sally Riffe, and Diadama married Maranda Arnold and raised a large family in West Virginia, who came to Grays Harbor and Mason Counties after 1905.

The Charles (1869-1954) and Reedy (Stiltner) Clevenger were the parents of a large family of early settlers from West Virginia which came to Glenoma between 1905 and 1915. Their marriage united another branch of the Clevenger-Stiltner families. Reedy was the daughter of Milburn Jackson Stiltner, the head of a large clan of Stiltners, whose story is told later.

Charles was born in Virginia and moved northward to West Virginia where he worked in the lumber and logging industry and with his sons was prominent in the same kind of work in Eastern Lewis County.

Charles and Reedy's family of eleven children form a large branch of the Clevengers, most of whom stayed in this area. Their children are Dewey, who married John Weslie Stiltner and had a large family in Morton, Eliza, Martha married Dwight Chapman, James "Jim" married Martha Hugh, Elmer married Minnie Davis, Emery married Mildred Blakely, Opal married Frank Paul, Mabel married Merwyn Johnson,

WILLIAM K. AND PRISCILLA (ADAMS) CLEVINGER had their first three of eight children while in Kentucky. The children in this 1910 photo are: Kemper L., Ethel Maude, and Arnold S.

Dorothy married Floyd Davis, Ralph married Ruby Clark, and his twin, Ruby, married Clem Reynolds.

Continuing the line from Nelson and Mary (Childers) Clevinger was their oldest son, William Keenus Clevinger, born in 1882 in Elkhorn City, Pike County, Kentucky. William married Priscilla Adams in Kentucky in 1901. William sought work outside the Cumberland Mountains as a log driver on the Big Sandy River, but discontented with the poor pay, he joined his father Nelson in moving to Missouri, then on to Grays Harbor and finally to Morton in 1910.

William was active as a property owner and carpentry contractor and built many frame houses in Morton's early days. He developed a farm in Davis Lake Valley and was a very active citizen as a Democratic Precinct Committeeman, School District Director, and County Road Supervisor from 1930 to 1959. Owning property in the town, he was one of the signers of the petition to incorporate Morton.

William and Priscilla's children were Ethel Maude, Kemper, Arnold, triplets that died at birth, Woodrow (the family researcher), Vivian, Eugene, and William Keenus, Jr.

PRISCILLA (ADAMS) CLEVINGER, along with all the women who came from the Appalachian Mountains, brought her skills in quilt-making and other mountain activities to Washington.

THE STILTNERS

The many large families bearing the name of Stiltner in the states of Virginia, West Virginia, and Washington are the descendants of Frederick Charles Stegler. He was born in Germany and migrated to Virginia just before the Revolutionary War. It is believed that he Americanized his name to Stiltner about 1790-1800.

Frederick's oldest son Elijah was the father of Milburn Jackson Stiltner, his fourth son, born in 1848. Milburn married Sarah Wood in 1867 in Virginia; they were the earliest of the Clevenger-Stiltner families to emigrate from the Cumberland Mountains to the Cascade Mountains.

They moved westward in 1888, taking part in the land rush into the Cherokee Strip of Oklahoma in 1889. Disappointed with their homestead near the present Woodward, they sold out and moved to the Yakima Valley in 1898. Discontented with the hot, dry climate of eastern Washington, Milburn rode his horse over the Cascades to the Big Bottom Country. Here he found green timber, good land, and friendly pioneers, including the Meades and Peters who were Regular Baptists from Kentucky.

Milburn staked out a homestead near Randle in the bottomland of upper Kiona Creek and Rainey Creek where he moved his family in 1898. His homestead cabin was a friendly stop on the Big Bottom Trail between Randle and Morton.

Milburn influenced other Stiltner and Clevenger men to leave Virginia and Kentucky for this area. He dedicated part of his homestead as the Rainey Valley Cemetery for his kinsmen, neighbors, and members of the Regular Baptist Church in Glenoma.

Milburn and Sarah had six sons and five daughters in Virginia and Oklahoma. Their children were Bery, Nelson, Victoria, Reedy (who married Charles Clevenger), William, Ross, Vicy (who married Clarence Dunaway in Glenoma), Almeda (who married Benjamin F. Meade in Glenoma), Grover, Martha, and Dewey.

Returning to the original immigrant, Frederick (Stegler) Stiltner's family line, we find his grandson Franklin Pierce Stiltner was born in 1856 in Virginia. The son of Frederick, Jr., Franklin became the patriarch of a very large family in the early history of Morton. Franklin married Anna Rosetta Cutlip about 1877 and with their oldest children moved to West Virginia where the rest of the children were born.

Franklin and Anna's children were Samuel, Mary who married Hiram C. Bell (who was active in the early formation of the City of Morton), John Wesley, who married Dewey Jane Clevenger and was a leader of both families,

GRANT STILTNER'S 1923 SCHOOL BUS picked up the children living at Lindberg, a thriving mill community then. A row of brick houses is all that remains today.

Grant married Sena L. Clevinger, daughter of Joseph C.; Edward J. "Pete" married Oma Ware; Lucinda married D. L. Cutright, and McKinley "Mack" married Pearl Peer, and he became the spiritual leader of the Stiltners, Clevengers, and their related families. Mack was an elder in the Mount Zion Old Regular Baptist Church in Morton. The last two children were Granville Burton, who married Margaret Lantz and was a historian of the families, and Donna, who in 1920 married first Morton's only doctor, Dr. Joseph Pine, who died young. Secondly, she married Earl Donahue, who also died young. Her third marriage was to Russell Seaton, and later she married Lt. Colonel Vernon Wildman. She was a long time secretary and booster of the annual Clevenger-Clevenger-Stiltner Reunion, and she worked tirelessly for the Mount Zion Church.

By 1908, logging and sawmilling on the Elk River in West Virginia no longer presented opportunity for steady work and good pay, so Franklin and Anna's children began the migration west. Grant, Sena and her mother Virginia arrived first, followed by John and Mary in 1910. By 1918, Franklin and his sons, who now had families of their own, had all reached Eastern Lewis County.

Most of the family settled on the northern edge of Morton on a site often called Stiltner Flat and Stiltner Hill. Franklin and his sons cleared stump land and built homes in the area.

By 1930, the Stiltners were the largest family in Morton. However, in more recent years the Clevengers have had more of their families remain in Eastern Lewis County, so they now outnumber the Stiltners. Both families have contributed much to the settlement and development of the area and continue to be valuable citizens.

Chapter 10

REEDY (STILTNER) CLEVENGER
ELEVEN CALLED HER MOTHER

Reedy Stiltner met her future husband Charles Clevenger when he came with two friends to hunt deer with her father. Deer were plentiful in West Virginia then and were an important part of their diet. The young men stayed with Jackson Stiltner and his family in Elk Lick Bottom for about two weeks while they got their meat supply. Pretty teenage Reedy, one of eleven children of Jackson and Sarah (Wood) Stiltner, attracted young Charles, who began writing to her after his return to his home. They corresponded for several months which developed into a romance. Occasionally Charles visited Reedy, but that involved a walk of 30 miles.

Charles and Reedy were married Feb. 10, 1892, in Greenbriar, Nicholas County, West Virginia. Charles was 22 years old, born Feb. 27, 1869, and Reedy was 16, born Sept. 4, 1875, in Buchanan County, Virginia. After their marriage they stayed with her folks for about a week, then

they set off on foot for his parents' home. Charles had two sisters who did not welcome his new wife; it wasn't long before Reedy decided that she and Charles must have a home of their own. The spirited young lady announced that she was going home to her parents until her husband found them a house of their own. In about a week he came for her and took her about three miles to a place on Williams River, which was their home until they migrated to Washington. Their first four children of their eventual family of 11 were born there in Webster County: Dewey, Eliza, Martha, and Jim.

In the meantime, Reedy's parents went to Oklahoma for a while. After their return, they heard about the homestead land available in this state. The Stiltners decided to move west with Harvey Blankenship to the Randle area. However, after Jackson Stiltner looked over the land open for homesteading, he decided that the

CHARLES AND REEDY (STILTNER) CLEVENGER were married in 1892 in West Virginia when he was 22 years old and she was 16.

SIX OF ELEVEN CHILDREN of Charles and Reedy Clevenger are: in back, Elmer, Martha, and Emery; in front, Opal, Mabel, and Dorothy.

TWIN BABIES RALPH AND RUBY CLEVENGER were born in 1917 to Charles and Reedy Clevenger. They are the youngest in their family.

timber was entirely too thick and heavy to clear; instead he bought a place at Rainey Valley near the present location of the Rainey Valley Cemetery.

The Stiltners wrote back to Charles and Reedy describing the country, which sounded good to them. In 1901, they arrived and settled near the Rainey Valley Cemetery near Reedy's parents. There were less than a handful of settlers in the area at that time. The next few years found them moving to Verndale (now Glenoma) where Elmer, Emery, Opal, and Mabel were born. In 1913, they moved to Blodgett, Oregon, for a year, but Charles could not find work close enough to their home to live with his family. Dorothy was born there before they moved to Cinabar. Next they found a place in back of Gus Thommen's about a mile south of the Glenoma School toward Rainey Creek where their last children, twins Ruby and Ralph, were born in 1917.

The Clevengers attended church that was held first about once a month in an old house in Glenoma. The Old Regular Baptist Church brought from back east was the only church around there in those days.

Charlie worked on several shingle bolt drives that started near Randle. The cold, miserable job was to break up jams where the river was full of bolts. The drives had to be during the flood stage in early spring when the Cowlitz River water came from the melting glacier and cold rainfall. It took two to three weeks to reach the shingle mill at Kelso with the highest pay being only one dollar a day.

During the years she was raising her big family, like all the pioneer women, Reedy canned from 800 to 1000 quarts of fruit, vegetables, and meat besides filling the root cellar with potatoes, apples, turnips, carrots, rutabagas, etc. from their large garden. Even during the Great Depression years the family always had enough to eat.

They obtained their sugar and flour from Chehalis during a five day round trip. They raised some wheat that they took several times a year to Cook's Grist Mill at Riffe to be ground into flour where the miller kept a share of it.

Reedy was an active member of the New Home Baptist Church in Mossyrock for many years. She remained active and in good health until shortly before her life ended in January, 1975, at the age of ninety-nine.

Chapter 11

SENA (CLEVINGER) STILTNER (MRS. GRANT), MOTHER OF TWELVE

From a tribute written by her children on her 82nd birthday

Sena (Clevinger) Stiltner vividly recalled the early spring day in 1908 when she, her young husband, small daughter, and baby boy arrived near Morton in a downpour of rain. The train stopped near West Fork where they continued into town by horse and wagon to Knittle's Boarding House.

Sena remembered the experience because this held the excitement of a whole new life for a young girl, not yet 19 years old, and her husband Grant, who were born and raised in the hills of West Virginia. When they sold their belongings, packed a trunk, and headed west, they believed that it was Indian territory, and it was months before she overcame her fear that at any time a savage might leap from the thick brush to scalp her.

All but her first two children were born in Morton; at one time she had six children enrolled in school. Although she and Grant had very little formal education, in fact Grant taught himself to read and write after he was grown, they desired a high school education for their children. In order that her family might have coats and shoes for school, Sena wore the same "Sunday-go-to-meeting" dress and coat year in and year out.

With so many children, she must have needed much help since her days from late spring until early fall were a continuous round of planting, hoeing, and working the garden, picking wild berries, and canning and preserving well over a thousand quarts of fruits and vegetables to see her ever-growing family through the winter months. Laundry was done on a washboard, boiled on the stove, and ironed with old flat irons heated on the stove. The help of having electricity in the home did not arrive until her youngest child was eight years old, but she never com-

GRANT AND SENA (CLEVINGER) STILTNER from West Virginia arrived in Morton in 1908 with the first two of their ten children, which were reared in Morton.

plained. Nor did she complain when three sons went away to war or when she lost two young sons and her husband.

Sena's love for her neighbors was often demonstrated. The bounties of her garden were garnered as well as the milk from her cow were given to one of the children to take and share with the less fortunate. If anyone, child or adult, was in the home at mealtime, he or she was urged to eat with the family. Knowing Sena was

TEN OF THE CHILDREN OF GRANT AND SENA STILTNER are in front: Mary Lee, Virginia, father Grant, mother Sena, Ann, and Jean. In back: Ron, Forrest, Carmen, Maybelle, Cliff, and Jess.

a good cook and there was plenty of food, the invitation was never refused.

Sena was content to live quietly at home. Bill Fairhart once said to her, "I always know when it's Christmas. That's when you come to town." He was right, she made her annual shopping trip to purchase gifts for her six sons and six daughters, who never gave her more trouble than could be taken care of by a few lashes with a switch. That was the only time the family heard her complain.

On her 82nd birthday her children placed this article in the Morton Journal in which they concluded that she was a remarkable woman; although poor in worldly goods, she gave them a rich heritage of love and closeness that did not come by accident. They wrote, "She has given us this and all the money in the world cannot buy the happiness her life has made possible."

Signed,
Cliff, Jess, Forrest and Ron Stiltner
Virginia Wheeler, Anna Best, Maybelle
Ashby, Mary Lee Talbott, Carmen
Ceccanti and Jean Longmire

Chapter 12

SHADE COMBS
A BOY IN EARLY DAY MORTON

It was a long and tiresome trip from Buchanan County, Virginia, for the E. C. Combs family. During the four days and five nights on the train, they had to care for and feed eight children. They didn't have much money to buy food, and their lunch basket was about empty when they pulled into Chehalis early on Thursday, April 4, 1907.

Shade Combs, who was interviewed for this article, was then just past ten years old (born August 24, 1896), his older brother Edgar was 13, Walter was almost 12, the other children were between them and the youngest, Riley, who was just 19 months old.

After their arrival in Chehalis, their father E. C. started looking for a hack or large buggy to transport the family to Riffe, a little town east of Mossyrock that was inundated by Riffe Lake when Mossyrock Dam was built. Although it was raining, he had to settle for a three-seated hack with no top which he rented from a livery stable for $15.00. When they got to Salkum at 2 p.m., the children were starved. A Fuller family fed them, then they went on to Winston Creek where they spent the night with the George Fuller family. The next day the hack broke down at Mossyrock, delaying them for two days before resuming their trip.

From Riffe they started out on foot up the trail to Highland Valley just west of Morton. Their destination was the home of the Joe Dotsons, their mother's brother; also there were several other relatives who lived in the area. The Combs bought 80 acres with a log cabin from Sherd Toller, property located between Dotson and Emery Tiller (the Tillers were cousins). "They had heard fabulous tales about the West," Shade said of his parents.

Settlers already in Highland Valley included the Frank Shorts, the James Rockwoods, the George Woods, the Esteps, the Ed Chapmans, and a bachelor Bob Chapman, in addition to the Dotsons. Along the wagon road to Morton were the George Chapmans, bachelor Fred Mienars, the Elbert Coopers (the parents of Gladys, who became Shade's wife), Billie Sherman, the Sheltons, the Rosses, the Crumbs, and the Stouts.

Frank Short went to Chehalis with his team and wagon to get the baggage, boxes and trunks, but no furniture, that had been shipped by rail from Virginia. To reach Chehalis he had to go first to Morton, then down the Bremer road to the Harmony road, since there was nothing but a trail between Highland Valley and Riffe. Even the primitive roads west of Mossyrock were no more than wide trails with deep ruts and mud during all the rainy season.

Early in 1907, as Shade remembered, "Our first spring there was rather slim pickings for us with a large family and no stored or canned food put up, although Dad had shipped a rather large box of cured pork from Virginia that came in mighty handy. We picked fresh greens in the woods. I went to Shorts and got a sackful of rhubarb which was delicious. We bought the best of apples from George Wood for 25 cents per bushel."

Combs, Dotson, and the Chapmans cut cedar shingle bolts during the winter of 1907-8 off the Dotson place. Jim Compton loaded the bolts on a sled then dumped them into a chute that ended in a pond formed by a splash dam on Highland Creek. All winter Dotson was in and out of the "snow" water. Shade said, "He didn't do nothing but hard work," and that was drudgery. The job "broke his health" with the result that he was back and forth to a Tacoma hospital before he finally died young in 1916.

The first school was built of split cedar boards located on the top of the hill between Highland Valley and Riffe, three-fourths of a mile from the Combs' home. Shade's father was a clerk on the

THE TACOMA EASTERN TRAIN first reached Morton in July 1910, which called for celebration. The railroad opened a way to market the abundant trees in the area which set the stage for growth of the town.

school board when in 1911 another school was built in the valley.

The first school teacher the Combs children had in 1907-8 was Tom Osborne, a young man from the Osborne family of Riffe, who was just beginning to teach. The next term, Nettie V. Wage taught Highland Valley school; she was old enough to be classed as an old maid, but later she married John Linder. He was a homesteader on Section 10 located above and back of Cottler's Rock, which during the 1930's came to be called Peterman Hill.

DR. HARRY FEAGLES, one of Morton's first doctors, was a good friend and hero to Shade Combs. Feagles' "crack team" had been purchased from Comb's father.

Their next teacher was Olive Session, a young lady who also married a homesteader from Section 10, John M. Jones. The next three years Alex Justice taught; he was from the family who lived between Highland Valley and Riffe. Another teacher was Nancy Hudson who married a Peregrine. Because Shade was nearing the end of his schooling then and was one of the older boys, he assisted the teacher. She boarded with the George Wood family as the practice for teachers was in those days.

Shade and his brother Walter once went to Riffe to pick up an old second-hand mowing machine. They loaded it in a wagon, drove up the Cowlitz River through Nesika, came through Fern Gap, back along the hill by Cottler's Rock, and up to their home in Highland Valley. They traveled 20 to 22 miles to come within three miles of where they started.

In the summer of 1909, 13 year old Shade helped survey the wagon road from Highland Valley to the ferry at Riffe. His job was to cut brush so that the County Surveyor could lay out the roadway. The road, just barely wide enough for a wagon, was finally opened during the summer of 1911.

Shade, almost 14, worked for the railroad construction gang when the railroad line was being brought into Morton. The camp was located where the Tubafor Mill is now. He worked in the cookhouse tent where one day he was severely burned. He received extensive treatment by the doctor that was here before the well-known Dr. Harry Feagles. When he was recovered from the burns, he worked for a while on the railroad grade that went by the Knittle homestead just east of Morton.

There was a horse and buggy mail route through Highland Valley that was started soon after the wagon road was opened; it ran from Nesika to Morton. Where the road crossed the Cowlitz River at Riffe, there were a ferry and a swinging foot bridge until the automobile bridge was opened in 1918. Shade did not attend the Riffe Bridge dedication, but he remembered it was arranged by the dedication committee chairman Frank McMahon. During this time Shade was helping build a sawmill at the top of Lake Creek Hill. Those days a mill was constructed in the woods, then when the area was logged off, the mill was moved to another location which was frequently every year or year-and-a-half.

The ferry at Riffe was the scene of a tragedy in 1915. Shade and his brother Alfred talked to the Bergen family as they went by on their way to the Catholic Church at Harmony. Within an hour someone in the family picked up the telephone when it rang on the farmer's line that the early settlers had constructed, and they heard the word that several of the family had drowned. Anna Bergen, Mrs. Louise Herselman, and three Bergen children drowned when the ferry swung out from shore as their horses and wagon were driving onto it.

Later in 1915 a horse stepped on Shade's eight year old brother Frank, cutting him from behind his ear to his chin. Shade and a brother had just finished plowing and watering the horse in the creek near the house; Shade was throwing hay down from the haymow when he heard a terrible scream. He rushed to the house where he saw Frank lying across his mother's lap. One quick look and he ran to get his "little old cayuse" which fortunately was down in the swamp where he could catch it. At a gallup he headed for George Stout's where he could call the doctor, because the Combs' telephone line was down.

By this time Dr. Feagles had a Model T Ford in which he and his nurse Anna Mulligan came quickly. The doctor put the boy on the kitchen table to sew up the severe cut. It was only a week later that Shade took his brother to have the stitches removed; Frank missed only seven or eight days of school. For the doctor's trip out to

the Combs', his services, and his nurse he charged only $15.00.

Before Dr. Feagles got his first car, he had a high-spirited team which it was said "went out and got there." He had bought the beautiful bay horses from E. C., Shade's father, for $35.00 each. Fourteen-year-old Shade drove the team to Morton where he showed them off by dodging stumps in the city streets.

After the doctor and Shade became good friends, Feagles often entertained Shade with stories of his adventures in Alaska where he had been before coming to Morton. He told of having a sway-backed horse without enough hay to feed it through the winter. Because it was nice and fat, he had it butchered and cured for his winter meat.

One time Dr. Feagles had a patient with a ruptured appendix, a Mayfield boy who was too sick to take to the hospital in Chehalis. Feagles operated on the kitchen table with light from the carbide lamps off his buggy. Assisted by the boy's mother, he saved the boy's life. Later Shade worked at a camp at Lindberg with the boy, who was working to pay the doctor bill.

According to Shade, Feagles was fascinated with Ford cars and he obtained an agency to sell them, which proved to be a financial mistake. Because of other money troubles and the fact other doctors were coming to the area, Feagles eventually moved to Chehalis. Shade said that all together Feagles was "quite a guy."

For the four years before the railroad reached Morton in July, 1910, the tracks ended on the side of the hill between the East and West Fork of the Tilton River. The station was called Glenavon where there was a small hotel and a railroad car for the depot agent to live in. Bart Bergen met the train each day with his team and hack to pick up the Morton mail and any passengers. Shade was there with his father when fat hogs were loaded on railroad cars to be shipped to Tacoma and Seattle. They had been driven from the vicinity of Riffe and Nesika over the trail through Highland Valley to Glenavon.

Originally the railroad was to bypass Morton; it had been surveyed to go to Randle, but a combination of the financial panic of 1907 and a route impractical to follow stopped construction. In 1909, when building the railroad resumed, they dropped back several miles to what was known as the Tilton Spur, then they followed the

West Fork River down to Morton.

When Shade was still a boy, he met the train in Morton when a road show arrived. After he helped carry their luggage uptown, he got a free ticket to their show which drew a crowd, since entertainment from out of town was rare. There was a black man in the cast; Shade was fascinated with the dark skin he had never seen before. They ran a contest for "Queen of the Town", at a penny a vote. "Anything to get money," Shade remarked.

"I had my nose stuck in everything that was going on," Shade said of his youth. One time he took advantage of a free meal when a hotel and saloon were opened. When this state and Oregon went dry (Prohibition) on December 31, 1919, the saloon closed its doors. "I saw it opened and I saw it closed," Shade recalled.

On one of his last visits to Morton, Shade was talking to Bill Gillispie about the time in early 1918 that Bill was on Grant Stiltner's bus (one of the first school buses), when the school children saw Shade's father suffer an accident. Combs was loading a railroad car with "side cut lumber", which as surplus in the local mills was being shipped to California. When the bus came by with the side curtains "flapping like a crow", Combs' horses bolted. When he jumped off the wagon to hold the team, he broke his leg. Shade said, "Some school bus!"

Shade and Gladys Cooper were married in 1918. They moved to National in 1920, came back to Morton in 1923, left again in 1926. Then after going back and forth to California, they finally settled there.

Shade concluded, "I had the pleasure of seeing Morton hacked out of bushes, trees, and stumps from 1907 on." Although he moved from this vicinity years ago, he clearly re-called Morton's early days and enjoyed "remembering when."

Chapter 13

CLARENCE ROSS, NOT A FARMER

Clarence Ross reached Highland Valley west of Morton at three or four years of age by riding from Chehalis in the pannier of a pack saddle. He was balanced on the pack horse by a sack of flour on this the last leg of the trip from the Midwest.

Clarence was brought by his adoptive parents Mr. and Mrs. Leander Ross from northern Michigan, because his birth father, who pioneered here, wanted him back. Mrs. Ross was his aunt as well as adopted mother.

The elder Ross couple settled on land that they expected to homestead, but they found it belonged to Northern Pacific Railroad from whom they bought it. Their property included what was later the Everett Rich farm, but their house was across the valley near where Highway 12 crosses the place. Later part of the place was sold to a Justice.

Their first home in Highland Valley was a little cabin with a roof of split cedar boards that was barely high enough to stand up in, but it wasn't long before they built another larger cabin.

Leander Ross was a veteran of the Mexican War, but he was so young at the time that he went as a flag bearer. Ross came from English nobility, but did not have a title because he was descended from a younger son. Only the oldest son inherited the title.

Leander was a skillful cabinet maker. The family has a beautiful large chest-of-drawers made of cedar that has four large drawers and two small ones with hand-carved wooden pulls that show his artistry.

Clarence Ross's real last name was Crothers and his parents named him James Clarence, but his adoptive parents changed it to Clarence James. An early Morton resident H. S. Crothers was his uncle who was the second president of Morton State Bank.

The first school in Morton had not been in existence for long when Clarence attended in 1894.

As a young man, Clarence was an expert at handling guns; he and Edward Dunaway, who lived near Davis Lake, often had shooting contests that proved they were evenly matched.

Clarence's daughter, Melba Ross Christian fondly remembered her father was a "whiz" at figures and he spoke four languages: English, French, German, and an Indian dialect. He loved to teach Indian lore which gave children an appreciation of the outdoors. Melba loved to teach, also; she taught school at Glenoma for many years.

Clarence had an ambition to be a medical doctor and he was working toward that goal when he attended high school in Chehalis, but he was called home to care for his parents.

He developed skill in photography, becoming sort of the official photographer in Morton. However, he was disturbed at being frequently called to photograph deceased people in a casket instead of being asked to take pictures of them while they were living. Consequently, he dropped out of the business, but his name can be found on old photos of Morton.

In 1911, Clarence married Donna Daisy Roberts, who following two of her brothers who came here first, came with her parents from West Virginia. Their father Jake Roberts had a pair of mules that had a reputation as a "crack" team.

Roberts specialized in buying old rundown farms, fixing them up, then selling them. He also took contracts to build bridges. The Roberts, who moved from Morton where for a time Mrs. Roberts ran a boarding house, finally settled in Rainey Valley east of Glenoma.

For quite a few years the Morton Modern Woodmen of America (M. W. A.) had a town band; Clarence not only played the coronet in the band, but also led the musical group. After his marriage, he and his wife played at dances with Clarence on the fiddle and Donna on the

CLARENCE ROSS, third from left, lead the Modern Woodmen of America band and played in it. On the far right is one time mayor of Morton Thomas Hopgood. Fifth from right is Dwight Chapman while George Engle is seated.

MR. AND MRS. LEANDER W. ROSS, who settled in Highland Valley, are shown with his brother Leonard. Mrs. Ross was Clarence Ross's aunt who adopted and reared him.

organ. One time when they walked to Cinebar and played for a dance there, a collection was taken that amounted to 25 cents.

Melba said her earliest memories were of being put to bed on one of the dance hall benches. The Wyatt family had a large home in the upper end of Highland Valley that had a second floor which was used for dances. Melba remembered being amused at one couple who danced with both arms stuck straight out from their sides.

Clarence ran the first planer in Miles Tower's sawmill. Later he went to work for Northern Pacific Railroad; he always said he was not a farmer. After the railroad job he went to work for Weyerhaeuser as a timber cruiser, eventually advancing to a vice-president in charge of reforestation. When planning for future forests was a concept that was just beginning, Clarence was a pioneer in the practice of leaving a few trees on hilltops to replenish the forests.

Melba recalled riding in the first school bus in Highland Valley, a truck with benches on each side and rolldown sides of canvas, driven by George Stout. She also remembered being at the dedication of both the Riffe Bridge and the Bremer Bridge. At the latter, there was a contest for the young men to climb a greased pole to reach the flag at the top and also there was a race to catch a greased pig.

Melba told of the time when she was quite small she went with her mother to bring in their cows while she waited at the bottom of a hill as her mother hunted the hillside. When it took a long time to find the cattle, Melba remembered how frightened she was before her mother came into sight.

Although the family moved to Tacoma when Melba was about seven years old, they visited here regularly, keeping close contact with Morton people. Eventually her Eastern Lewis County roots drew her back, so that she spent most of her adult life in the Glenoma area.

Clarence died young of hardening of the arteries and high blood pressure after a number of years of ill health.

Melba remembered visiting the Southwest Washington Fair in Chehalis with her father where they watched a demonstration of a new invention—farm tractors. As far-sighted and talented as Clarence was, he was sure they would never catch on because they gave off gas fumes that would surely kill the crops.

Chapter 14

HERSCHEL WILSON, SR.
HOPS AND CEDAR BOLTS

It was an unusually cold spring day in 1916 when Herschel Wilson, Sr., and the rest of the crew of men driving shingle bolts down the Cispus River were thoroughly chilled; it was time to take their lunch break. They spent the morning in the icy river guiding the chunks of cedar destined for a shingle mill, keeping the bolts moving down the river, so that they were looking forward eagerly to a hot meal. The cook for the crew Otis "Oat" Gillispie met the men with a big pot of navy beans and biscuits, but both were as cold as the day.

Wilson was so disgusted with the offered cold meal that he quit on the spot, even though it was only the third day of that drive. He went into Randle where he got dinner at a cafe and charged it to his former employer, the Lake Creek Lumber Company. The owner had a mill at the mouth of Rainey Creek in Glenoma as well as the mill at the mouth of Lake Creek on the west edge of Morton.

Wilson was born in Harmony, but his family moved to Morton when he was one year old. His father Francis Marion Wilson was the postmaster of Morton from April 15, 1896, to September 27, 1898, when the post office was located just west of the Tilton River Bridge. The senior Wilson gave up the postmaster's job when the family moved to Olympia. They later moved to Oregon.

Back in Washington about 1912, Herschel Wilson worked in the hop fields at Harmony, bailing the hops after they were picked by families from Mossyrock, Silver Creek, and Cinebar. The hops, used in brewing beer, were sold in Chehalis. The early settlers of these nearby communities depended on earning enough cash during the harvest season in early September to get in their winter supplies of sugar, flour, and coffee (which came in the form of roasted green beans).

The hops were grown on twelve-foot poles which were let down at about a 45 degree angle, enabling the pickers to sit on a box or barrel as they filled huge boxes that held 30 bushels. They received $1.00 per box; good pickers could fill two boxes in a day's picking. All the children over the age of toddlers picked alongside their parents.

J. M. Dunn, an early settler who had a hop yard at Harmony, donated an acre of land for the cemetery that bears his name; it lies just east of the Mossyrock Bridge on Highway 12.

Wilson came back to Morton about 1913 when he got a job driving shingle bolts to the Peasely and Francis Mill. The previously mentioned drive in 1916 was one of the last shingle bolt drives in this area.

One year Wilson worked for Ernest Cooper in Bremer, an area west of Morton on Highway 508, sledding shingle bolts out of the forest. They used a 16-foot-long sled that held two cords of cedar pulled by a team of horses on a skid road which was made with poles eight to ten inches in diameter laid across the road about four or five feet apart. The sled was slid on the skid road to the top of a chute made of logs. Wilson's job was to keep the chute clear, so that the cedar bolts would keep moving in the two-block long chute that stretched from the hillside to the Tilton River just east of the Bremer Bridge.

Wilson lived in Morton continuously from 1916 on, except for one year in the service during World War I. In 1917, he married Mathilde Hugh and they had two sons, Herschel, Jr., and Nestor.

Another job that Wilson held was for Charlie Thompson's mill that was located above the Crumb place in Highland Valley; a partner in the mill was Charlie Waste, the father of Milton Waste who was a long time postmaster in Morton. From the mill there was a flume from the hill down to the flat east of the mouth of Lake Creek. Cut lumber was sent down the flume, then Wilson loaded it on a wagon and hauled it to the Tacoma Eastern Railroad terminus at the Morton Depot.

Francis and Broadbent later had a mill in the same location as the Lake Creek Lumber Company where the creek runs into the Tilton River. Broadbent had a dynamo run by a steam engine to operate the mill. Later he built a dam on the Tilton at the south end of the Chapman Road, and the dynamo there furnished the first electricity to Morton townspeople at a cost of $5.00 a month just for lights, as Wilson remembered.

Broadbent built a mill where Cowlitz Stud Mill is now located just north of Morton, later selling out to a local man who bought timber at

Ladd, a little mining town by a coal mine up in the hills west of Mineral. According to Wilson, the man did poorly on an operation with too much overhead, although he was a good businessman and prospered in later ventures, especially in the insurance business.

Until 1927 Wilson worked in the woods, but in that year he was crushed by a falling tree. His back was broken in five places. He was taken by a hearse that was used as an ambulance driven by Jess Crips to the hospital for a long stay. He was never able to go back to work in the woods, but he was able to work on the State Highway crew and help his sons in a service station until his retirement.

THE HARVEST OF HOPS grown in Harmony brought whole families to earn enough cash for winter supplies. Hops grew on the 12 foot poles strung with twine shown in the foreground. Herschel Wilson worked there in 1912.

Chapter 15

GEORGE ENGLE
HIGHLAND VALLEY PIONEER

When George and Mary Engle homesteaded in Highland Valley in 1890, they had to burn thousands of dollars worth of cedar to clear space enough for a house and garden. For their first several years they had to continue burning cedar until a market developed for shingle bolts. Wrenching cleared land out of the heavy forests challenged the toughest pioneers; George Engle, a big heavy man, was well equipped for the job.

George Washington Engle was born on the Fourth of July, 1857, hence the patriotic name. Mary Mienars, his wife, was born in 1860. Born in Nokomis, Illinois, George had a sister Alice who was several years younger than he. Also born in Nokomis, Mary was the only daughter in a family of seven sons. In those days it was believed that a girl did not need an education; the result was that Mary had only about three months of schooling; although she did learn to read, she could not write. One thing that interfered with her school attendance was that her older brothers were married and called on her frequently to help with their families; also her mother needed her assistance.

The Mienars with their eight children lived in a little sod house with a loft where the youngsters slept. They were noted for having the finest barn in the countryside. When asked why the barn was a much better building than their house, Mary's mother replied that their stock provided their income, while people could live anywhere without conveniences.

After George and Mary's marriage in 1880, they lived in St. Louis, Missouri, for ten years. Mary's brother George Mienars had been living in Morton, Washington Territory. On a trip back to St. Louis he urged the Engles to follow him to the land that could be acquired just for living on it and doing a certain amount of improvement each year. According to Engle's daughter-in-law Frances, the railroads were offering free passage

GEORGE AND MARY (MIENARS) ENGLE were married in 1880. Ten years later they homesteaded in Highland Valley.

for families moving west, hauling them and all their household goods for no charge as an inducement to settle the western states. Even for those who paid their railroad fares, the prices were low.

The Engles decided to take advantage of the offer. When they arrived in Chehalis, there was not yet a wagon road to Highland Valley, just trails from Mossyrock or from Cinebar. They chose a homestead on the north side of the valley, and they became some of the first settlers there. After developing the homestead, Engle received his patent (deed) for the property on November 18, 1907.

"Mary just believed in working," Frances answered when asked what Mary did. Engles' home was a hospitable place with people stopping by to stay overnight and having a meal; they knew they would get good food, because Mary was a wonderful cook all agreed. Their neighbors enjoyed visiting and eating with them, too. Mary did lots of embroidery and hand work in her leisure time, Frances said.

When George, a very heavy man, was 68 years old, he fell out of a tree in his orchard while he was doing the spring pruning. He was taken to the little hospital in Eatonville with a broken leg

and other injuries. In 1925, the hospital consisted of a few rooms over the drug store. The doctor set George's leg and put a cast on it, but within a few weeks he developed blood poisoning and he died. Mary kept the farm for four years, then sold out and moved into Morton.

At this time, Engle's son Bernard had finished a hitch in the Navy and he was working in the oil fields in Terlinga, California, where he met Frances. They were married the day after Christmas, 1930. Mary was vacationing in Long Beach with some friends. Since she was ready to come home, Bernard and Frances decided to bring her home. The Depression was in full swing. Frances said, "Instead of lines of men lining up to go to work, it was lining up for soup kitchens." Orange orchards were being torn down, giving men a few days work, but there was not any steady work. Bernard decided to come back to Morton, thinking there would be work here, but there wasn't.

They stayed with Mary for a month; then they moved to Packwood. "We had a 1926 Ford with little side lights and all fixed up with fancy trimming on it," Frances said. After they were living in Packwood, Bernard traded the car for ten acres of property across from the Packwood

THE MODERN WOODMEN OF AMERICA had a band in Morton for quite a few years. George Engle is on the right end of the front row. Pioneer merchant Thomas Hopgood is next to Engle. His brother-in-law Fred Mienars is second from left.

ENGLE'S HOMESTEAD on the north side of Highland Valley was one of the first there. After "proving up" on the land, they received their patent (deed) in 1907, the reward for 17 years of hard work.

Lumber Company. Frances remarked, "We had a lot of old cars, so we didn't need the car, anyway." They also owned the acre and a half where the mill is now which they traded with the Kerr Brothers for ten thousand feet of lumber to build a house.

Later Frances and Bernard moved to Morton, and they spent the remainder of their lives here.

Concluding the interview, Frances remarked, "George and Mary Engles came west in 1890 and it was Mr. Engle that cleared land and built the farm, built up his cattle herd and farmed until 1925, when he died." She emphasized that she hoped this account will help people remember our pioneers, many of whom led similar lives developing this country.

Chapter 16

ETHEL (COSTON) THOMMEN
and the W. B. COSTON FAMILY

When Ethel (Coston) Thommen started to school in the log school house where Backstrom Park is now, she and her older sisters and older brother walked from their home at the foot of Peterman Hill. The family lived for five years in the pioneer Pius Cottler's original homestead house located on the knoll across Highway 12 from the junction with Highway 7.

Until the 1930's when the Peterman Logging Company logged the hill south of the town of Morton, the hill was called Cottler's Rock. Before the Costons rented the homestead house, Cottler had moved to the two-story house on First and Division Streets, a house he built and that is still lived in.

To go to school the Coston children had to walk down a trail to the cemetery, cross a swamp and Lake Creek, then follow the main road into town (now Seventh Street). Before 1912, Lake Creek was located further north that it has been since it was rechanneled to drain the swampy area around Davis Lake.

The Coston family came from Texas; William Berry Coston was born in Paris, Texas, on October 30, 1877, and in 1897 he married Mattie Modena Rea, who was born February 4, 1879, in Alabama. Their first two children were Leola, who was born in Texas on November 17, 1898, and William Thomas "Tom" on November 19, 1902. Anna was born April 29, 1904, in Oklahoma when it was still the Choctaw Nation. They also lost two infant boys.

The family next moved to Washington in 1905 settling in Dryad, west of Chehalis, where Ethel was born on July 19, 1906. After they moved to Ajlune (east of Mossyrock) Carl Rea "Dick" was born May 22, 1908, and Lois on November 6, 1909.

Their final move was to Morton in 1910 where the parents lived most of the remainder of their lives. W. B., as Coston was known, died at age 70 in September, 1947, and Mattie lived to age 72, passing away in 1951.

When Morton was incorporated in 1913, W. B. served as town marshal; during that year his pay was raised from $35 a month to $60. Unexplainable today in the city council minutes for January 1922, it shows Coston was hired as marshal for $2 a month.

While living on the Cottler homestead, Coston built a large house on a big lot that took in the whole corner from alley to street on Fourth and Division, next door to the present United Methodist Church parsonage. That house burned later and another that stands today was built on the same foundation.

They had a barn on their property where Coston kept a team of horses and a milk cow and raised a sizable garden to furnish foodstuffs for the winter. Coston hired out with his team to plow fields for others, but preferred to spade his own garden by hand. He hauled lumber with his team and wagon for some time; then later he worked for Peterman Logging Company where he fired the donkey engine.

Coston was a hard worker, never idle, a good father to the six children he and his wife raised. He was noted for enjoying long hours of conversation with people.

Mattie was known as a good cook; Althea, Dick's wife, remembers outstanding meals in the Coston home and she often asked for recipes only to be told Mattie just "put things together." She always baked homemade bread on Saturdays and family members would "just happen" to visit that day.

Mattie was a devoted church worker in the Methodist Church, very active in the Ladies' Aid and lending her skill in cooking for church dinners.

In 1929, Dick took his parents to Texas where for three months they visited relatives and old

THE FOURTH OF JULY, 1914, celebration was allotted funds by the City Council for a community event. Flags flying across the street are in front of the Hotel Hilts.

friends, a highlight in their lives.

Coston's daughter Ethel spent her early life in Morton, moving to Glenoma when she married Gus Thommen in 1936. When Gus retired in 1960, they moved to Morton. Her last years were in Medford, Oregon, after Gus' death and her remarriage to Lois Coston's widower Willard Hunter.

As Ethel reminisced about her childhood, she told of going to the pioneer Gus Temple's home to play with his children, walking the horse trail that was the only connection then between the homes. She remembered trips to Chehalis by horse and buggy that took all day, then sometimes they would drive another day to Raymond to see her father's sister.

Ethel remembered Morton streets being made of puncheon (split logs) in the early days, later improved with planking; the first planks were laid on Main Street in 1915. However, much of the year the planks tended to float on the mud under them so that when a car hit them, the mud splattered all over.

She was amused at the memory of a Mrs. Buchanan's coming out of the Post Office that was in Tower's Store where the Fire Station is now. The lady stepped on the end of a puncheon log; her foot went into the mud when her galosh stuck and she stepped out of it. The children watching thought that was a big joke.

The main road by the cemetery also was puncheon; eventually many of them were broken, with the result that wagon and car wheels dropped into the mud underneath. There was a speed limit sign on the edge of town that read "12 miles an hour". One time Ethel's cousin had come to visit and as they were bumping along on the old puncheon, she remarked that the speed was limited because you would break your neck if you went any faster!

When Ethel was about 10 years old, she had an accident on a teeter-totter that whirled around. It was behind W. K. Clevinger and L. D. Childer's store (later Fairhart's) where she often played at Clevinger's home. This time her fingers got caught in the teeter-totter and some skin was stripped off. After Mrs. Clevinger put the skin back in place, it healed with no difficulty.

Coston's youngest son Dick worked in a Morton cinnabar mine after high school, later at a similar mine in Sutherlin, Oregon. While Althea Ellis was still in high school (she came to Morton in her Junior year), Dick started dating her. After going together for three years, they were married on March 20, 1932. Dick drove logging trucks for Peterman during the 1930's, then for Kosmos Timber Company for many years.

Their only child James was born in 1935. Tragically, he was killed in a logging accident when he was only 26 years old, leaving a wife and three small children.

The other Coston children all left Morton, except for Tom, who married and had three children. Leola spent most of her married life in Tacoma and had one daughter. Anna lived in Portland and had one daughter, while Lois was in Medford, Oregon, and had a son and a daughter.

Coming here in 1910, early settlers such as W. B. and Mattie Coston helped establish the town of Morton, contributing to its growth from a little village to a small city.

Chapter 17

THE PERIGO BROTHERS and LIZZIE

by Dorothy Grose

The four Perigo's: Elizabeth (Lizzie), Sam, William (Bill) and Peter who settled in Morton were from a family of eleven children born to Hiram and Harriet (Murphy) Perigo in Richland County, Wisconsin. Their ancestors came to the United States from Ireland.

Lizzie Perigo married Sam Richie and lived in Williston, North Dakota with her family. Lizzie (a widow) and her four children: Vernie, Roy, Clara, and Alice lived with Bill Perigo when they arrived in Morton. Later Lizzie had a home on the hill northeast of Morton across the road from the original Catholic Church.

Sam (a bachelor) had a farm near Tieton, northwest of Yakima, where he raised peaches, etc. Sam was quite a farmer and gardener; in later years he had a peach tree that produced fruit at the home he shared with Bill one mile west of Morton. Sam worked for Bill in his business and in the late 1930's and 1940's Sam and Bill cut and sold wood from the Otis and Margaret (Perigo) Knittle property and the Bell Brothers farm west of Morton.

Bill (a bachelor) settled in Morton on 38 acres of land just east of town across the road from the Knittle homestead. Bill and a partner had a blacksmith shop on the north side of this property and were the town blacksmiths. Bill also had an office on Main Street of Morton about where the present P. U. D. office is located. Bill owned a large bay team of horses and a big wagon with side racks; he would go to Chessers or Broadbent and Frances Mills and pick up wood and do home delivery. He also picked up freight at the depot and delivered it to stores around town. Bill was also a mason and built many chimneys around Morton. After Bill retired, he had a small blacksmith shop on the Otis Knittle farm west of Morton, and Sam and Bill had a rack in their woodshed where they sharpened saws.

The original house Bill built and shared with Lizzie and her children burned and Bill built a one room house that is the kitchen of the present house.

Peter Perigo married Annie Frawley in Wisconsin. After their marriage, they lived in Wisconsin, then moved to Williston, North Dakota where Pete's Aunt Amelia and family and sister Lizzie and family lived. They lived in the typical homestead shack. Margaret was born in 1910, after seven years of marriage.

In 1910, Annie, Pete, and Margaret traveled by team and wagon to homestead in the East Gap Section of Saskatchewan, Canada, where they lived in a "Soddee" and burned "cow chips". Later they built a homestead shack. Hiram and Peter Loren were born in Canada.

In 1920, the family left East Gap and moved to Smiley, Canada where Pete traveled for the Rawleigh Company.

In 1923, during a flood (they had to walk a log on the East Fork of the Tilton to get into Morton) Pete, Annie, and the three children arrived in Morton. They moved into a log house across from the Knittle homestead. This log house burned down in 1932 or 1933 when Alice (Knittle) Sloan and Delbert Sloan lived in it.

Because Bill was not making the required improvements on his homestead lease and was going to lose his claim on the 38 acres of property and one room house, Pete and Annie took over the lease. Pete and Annie tore down an old sawmill by the first creek on their property and built onto the kitchen and they built a barn out of the lumber and timbers. They stored the extra lumber in the top of the barn. The kitchen was not sealed and it had a wood board floor that Annie had scrubbed until the boards were

PETER PERIGO'S FAMILY about 1925-26 were Loren, Hiram, Peter, his wife Annie (Frawley), Margaret, and her future first husband Fred Adams.

smooth and white. The front room had a good board floor, but the ceiling was open (not sealed). Later they used the lumber stored in the barn to seal the ceilings of the kitchen and front room. Annie sold three cows for $150.00. They used this money to buy boards for the kitchen floor and cupboards and for linoleum for the front room.

They put electricity in the house in 1937 from the Morton Dam just west of Morton. There was a storm that year and they were out of electricity for three months, but it didn't bother them too much as they were used to that.

A creek that starts on the Perigo property was dammed by the town of Morton. It was three feet deep and by gravity was fed to a wooden tower which supplied water to the town of Morton. The present tower is located approximately at the same location.

Pete worked in the mills, drove a tie truck and he was a mill fireman and watchman until he retired.

Annie tended a big garden, canned, milked the cows, and had her orchard and berries.

Margaret married Fred Adams from Mineral and they had one son George. After their divorce, Pete and Annie legally adopted George.

Margaret married Otis Knittle and had four children: Alfred, Dorothy (Knittle) Grose, Irene (Knittle) Dean, and Melvin. Margaret and Otis celebrated their 50th Wedding Anniversary before Margaret's death.

Hiram married Birdie Ann Ulsh and had two sons: Michael and Donald.

Loren married, but never had any children.

George married Doris Denend. She had a son Terry by a previous marriage. Doris and George had one daughter Jennie Lee.

George married Mary Lou Romaine. They had two sons: George and Donald.

Lizzie (Perigo) Richie, Sam, Bill, Pete, Annie (Frawley) Perigo, Margaret (Perigo) (Adams) Knittle, Otis Knittle, Hiram, Loren and George are all buried in the Morton Cemetery.

Chapter 18

JAMES M. COMPTON
FARMER and MILL OWNER

by Ed Compton

James M. Compton, born 1886, with his new bride Celina Tiller left Buchanan County, Virginia in 1907 to come west to make their first home. They traveled by train to Chehalis, where they were met by cousin Emmett Combs with a team and wagon for the last of the journey to Highland Valley. His first cabin was built with hand split cedar and it was here their first child Hazel (Leyman) was born.

Soon after Compton's arrival in Lewis County, his desire to explore took him and Elbert and Ivan Tiller, brothers-in-law, on foot through the White Pass Trail to Yakima and then on to the Columbia River.

Some of Compton's early jobs were working for Broadbent rafting shingle bolts down the Cowlitz River. One time he was employed in Lindberg which required a walk of nine miles each way every day. Later he hauled lumber to Morton from Lindberg with his team and wagon; this meant he left home at 4 a.m. returning at 9 p.m.

Before long a deal was made with Frank Short to slash a 40 acre piece of land in exchange for a 40 acre place for his own. This land had a solid stand of green timber that he fell with an axe. The story is told of a circuit rider that came through and said he had been walking 15 feet above the ground on slashed timber.

The timber was burned and fields cleared for pasture, a barn was built for cattle and horses, a garden planted, and fruit trees were brought from Chehalis on horseback — thus establishing their first farm. The home built on the farm was made with hand hewn rafters and foundation, some of which can still be seen on the location. Part of the interior lumber was left over from the building of the Highland Valley School.

It was here the following were born: Bill, Julia (Clevinger), Ellis, Ruth (she died of appendicitis when five years old), and Ed.

Compton later obtained a 140 acre farm in Highland Valley from Elbert Cooper and Fred Mienars, where the youngest child Virgil was born. Virgil later farmed this land until 1968.

Since the hay was cut by hand, it was a great day of excitement when the mail-ordered, horse-drawn mower arrived in many pieces to be assembled.

His wife died at the early age of 33 leaving him the family to raise.

At one time a dairy was established on the farm and they furnished bottled milk door-to-door in Morton. It was on this 140 acres that Jim Compton built his first of many sawmills. He sawed many sets of timber on the hills near Morton. He was in the lumber business until his death in 1947 at 61 years of age. His love for the farm followed him through his life for he was never without a few cows to milk.

THIS SPLASH DAM was one of three on Highland Creek. It was built in 1907 to hold cedar shingle bolts until high water when they were floated down to the Tilton River on their way to shingle mills in Kelso.

SOME HIGHLAND VALLEY MEN who drove shingle bolts down the rivers called themselves the "Rutabaga Gang." The long poles were used to work bolts off gravel bars and out of log jams.

Chapter 19

Foreword to
HENRY CLAY TEMPLE'S DIARY

January 1, 1866

This day I propose to keep a diary for the year, with a description of the weather, such work as I may perform and such thoughts as I may think proper.

I was born September 18th, 1833, near Macomb, McDonough County, Illinois. When two or three years old my parents moved to Henry County, Iowa. In 1843 or 1844, we moved to Wapello County. In the spring of 1849 my father got the California fever and crossed the plains but being sick, he did not stay long in the gold fields but started home in December and took passage on a sail vessel. After a long passage he landed in New Orleans. He came by the Isthmus of Panama. Soon after getting in New Orleans he took something like the cholera and died.

I was left with a mother, five brothers and two sisters. One brother died sometime in the year of 1850, one died in the year of . . . . ? In the spring of 1851, I left home and went to Marion County, to the town of Pella and set in with a 'Dutch Uncle' to learn the blacksmith trade. Being like most boys I soon got tired of that and went home.

In the spring of 1852 I started for Oregon. My older brother came the same season. I did not see

ONE OF THE FIRST FAMILIES to homestead in Davis Lake Valley were the Temples, who arrived in 1883. In back are the four sons: Hugh, Golden, Gus, and Harry. In front are: mother Elizabeth Connelly Temple, daughter Grace Buchanan, father Henry Clay Temple, and Mart Broadbent. Lillie Mae, another daughter, is not pictured.

him on the road until I got to the Cascades. I came with a man from Des Moines by the name of Allen, an old 'bach' and he had his mother and two sisters with him. The sisters were large fine looking girls, one of them took a man before she got through. (The man had lost his first wife on the road). The other was thought to be in love with me but I could not see the point.

After some ups and downs but nothing desperate, I got to Portland, Oregon, October 10th, 1852 and looked at the town a day or two. There was a farmer that wanted a hand so I went to work for him. His name was George Ritridge, a Yankee and he liked to boast of it. He was a sort of a dairyman and kept some cows. I took the milk to town, it was not all milk but one fourth water. I stopped there until April. Having heard what a great place Puget Sound was, I thought that was the place for me, so a man by the name of John Smith and I started. Took passage on the steamer Vashon for Monticello, then we footed it to Steilacoom. After looking around for a few days we went to work for a Company of men by the names of Campbell, Guile and Berry. Was to get $65.00 per month. Campbell became paymaster for which I never got all my pay. Campbell took a squaw to live with and he became degraded below an Indian.

Sometime in October, G. D. Stratton, James Van Winkle and myself thought that getting out timbers and piles was a paying business so we came to Hood's Canal and went to work. Had worked but a few days when Stratton met with a serious accident. He and Van were chopping when Van's axe glanced and split Stratton's knee cap by which he lost his leg and very nearly, his life. So Stratton sold out to a man by the name of Norman Dilly. We got out a lot of square timber but found no sale for it.

Sometime in the year of 1854, my brother, William, came over and bought Dilly out. After that we got out some saw logs for a Port Gamble Company. In the spring of 1855 we loaded a vessel with spars for San Francisco.

BACK HOME 1855 - 1862

I started home (to Iowa) in June, left my part of the team with William. Landed home July 16, 1855. Spent the winter carelessly, making love with the girls until the 26th of April, 1856 when I took Elizabeth Connelly as my wife. (Known as Betty, she was Amish.) After farming for several years I started for Washington Territory.

Started April 22, 1862 and landed at Seabeck, Hood's Canal, August 22nd. Worked at Seabeck Mills for one year and then moved to Seattle, Washington Territory. Worked at Freeport mills until March 18th, 1865 when I got an appointment as carpenter, on the Skokomish Indian Reservation in Mason County, Washington Territory.

Since I have married, my wife has had six children, the first a boy, second a girl, third a boy, fourth a girl, fifth a girl, and the sixth, a boy. The first three are dead.

(This was followed by Temple's daily entries for 1866.)

Chapter 20

HENRY CLAY TEMPLE'S STORY CONTINUED...

When Henry Clay Temple wrote his 1866 diary, he and Elizabeth "Betty" already had two daughters and a son. Ella was born March 6, 1862 and Etta was born March 28, 1864.

Etta married Will Starkey and they had four children: Leona, Clarence, Myrtle, and Bernice. Etta contracted tuberculosis and died while her children were young. Starkey reared Leona and Clarence, while Etta's younger sister Lillie Mae, adopted Myrtle and Bernice.

Temple's diary was kept 20 years before his move to Morton. An entry in his diary for February 7 reads: "Last night, about one o'clock, I was called up by my wife. She was sick so I called in Mrs. Knox and Mrs. Leak and Mrs. Ford. About three o'clock my wife was delivered of a fine child, a son. The child is as smart as could be expected. As there is no woman, anyways nigh, that I can get to wait on my wife, I will have to do it myself. If Mercer's girls were here, one could find employment for two or three weeks. I was not expecting a boy, so have no name for him." (He was later named Harry.)

From the copy of the first six months of Henry Clay's diary, it is seen that he did a variety of carpenter jobs on the Skokomish Indian Reservation. He made fancy doors for cabinets, axe handles, a tool chest, a cart tongue, gates, churn, cradle, checker board, coffins for Indians as well as building a scow and mending shoes. He was paid $4.00 a day or $250 a quarter. He paid taxes on an assessment of $300 and he paid a poll tax of $2.00. One day he paid $4.88 for 13 yards of calico for his wife.

Before the family moved to the Puyallup Valley, Hugh was born on August 16, 1868 while they spent a short time in Linn County, Oregon. The Temples were among the very first families to settle in Puyallup. Henry Clay operated a hardwood mill at Maplewood Springs which is now part of the Western Washington Fair Grounds. He was active in local affairs; he served on the school board with Ezra Meeker, who arrived in Puyallup ten years after Temple.

Hugh first visited Morton in 1883 and he moved here with the family in 1886. On July 5, 1900 he married May "Mazie" Garvin. They established a home four miles north of Morton on what is now the Resort of the Mountains. They had one daughter.

The Morton Mirror for September 26, 1930 reported Hugh's death in an article as follows: "In 1915, he was elected a director of the State Bank of Morton, which position he held continuously from that time. He was Republican Chairman of Temple District practically from the time of its organization and served many years on the election board, always being one of the first to report returns of balloting. This spring when A. L. Patterson of Seattle sold his interests in the Hi-Carbon Coal Company, the board of directors honored him with election to the presidency of the company. He had always been active in business affairs and was one of the major stockholders in the Hi-Carbon mine."

During the years the Temple family lived in Puyallup, their last four children were born: Gus, Lillie Mae, Grace, and Golden.

Gus was born May 20, 1870. His first wife Tilly suffered from tuberculosis. Searching for a cure for her, they went to Arizona, but she died from the disease leaving three children. Later Gus married Zeda.

Lillie Mae was born May 29, 1874; she married first Fred Broadbent, who was a prominent mill owner and businessman in Morton. As previously mentioned, she and Fred adopted two of Etta's daughters. During her second marriage to K. A. Hendricks, she and her husband lived in Hawaii during the 1930's.

Born November 16, 1879, Grace Adela married Fred F. Buchanan on July 1, 1901. She was very active in the Morton Community Methodist Church and was president of the Morton Ladies Aid for several years, also she had been one of Morton's early school teachers. Grace and Fred had one son and four daughters, one of whom is a lifetime resident of Morton, Jessie Buchanan Sword. Grace suffered a stroke just after Christmas Day, 1938 and died a few days later.

Temple's last child, Golden was born June 11, 1881. Edna Violet Sexton, a member of a pioneer family living near Chehalis, married Gold on November 4, 1906. They had three sons: Clyde and Golden, and one who died as a baby. According to his obituary in The Morton Mirror of March 1932, "He was engaged in the sawmill business most of his active life and was always interested in public affairs, a good citizen, a splendid neighbor, and one of the most respected men in the community." During his last two years of life he suffered continuously from a painful intestinal infection, as a result he took his own life.

Three years after the birth of their last child, Henry Clay Temple filed on a homestead in the spring of 1884 which was located in Davis Lake Valley. The two older sons Harry and Hugh helped him build a log house complete with a puncheon floor from split logs hewn smooth during the fall season. Their furniture was handmade using a skill Henry C. exhibited previously. He had made a rocking chair and butter bowls that they brought on the covered wagon on their trip west when Harry was a babe in arms. His talent for woodworking was also displayed in the fancy carved doors he made.

On April 23, 1906, Henry C. was appointed Post Master at Morton, and he served until November 9, 1908. By this time he had moved into town where he had the post office in his home on the Bear Canyon Road just north of Main Street where he set aside a room for it.

He and his son-in-law Frederick Broadbent established the Davis Lake Shingle Mill. "He brought the first farm wagon and the first cooking stove into the valley loading them onto pack horses and traveling a winding trail for 18 miles. The first Fourth of July celebration was held in honor of this event. 'All' the neighbors, consisting of a man and his wife and a bachelor, were invited in and dinner with bread baked in a real oven was served," according to The Morton Mirror. He passed away on December 27, 1920 at age 87.

Henry C.'s wife Elizabeth "Betty" had died at 78 years of age on April 17, 1917 just five days before they would have celebrated their 61st anniversary.

The Morton Mirror also wrote, "He had watched this section develop from a wilderness to its present state and his memory spanned a half century of progress, so that he often remarked that despite the present day advantages over many aspects of the early pioneer's life, there was nothing in this day and age that could compare with the zest for living inherent with the people who settled this section."

Chapter 21

GUS TEMPLE'S FIRST TRIP TO DAVIS LAKE VALLEY

Written in 1935

In the spring of 1884, my father, Henry Clay Temple, filed a homestead entry on the northwest quarter of section 18, township 12, range 4 east of the Willamette Meridian. This land lay in the Davis Lake Valley. That fall in late October he, with my older brothers Harry and Hugh, came in and erected a log cabin on this land. At that time the only known access to the Davis Lake Valley was by a trail leading up the Cowlitz River from the end of a wagon road on Klickitat Prairie. This trail left the Cowlitz River near the mouth of Rainey Creek, thence up through Fern Gap leading down through the valley about two miles. Being an old Indian trail, naturally it was very crooked. There were so many logs to climb over and the crossing of the Cowlitz River was a decidedly hazardous undertaking. So those early settlers were highly desirous of finding a better and shorter route to Chehalis.

When the cabin was completed, Harry took the horses back out over the Cowlitz Trail to Chehalis, and on to our home in Puyallup. While father and Hugh, together with H. M. McCune and A. M. Green, the only other settlers in the valley, set out on foot heading westward down Lake Creek and on down to the Tilton River, then a totally unknown country. In the afternoon of the second day they came to the cabin of the first and only settler in the Tilton River Valley. His claim was about one mile east of Bear Canyon and he had a sort of a trail out across the canyon to Cinebar.

They continued their journey on to Chehalis. McCune and Green returned to their homesteads for the winter by the Cowlitz Trail and Hugh and father took the train to Puyallup. So far as I have been able to ascertain, they were the first white men to ever make the trip over the Tilton route.

Fifty years ago, on March 27, 1885, H. C. Temple, my father, and myself (Gus Temple), then a boy of 14, and a big black dog left our home in Puyallup bound for the new homestead in the Davis Lake Valley, then a part of the wilds of eastern Lewis County. Having but one pony we took turns riding — 'one walk, the other ride'. That first day we made about 35 miles and camped that night four miles south of Tenino at the 'Old Tilly' place on Grand Mound Prairie. In the days before the Northern Pacific was built to the Sound, this place was quite a famous inn or relay station for the stage coaches running between Monticello and Olympia. We slept in an old barn that first night of our journey.

March 28. Up at break of day. Cooked our own breakfast over a camp fire and soon were off on our journey again. Passed through Centerville, then a small town of four or five stores, and probably about the same number of saloons, a livery stable and a few dwellings. The name was later changed to Centralia, and in the 50 years that have elapsed, it has grown to be one of the larger town (sic) in Lewis County.

Arrived in Chehalis about noon. Chehalis, at that time the county seat, boasted of two general stores, carrying a very limited stock; a drug store which was also a post office; hotel, bank, newspaper, livery stable, and, of course, a saloon or two; also a tin shop, which carried some hardware. I remember this tin shop particularly, as father had the man there make a reflector for him. A reflector is a tin contraption used to bake bread by setting it before an open fire. We also purchased a brush hook, which came in very handy before we reached the end of our journey.

Then we went to one of the stores operated by a man named Long. Here we purchased a supply of groceries, to the limit of what our pony could carry. These consisted of flour, sugar, bacon, beans, coffee, and so forth, about 150 pounds in all. These we packed on the pony, a process that attracted very little attention in Chehalis in those days, as pack horses could be seen on the street at most any time. After the pack was on and securely tied with the packer's famous diamond hitch, we again were on our way, this time both of us walking. That night we camped at the Dilenbaugh place, four miles South of Chehalis, and had hot biscuits, baked in the new reflector, for supper.

March 29. Up at dawn, breakfast by our campfire and we were soon traveling, leading the pack horse. Four miles farther on, we left the old stage road and turned east on a road leading through the Alpha Prairie and to the Lovell place east of Cinebar Creek, where the road ended. After an uneventful day's traveling we camped at the Burnside place, three miles east of Alpha Prairie. Weather was wonderful and the roads dry and dusty. A barn furnished the shelter, but this one was minus the hay.

Friday, March 30. "Lost in the Forest." Hit the road early, as usual, and were soon at the road's end at the Lovell place. We stopped and purchased some seed potatoes and honey, which added more to the pony's burden. We then headed for the wilderness of Bear Canyon and Tilton River Valley on a so-called trail. This trail had been used very little and was hard to follow. Several times we lost our way altogether. Then there were many logs that were too large for the pony to climb over and we had to find a way around these, so naturally our progress was very slow. However, by late afternoon we arrived at the new homestead of a Frenchman by the name of Antone Leurquin. He had been there but a short while and his domicile was made by splitting out cedar boards and leaning them against a very large log. This place was a short distance below the present Bremer Bridge. There were no settlers farther up the river, so this was the "end of the trail". That night we spread our blankets under a large cedar tree on the bank of the Tilton and soon were lulled to sleep by the gentle murmur of the river.

The next morning we continued, following the trail of a cow and a calf that had been taken through a few days before by William York, first settler in the Big Bottom Country. Our course led along the side of Bald Mountain, which was so steep in places we had to do a little grading in order that the pony could pass without sliding down the side of the mountain.

We finally reached the North Fork of the Tilton, which we forded. Then we followed along up the river, often zig-zagging through vine maple thickets. Finally we came to Little Mountain, where the river ran close to its rock edges. Here we camped for the night under a large cedar, having been all day making six miles.

Sunday, April 1. We were up at the break of day, and after breakfast of biscuits and bacon, we packed our provisions on our backs up along the river where the pony could not go. Dad returned to swim the pony across and take it up past the ledges, and forded it back again. We repacked the pony and headed on the last leg of our journey, with the homestead only a few short miles away. We were nearly home.

We made faster progress as the brush was not so dense now, and soon we were to the place where he had to ford over the south side of the river, just above the mouth of Lake Creek, and there we found a trail that had been blazed and partly slashed. This trail was the work of H. M. McCune and A. M. Green, who were the first white men to winter in the Davis Lake Valley.

About two miles up the trail we were pleasantly surprised to meet these men on their way to cut more trail down the Tilton to meet the end of the road at the Lovell place. They turned back with us and we all had dinner at McCune's on his homestead — and that was some dinner, as I now remember it, as McCune was an excellent cook.

Later on we went to dad's little cabin on the homestead, where I spent my first night in Davis Lake Valley. Since that day, half a century has slipped by, and I am still living in the same Davis Lake Valley. But when I look around I see many, many changes.

Chapter 22

BREMER, WHO OR WHAT'S THAT?

A nearly forgotten gravestone with the name Adam Bremer has prompted research into the settling of the eastern Lewis County area still known as BREMER, pronounced with a long "E". The large monument inscribed "Adam Bremer, Died February 28, 1905, Aged 75 years, 10 mo. and 9 days," is found on one of Rudy Wetzel's places on the Butts Road, nine miles west of Morton.

Located in the Tilton River valley along Highway 508, Bremer once had a post office, a school, and a community hall, and it was home to around 20 families of pioneers. The first settlers came in after the area was surveyed in 1880.

The Bremer area is generally designated to extend westward from the Bergen Bridge (the second bridge over the Tilton River west of Morton) near the former Indian Hole Campground to Bear Creek Canyon. The Butts Road follows about the same route as the original Bremer Road, the main road west from Morton, but it is below the hills instead of on the sidehills. It was a puncheon road of split timbers in the swampy places, and the main sections were just a graded, often muddy, trail for many of the early years.

Adam Bremer was a brother of George Bremer, who lent their name to the valley, the community, and the mountain on the north. Both men received title to their farms in 1901: Adam with 80 acres and George with 160 acres, both in Section 22, of Township 13 North, Range 3 East, which is along the Butts Road.

As throughout the West, Northern Pacific Railroad was granted alternate sections, so that the pioneers either bought railroad land or homesteaded United States property, depending on which section they settled.

Homestead land had to be occupied and developed (proved up) in a certain number of years, then the patent (as the deeds were called from the government) was issued by the Presi-

THE GEORGE BREMER HOUSE was built by one of the first settlers on the present Butts Road. Built of split cedar, it burned in 1920 while the J. H. Butts family lived there.

dent of the United States.

Because of the impossibility of determining the time needed to prove up on their land, it can not be determined by the early property records in the County Courthouse just when the pioneers first lived on their places, only when they got either their patent or deed.

The establishment of the first homesteads in Bremer was in the 1880's, but by 1895 there still were only five married couples and four bachelors living there. The couples were: the George Bremers, the Adam Bremers, the Ed Coopers, the Albert Murrays, and the Robert Pickens.

The George Bremer family lived on the upper side of the Butts Road where there is now an unoccupied house and an old orchard, across the road from the Raintree Nursery. Adam Bremer lived about a mile west on the place J. H. Butts bought later, which went to a son, Millard Butts, and now belongs to the Thomas Blums.

George and his wife had the post office that was named after them in their home and eventually served about 20 families. The name of the Bremer Post Office was changed in later years because of confusion with Bremerton; then later Bremer became a rural route out of Morton.

The George Bremers had four children: Tom, Fred, Kate, and Lida. In 1906, Thomas, the son, bought the farm that is part of Sidney Butts' property at the east end of the Butts Road. After the elder Bremers died, the family moved away from the area.

Ed Cooper was among the first settlers, coming to the Harmony district (north of Mossyrock) in 1892 with his father, James A. Cooper, who homesteaded in Section 32, receiving his patent in 1905. Ed bought 40 acres from the railroad in an area so remote that he had to follow an Indian trail to the Tilton River; then he had to cut a trail through the woods wide enough to get his pack horse in to his chosen place.

Ed Cooper built a house, part of which is still standing as the kitchen section of an existing home, which is located just east of the Butts Road on Highway 508 and now belongs to Steven and Janet Hoddinot. Black walnut trees that were planted by the pioneer Cooper still stand.

Ed Cooper married Enoch Casto's daughter, Emma Pearl, in 1897. They had only one child, Harry, who with his wife, Katherine (Studhalter), lived in Morton for many years.

Emma Pearl, known as just "Pearl", came with her father Enoch Casto who came by covered wagon from Missouri with his wife Barbara and their five children: Pearl, Ed, Myrtle, Viola called "Vida", and Mary. They settled briefly in

BERGEN'S HOUSE was near the Bergen Bridge, the second one over the Tilton River west of Morton. Thomas Bergen is on the left and Ed Cooper on the right. The style of house was typical of the early 1900's.

Oregon, then came on to Washington. Arriving in Harmony, just at the end of the hoppicking season in September 1895, Casto set out to locate his son Ed's property over the hills in the Tilton Valley. Ed had come ahead of the rest of the family.

Enoch Casto bought 160 acres with his son-in-law Henry Randles from the railroad for $1.25 an acre in Section 21 in 1899 and more in Section 27 in 1900. He was a Civil War veteran who received a pension of $30 a month, a healthy sum in those days. He traded a rifle he didn't need for a milk cow and two heifers and built a house of split cedar boards as most of the pioneers did. Casto's home site was across the Tilton River just west of the Bremer Bridge (the third bridge west of Morton).

The Albert "Bert" Murray farm was the first place after one turns off the highway onto the Butts Road. His mother came in 1886 from Iowa as a widow with four children: Albert, Elmer, and Nellie Murray, and Charles E. "Ed" Holden, a son by a previous marriage.

Ed took his own place and was counted as one of the first bachelors in Bremer. Nellie became a public school teacher before Washington was admitted as a state. She later married Robert Pickens, thus forming one of the five first families in the area. In 1902, they bought land in Section 27 that had been railroad property.

THE PICKENS FAMILY OF BREMER were early settlers. Robert and Nellie (Murray) Pickens children were: Lillian, Loma, Beulah, Florence, and Robert.

The Murrays lived first in a little split cedar cabin on the Bremer Road and later moved to the valley where in 1908 they built a big square house located just west of the Bremer Bridge.

The last of the families of earliest settlers was the Robert Pickens, as previously mentioned.

Pickens was born into a large family in Tennessee shortly before the Civil War. As a young man he went to Texas to work for a relative, but repeated attacks of malaria prompted him to move north to Washington.

The only social life the early settlers had was an occasional house party. At one of these parties, Pickens met Nellie Murray (Albert's daughter), and they were married on May 13, 1888.

Their first home was a log cabin on a 160 acre homestead in Cinebar west of Bear Creek Canyon. Their first child, Lillian, was born there in 1889; then they moved to the Bremer valley on 160 acres bought from the railroad. The property is located below the road about midway on the Butts Road.

Pickens built a two-story home where their other children: Loma, Beulah, Florence, and Robert were born.

The bachelors in the valley in 1895 included, in addition to the afore mentioned Charles "Ed"

Holden, Antoine "Anthony" Leurquin, William "Billy" Stocking, and Samuel Ezra Conger.

Ed Holden got his patent in 1899 from the U.S. Government and Leurquin, a Frenchman, got his in 1902 in the same Section 26; then in 1900, Leurquin bought railroad land in Section 27. In 1904, Hubert Leurquin, who was probably Anthony's brother, bought both pieces of property. Hubert had three children: Emil, Evangeline, and Lucy.

William "Billy" Stocking who was distinguished by having more than the average education, homesteaded in Section 34, Township 13, Range 3 East on the land that is now the Compton's Tree Farm.

Samuel E. Conger homesteaded in Section 28 and bought from Northern Pacific in Section 21 in 1901. He was noted for having numerous cats.

When the white families came to Bremer, there were two Indian homes along the Tilton River, just downriver from the Bremer Bridge; the Louis Satanis and Jack "Jake" Castema families.

Thomas Bergen was an early homesteader, too, receiving his patent in 1899 in Section 30, Range 4 East and another 160 acres in Section 32 in 1900. Shortly after the turn of the century he deeded 6/10 of an acre to School District No. 127,

HORSE LOGGING by Millard Butts supplied timber for Butts' mill on the Dodge Road.

the Bergen School, near the bridge that was also named after him. The Bergen Bridge is the second bridge west of Morton.

The Louis Studhalters came in 1912 and lived just east of the junction with the Butts Road, on the south side of Highway 508.

They purchased 80 acres from Mrs. Studhalter's brother, Ed Kunz, later adding 120 acres. After seven years in a cedar "shack", they moved to the Dodge Road to a large home they bought from Elmer Murray, the property now owned by the Robert Whannels.

The Dodge Road, which is part of the original county road, took its name from Phineas H. Dodge who bought 160 acres from Northern Pacific in 1895.

The Butts Road acquired its name from J. H. Butts who came to Bremer in 1918 and bought extensive property that included as much as 360 acres, mostly timber land. Part of this was the George Bremer place where they lived for two years before the house burned down. The fire started in the chimney that was built of home-made bricks, and the cedar building "went up like a torch."

At the time of the fire, the children were at the empty Pickens house that Butts was renting for the hay and a garden. The children were "stomping beans"; dried beans in the pods were spread on the floor of a bedroom, and the children were shelling them by jumping on them. After the fire, they moved into the Pickens house.

One of the reasons the Butts family moved from Vashon Island was Mrs. Butts' reaction to seeing 12 and 14 year old children working full time in Seattle. She did not want that for her eight children (two more were born in Bremer). They saw an advertisement in a newspaper for the Bremer property and bought it.

Butts was a sawmill man, and he had several sawmills in the area. One sawmill was located next to Studhalters where he cut timber on Ed Holden's land; another was up a hill on the North Fork of the Tilton River and several locations on Butts Hill. The whole family worked in the garden and in the mills "as soon as we were old enough to pack a slab," Clifford Butts said.

The pioneers were concerned about the education of their children, and in the early days they built a split cedar school house between two creeks on the Butts Road near the present Sidney Butts' farm. At that time, each student had to furnish his own bench, but Harry Cooper was allowed to share one with his aunt, Vida Casto, who was a few years older. Harry went to the Bremer school only three months; then a new

ONE OF BUTTS' SAWMILLS was on Butts Hill in 1930. When an area was cut over, the mill was moved.

THE BREMER SCHOOL was about ten years old in 1916. The students were: Evangeline Leurquins, Josie Santinus (Indian girl in back), Hattie Greer, Lillian Greer, Lenora Maack, Elsie Studhalter, Nellie Reasoner, Louise Studhalter, Grace Reasoner, Cordelia Greer, and Katherine Studhalter.

building of sawed lumber was built near the Bremer Bridge and the local children went there in 1906.

The first school terms were only five months in the summer, later six months. There was very little money to pay the teachers, according to

BREMER BASEBALL TEAM included: (seated) Harry Cooper, Louie Studhalter, Vernon Randle, Billy Casto, John Sword, and Arthur Cooper. Standing were: Ed Studhalter, Charlie Thompson, Allen Casto, Jack Thompson, and Grant Randle, all sons of homesteaders.

Lillian Pickens. She wrote, "Only very 'missionary-minded' people were willing to spend their vacation on a job like that where they boarded around (with different families). As I remember, we forgot during the winter all that was learned during the summer. At the age of twelve, I could scarcely read and decided to go to Chehalis and work for my board in order to go to a real school."

Eventually Lillian and her sister Loma went on to complete college and both taught school for many years; Lillian taught in Japan for 25 years.

Bremer had no religious services until Nellie (Murray) Pickens started a Sunday School in the school house. She purchased a hand organ which was the first musical instrument in the valley, and the children learned many of the old songs. Nellie's first lesson on the organ was "Haven of Rest" and daughter Lillian said, "We kids declared we never had any 'rest' after that."

Because the Bremer School was located too far from the west section of Bremer for the children to walk, a school was started just this side of Bear Creek Canyon, near Alder Creek, that is now Burton's Tree Farm. The teacher was Anna Reasoner, whose family lived in the Albert Murray place on Butts Road; she taught her sisters and brother, the children who lived close by, and several of Fred Wilson's children.

Anna's father Ernest Reasoner carried the mail from Bremer to Alpha with his team of mules in the early days.

Other early settlers in the Bremer area were: Alexander Milligan, Jesse O. Casto, Thomas H. Greer, George Stout (before he moved to Highland Valley), Ernest Cooper, Charles S. Jackson, John G. Little (Bill Little's father), Classe Hinrich "Henry" Maack, John LeVexier, and many more. These pioneers we know nothing about except that they left their names in the County record books as homesteaders or buyers of Northern Pacific Railroad land, in the last of the 1800's and early 1900's.

Adam Bremer's gravestone that prompted this Bremer history research is an example of the pioneer custom of sometimes establishing a graveyard on private property. The monument and several unmarked graves sit among the ferns and brush now, the only reminder of how Bremer got its name.

Chapter 23

THE CITY OF MORTON'S EARLY DAYS

When it comes to the City Council of Morton, the old saying applies — "The more it changes, the more it stays the same." According to the original minutes of the council in the first year of incorporation, one of the very first ordinances dealt with the problem of dogs running loose, a familiar problem today.

The town was formally founded after sixty-three residents of Morton petitioned the county for incorporation late in 1912; the hearing was held Dec. 16, 1912, when the population was 300. The petition was signed by the following citizens residing within the boundaries: F. M. Broadbent, Mrs. Olive Jones, Jno. M. Jones, M. McEntee, Mrs. M. McEntee, L. F. Phelps, Mrs. L. F. Phelps, C. W. Winsberg, Mrs. Louise Winsberg, Dr. F. O. Wilkinson, and Dr. Harry Feagles, A. D. Estep, and J. G. Keen.

Also John Bingaman, Frank Bingaman, J. Hogan, T. Dunston, J. W. Robbins, Ella Chapman, Emil Carter, Ray Thompson, Wm. Swanston, W. Collins, Mrs. Ida Collins, Arthur Voight, A. Russell, O. S. Wingrove, W. M. Estep, S. W. Jordan, and Mrs. S. W. Jordan.

In addition, Elvin Curtit, M. C. Hopkins, Josephine Nicolai, W. W. Keen, E. J. VanKeuren, R. L. Herselman, L. F. Adkins, Chas. E. Waste, Ella M. Waste, A. E. Kerr, G. L. Kerr, L. D. Childers, J. F. Fowler, C. W. Morris, N. G. Morris, C. B. Smith, Mrs. C. Smith, W. K. Clevinger, Tina Clevinger, Frank Bergen.

Also Nils Sundstedt, P. Cottler, Mrs. P. Cottler, George Nicolai, M. W. Grinnell, Dorothy Treutle, N. D. Tower, Alice M. Tower, J. M. Bell, Mrs. J. M. Bell, E. E. Temple, Edna Temple, and D. L. Clowers.

An election was held Jan. 4, 1913, to authorize creation of a fourth class town. The next day Morton with an assessed value of $40,101 became a city, with Thomas Hopgood as Mayor.

The election officials, judge and clerks, were H. Randles, G. G. Temple, and W. A. Collins, but the council did not get around to paying

MAIN AVENUE IN MORTON was planked in 1915, the second attempt by the City Council to improve the street (it had been partially graveled). C. B. Smith's Hardware is on the corner.

them until May 3, 1913, after a bill was presented on the following letterhead:

"The Club"
Largest Pool and Billiard Hall South of Tacoma
Complete Line of Smokers Sundries
Confectionary and Fruit

The statement was acknowledged resulting in the election board being paid $4.50 each.

The first council meeting was held February 21, 1913, with Mayor T. S. Hopgood and Councilmen C. B. Smith, N. D. Tower, C. W. Winsberg, and Geo. D. Kerr. The first ordinance fixed the time and place of council meetings to be the second Tuesday of each month at a place known as Winsberg's Hall, where there now are apartments in the Lindley Building.

Ordinance 2 fixed the amount of the bond for the Town Treasurer at $1,000. Ordinance 3 dealt with misdemeanors while number 4 concerned "the Regulating and Governing of the sale and traffic in intoxicating liquors within the corporate limits of the Town of Morton." The problem of dogs was covered in the very early days with Ordinance 5 entitled "An Ordinance to Provide for the Taxing and Killing of Dogs." Sound familiar?

The liquor ordinance said in Section 1, "That the words intoxicating liquors whenever used in this ordinance shall be taken to mean and include spiritous, vineous, fermented, malt, and every kind of intoxicating liquor or liquors." The second section required a license to "sell, dispose of, give away or traffic in" intoxicating liquors, and the third section set the license fee at $1,500, a large sum in 1913 dollars.

On March 18, 1913, the dog control ordinance became law providing firstly "That no dog shall be permitted to go abroad in any of the streets, squares, alleys or public places within the Town of Morton, without a collar of leather or metal properly secured about its neck; with a number stamped upon metal or engraving thereon, the tag number to be furnished by the Town."

The remaining sections called for a $1.00 license fee for male dogs and $2.00 for females; the Town Clerk was to keep a record and inform the Town Marshal when licenses expired. If citizens of the town did not meet the requirements, "It shall be the duty of the Marshal or his deputies to seize, kill and properly bury in some suitable place, any and all dogs running at large." "Vicious or mad dogs" could be legally killed by any person, whether the dog was licensed or not and the owner fined from $5 to $20.

The second Council meeting on March 11 resulted in a committee being appointed to locate a lot for a "calaboose" (jail) and to investigate the cost of construction. In April it was reported that a lease on the C. M. & P. (Chicago, Milwaukee and Pacific Railroad) right-of-way could be secured for $10 a year. E. H. Head was given the contract to build the calaboose, the cost of which was $198.

Town Marshal J. Johansen was hired for $35 a month in March but resigned in May, then in June the wages were raised to $60 per month for W. B. Coston who was hired for the job.

Another problem encountered in the first meetings was the condition of the power lines; the solution was to hire A. J. Weeks to take care of loose wires of the Rainy Valley Electric Company; he was paid $10.60 for the job.

Shortly after that, the franchise for "electrical purposes" by A. W. Vanarsdall was revoked, and a franchise for a "Rural Telephone" was granted with the provision that "the city officials be allowed free service for city business only."

A few months later the application for "electrical purposes" was accepted from F. M. Broadbent and M. Broadbent. In the meantime, the Street and Alley Committee were to look after "electric lights for the jail and street lights and the same to be installed."

The meeting on May 13 resulted in passage of Ordinance 6, imposing a license on "theatrical performances, concerts, circuses, shows, menageries, merry-go-rounds, riding galleries, shooting galleries, lectures, peddlers, hawkers, draymen, auctioneers, bill posters, billiard, and pool tables." Apparently our founding fathers wanted to cover everything!

All of the above were to obtain a license to do business or be fined from $5 to $50. The ordinance goes on to set license fees of $1 to $5 per performance, or in the case of draymen there was a fee of $8 per year for one horse and dray or wagon, more for two outfits.

Bill posters were to pay $3 per day, $5 per week, or $12 per year. Ordinance 6 says, "Every person, firm or corporation who shall do the act or work of painting, posting, sticking, stamping, tacking, affixing, exhibiting or distributing any advertising matter, bills, circulars, posters, cards, handbills, dodgers, signs, devices or other matter used to advertise and calculated to attract the attention of the public within the town of Morton shall be deemed a bill poster, within the meaning of this Ordinance." Again our first Councilmen covered the field quite thoroughly.

In June a special meeting was called for the purpose of purchasing the first fire apparatus for the protection of the town. They voted to buy a "Chemical Engine" from Columbia Engine Works of Portland, Oregon, and decided "payment be ordered at the same meeting in a three

MORTON'S FIRST SERVICE STATION was owned by Steve Bergen, who served once as mayor. He sold Red Crown gas at this "modern" station located at the site of Roy's Motel.

to five year warrant at 6 percent interest for $602.29."

On August 28 a special motion was passed "that a 10 mill levy be made for maintenance of the City of Morton." The budget for the next year was $2,000, which included fees for a clerk and an attorney, both for $180, plus hall rent of $20. Compare this to the 1989 budget of $730,206.52.

In October 1913, the problem of street maintenance surfaced with a motion to match the Commercial Club's offer to put $50 worth of gravel on Main Street; then a year-and-a-half later, on March 1, 1915, a contract was let for grading and laying planks on Main Street. Because the first men awarded the contract for planking could not furnish a $3,000 bond, the job went to Ralph R. Wheaton for $2,675.

Another job completed about the same time was for a "walk and railing fixed between Tower's Store (now the Fire Station) and the schoolhouse" which was in the present location. This walk was for the school children to cross the gully that existed then.

The year 1914 began with the problem of a water system. A proposed franchise to J. P. Nevins was to include a wooden reservoir 16 ft. by 24 ft. to hold 50 thousand gallons, a pump with six inch "succion" (sic) and 5 inch discharge. The mains were to be circular along Main Street to Third, along Third to Division, along Division to First and along First to Main; beginning at

Third a line was to be run to Old Town with 60 pounds pressure at any hydrant. The hydrant rental was to be $3 each per month the first year, then $6 with users to install their own Corey hydrants at $45 each.

In March 1914, Dr. Harry Feagles presented a "communication regarding the epidemic of diptheria." A motion passed to have Morton Drug Company order sufficient antitoxin to administer to all the school children. Also they decided to "ascertain from P. J. Orr (school superintendent) whether the children will submit to same." Previously there had been at least two deaths from diptheria; Gertrude Casto, aged 16 years; and her sister Gracie, 13 years, who died during the winter of 1911-1912.

At the June 9, 1914, meeting the Council hired a watchman for the evening of the Fourth of July and passed a motion to "allow the Executive Committee of the Fourth of July control of the city under City Marshal during July 3, 4, and 5."

On July 14 a report was issued by the Department of the Auditor of the State covering the first one and a half years of the town's existence. The city officials were: T. S. Hopgood, Mayor; J. M. Bell, Treasurer and Clerk; J. M. Jones, Police Judge; and Dr. Harry Feagles, Health Officer.

The report begins, "The financial condition of the town is all that could be desired..... to date not one cent of interest has been paid." The report continues, "In the year and seven months the town has been incorporated they have never held an election or opened the registration books. The fall election was neglected — in fact no one thought anything about it until asked for returns from the election."

The financial report for this first period showed:

Cash account Jan. 1, 1913 nil
Jan. 1, 1914 $38.78
July 31, 1914 $834.41

Police Court "during the period covered by this examination, the police judge has tried 24 cases and remitted $191.60 in fines to the town treasurer," the Auditor reported.

Ordinance 13 was passed August 11, 1914, to "prevent Running at Large of Domestic Animals." Section 1: "That it shall be unlawful for the owner of any horse, mare, mule, colt, bull, ox, steer, sheep, goat, swine, or cow to allow the same to run at large within the town of Morton at any time."

However, Section 2 called for impounding any such animal, "except for one cow per family without a bell on ....."

This ordinance remained in effect until 1922 when cows were no longer permitted to run at large in the streets of Morton, thus our present Councilmen do have some different problems to challenge them, but some remain the same.

Chapter 24

THE BEGINNINGS of the BUSINESS COMMUNITY OF MORTON

Every community has had a beginning with a few hardy souls who pioneer an unsettled area, but a town does not develop until enterprising businessmen set up stores to provide goods the public needs. The City of Morton is no exception.

Beginning with the first homesteaders in the early 1880's, the region grew until in 1912 the residents felt the need to organize a city government. Sixty-three citizens signed a petition to incorporate, and Morton became a town in January, 1913.

The history of Morton businesses seems to be naturally divided into the pioneer years from 1880 to 1913, and the building by the early merchants from 1913 until the disastrous fire that wiped out the main business district in 1924.

The next period included constructing new fireproof buildings and expanding businesses. Since then a number of businesses have come and gone; this account is an attempt to chronicle some of the earliest ones.

The 1924 fire in the business district has historical significance in that all Morton history dates from that event; in any research about the city, reference is always made to "before" and "after" the fire.

The Hotel Hilts, located on the west side of Second Street across from the present Union station, gained notoriety as the place the fire began. During the early morning hours on July 24, 1924, fire erupted in the two-story frame building. The volunteer firemen were hampered by water pressure too low to effectively fight the blaze. To compound the problem, the fire hose attached to a hydrant near the hotel burned in two. As the firemen stood by helplessly, the fire spread rapidly until the whole downtown business district was destroyed. The damage was estimated as a loss of $250,000.

The first commercial building in Morton is generally believed to be George Hopgood's store; certainly it was the first building of any size. Before that time, the first little store and residence were established in a building made of split cedar boards in conjunction with a post office by James Kelso, the first postmaster. It was located about three-fourths of a mile west of the present Tilton River Bridge.

There were enough settlers in the area to apply for a post office in 1889. The application had to include a name for the post office and the story goes that a Mrs. Boomhauer wanted it named for her because she was the first white woman to live in the Davis Lake Valley, which was the name used for the locality.

However, the name of McKinley was submitted, but was refused by the postal department because the state already had a post office by that name. Instead, the postal service assigned the name of current President Benjamin Harrison's Vice-President, Levi P. Morton, to the new communtiy.

After six months, Kelso sold his store to Lewis F. Reed, who became postmaster for the next five years. He moved his little store to about 150 feet from the Tilton River Bridge. For the next two years, Francis M. Wilson served as postmaster from his residence located at the west end of the bridge.

George Hopgood was appointed postmaster on September 27, 1898, moving the office to his residence on his homestead on the O'Neill Road where he also had a small store. In the summer of 1903, he moved into his new large building on the southeast corner of Main and Seventh Streets, later known as Old Town.

Hopgood's new store building is the one remembered by many old-timers as the first store in Morton. The building had two stories with rooms above. Hopgood was postmaster until 1906, when another pioneer, Henry C. Temple, was appointed.

MORTON'S FIRST HOSPITAL was located where Bob's Boot Barn is now. Dr. Joseph Pine had an office and a couple of hospital beds.

THE STATE BANK OF MORTON was established in 1911 by local businessmen. The frame building was on the northwest corner of Main and Second. Rebuilt of tile blocks after the fire, it is now part of the Coast to Coast Store. The firebell tower is in back.

THE MORTON DRUG COMPANY occupied the lower floor of the Masonic Temple completed in 1914; it is still in business next door. The sign in the window says, "Tacoma Ice Cream today".

In 1909, George Hopgood's son, Thomas S., and Robert L. Herselman bought the Fred D. Reed homestead in Section 2, Range 4E, Township 12, and had it platted with streets and lots as the Town of East Morton.

When the Tacoma Eastern Railroad was completed to Morton in 1910, the business district grew in East Morton nearer the depot than were Hopgood's store and the first homes. In 1911, Pius Cottler had part of his homestead on the southwest edge of town added to East Morton, called Cottler's Addition.

In 1909, Hopgood and Herselman held a raffle for a lot on the southwest corner of Main and Second Streets where Fairhart's Store was later located. The winner, Nelson Clevinger, turned it over to his son, William K., who with his brother-in-law, L. D. Childers, built a frame building for a store and residence.

About this time, another enterprising merchant arrived in Morton from Ladd, the little coal mining town west of Mineral. Charles W. Winsberg had been postmaster and company-store keeper there after coming from the Burnett-Carbonado region. His wife worked in the cookhouse at Ladd. She was Louise Setula, who came from Vassa, Finland, to New York as a girl in her late teens. She worked there several years before starting West.

Winsberg first set up a business in a tent where the Morton Auto Parts is now located in the middle of the block on the north side of Main Street between First and Second Streets. He had a large frame building constructed in that location, operated as the Farmer's Exchange, carrying a large variety of goods, including hardware, feed, coal and briquets. In the back was a livery stable.

Winsberg conducted business there for several years, then built a store with fireproof walls on the southeast corner of Second and Main Streets. It has been known as the Lindley Building since being acquired by the dentist, Dr. Ross C. Lindley, in 1926. Lindley converted the large second story hall into apartments.

HOPGOOD'S STORE was the first building constructed for that purpose in Morton. Located at Main and Seventh streers, it stood for many years. The bandstand in the intersection has been duplicated in Backstrom Park.

THE MORTON CAFE was located in a false-front frame building typical of the era.

Winsberg's warehouse was the large frame building across the railroad tracks on the First Street that is known locally as the Western Farmer's building, now being used by B and C Recycling. He bought coal in railroad gondola carloads and sacked it in canvas bags to deliver to his customers.

In the 1924 fire the Lindley building was gutted, but because the walls were intact, the interior was rebuilt. Several businesses have occupied the space since, including George Long's and William Klat's clothing stores, and Earl's restaurant. Presently there are Family Fashions clothing and the Sewing Room in front and a florist, book store, and deli in the west side of the building.

Winsberg had a severe case of Spanish influenza during the epidemic in 1919. Before he was fully recovered, he went to the store to check on his business, suffered a relapse, and died while he was yet a young man. His widow was left with three small children: Marie, seven years old; Mike, five; and Rose, just one year old. About eight other Morton residents also died from the "flu," according to Mike Winsberg.

Escaping the devastation of the fire on Main Street were Barnum's Cafe next to Winsberg's store, and next to Barnum's was Chesser's Ford Agency. The Wheel Cafe is now located in the former Barnum's building.

George Chesser came to Morton about 1916 and ran a sawmill located on the Davis Lake Road about two miles out of town. That mill burned while Chesser was building the Chesser Lumber Mill in 1919 where the Tubafor Mill is now on the north edge of town along Highway 7.

He bought the Ford Agency from L. St. Johns of Chehalis in 1922, but he didn't sell the mill until 1928. By then most of the machinery had been sold.

Although Chesser's tile block building did not burn until years later, the plate glass window was broken from the heat of the burning stores across the street during the big fire. He sold the car agency in 1943 and retired until his son, Lewis, came home from World War II; they went into sawmilling together.

Chesser's wife, Margaret, was an independent businesswoman, operating a grocery store just north of the present Cowlitz Stud Mill office from 1939 until she sold it to Mr. and Mrs. Charles Dull about 1947. Previously, she had farmed with Lewis, raising a big garden, milking cows, and selling milk, eggs, and chickens, having as many as 5,000 laying hens at one time. Besides her son, she raised two daughters, Thelma and Georgia.

One of the early boosters of the town was M.

C. Hopkins, who established the first newspaper, the Morton Mirror. He had a heavy linotype machine and printing press shipped here by Tacoma Eastern Railroad and he installed them in a building behind L. D. Childer's store (later Fairhart's now Family Furniture). His first edition was dated June 7, 1912, thus preceding the incorporation of the town by six months.

The Mirror was published by Honeywell and then Knapp in the early years. Briefly the Lewis County American was published by Chester Kimple in the late 1930's. For 22 months Morton was without a newspaper, then the Morton Journal came out in 1945 published by Archie Watts. Editors from 1960 to 1971 were Juanita and Merlin Rosin. For the next sixteen years, The Journal was published by Jim and Mary Beth Marvin, and presently it is published by Frank De Vaul.

In 1913, Childers and Clevinger sold out to Esper M. Fairhart, a Lebanese who had begun as a traveling salesman, carrying a pack of dry goods on his back, visiting customers from his home in Tenino as far as Packwood. Within a couple of years in the dry goods store, he was joined by William M. Fairhart, his brother. Known as Billy or Uncle Bill, he added groceries to the business.

In 1920 Esper was called back to Lebanon when his father died. He and his wife took their children with them: Mamie born in Tacoma; Marcel and Madeline, who were born in Tenino; and Messina (Mike), Marguritte and Melberna, born in Morton. Three more children were born in Lebanon before Mrs. Fairhart died in 1934. After Esper died in 1943, bachelor Billy began sending for his nieces and nephews to come to the United States and work in the business with him.

In the early 1920's Fairhart had a block building constructed that was supposedly fireproof. However, when the big fire hit, the building simply crumbled. Billy went to Tacoma, his good credit obtained a load of groceries, and he was back in business within days of the fire. It wasn't long before he had another bigger building on the corner with a hotel in the second floor and eventually had several business buildings in the same block.

The Fairhart store remained in the family; it was the only establishment that continued in the same place and the same business from 1913 to 1986.

Another business on Morton's main intersection, located on the northwest corner was the State Bank of Morton. The bank was chartered in 1911 in a frame building that perished along with most of the business district in the fire of 1924.

The original subscribers of the bank were: A. Cheney, Hilda and Maren Rosten, C. A. Cook, J. M. Bell, J. F. Fowler, R. L. Herselman, Fred Scott, A. W. Wanarsdall, Pius Cottler, C. W. Winsberg, E. Edlund, and J. C. Van Anken. The original capital was $11,000.

The bank vault survived the fire, and after it cooled, Mike Winsberg was there when the vault was opened with a blow torch to find the contents only lightly scorched. Four days after the fire they began writing drafts at a temporary location, and within five days paid off the losses of their policy holders. The vault still stands in the Coast to Coast Store.

The bank was rebuilt with hollow tile blocks plastered inside and out. The fireproof building was used until a new building was completed in 1965 located on Second Street next to Winslow's Shopping Center. In 1973, the State Bank of Morton became part of the Puget Sound National Bank group.

Winsberg, who was one of the main sources for this account, went to work in the State Bank of Morton in 1935, bookkeeping, posting accounts, and keeping a fire going in a wood stove. He retired as Vice-President and Manager in 1976.

Completing the businesses on the four corners of Second and Main was the hardware owned by C. B. Smith and C. W. Morris. A complete line of hardware was carried in the large wooden building that extended from Main Street to the alley on the north. Smith was also a mortician and had a mortuary in the back of the store; old-timers remember that bodies were "laid out" upstairs.

Completely destroyed in the 1924 fire, the hardware was not rebuilt. Instead, the business moved across the street and down the block to where the Two Brothers Trading Post is now. Later the Smith and Morris Hardware was Clarence Lillegard's for many years, then Ernest Sparkman's Ace Hardware.

Sometime later the empty lots on the main corner was used by Jess Klasey for used cars; then after 1938 a Maxwell gasoline station was built, followed by a modern station in 1966, operated for 20 years as Sparky's Shell Service by Elmer and Richard Sparkman now Ron's Service Center.

Across the alley to the north of the Union station, there was a livery stable before the fire. Afterwards Steve Bergen operated a service station in a new building. Previously, he had had a pool hall in the Hilts Hotel. Reg Lester took over the Union Station in 1935, then moved across the street in 1941 to a new building that incorporated part of a brick building that had been Dr. Joseph Pine's office. Lester had a Mobil service station, garage, and Buick-GMC agency for many years. Several businesses have been there since then.

In 1919, after Dr. Pine's military service during World War I, Pine bought out the first doctor in Morton, Dr. Harry Feagles, who moved to Chehalis. Pine's first office with a couple of hospital beds had been in a frame building on Main Street where Bob's Boot Barn is now on the north side of the middle of the block between Second and Third. Pine married his nurse's aid, Donna Stiltner. He left Morton in 1925.

Before the fire, Lars F. Phelps had a small clothing store next to Smith's Hardware, where the Morton Tavern is now, and afterwards had a larger building next to the State Bank of Morton. The Coast to Coast store has occupied the building since 1966, owned for about 20 years by Neil and Elva Wright, now owned by Bill Whitfield.

Going back to the northwest corner of the main intersection, just west of the bank was the tower that held the fire bell. Next was Rice's restaurant that burned. Within a few days after the fire, Rice had a small wooden building thrown up, and with a few rough tables on a dirt floor, he was back in business.

Rice rebuilt the cafe and added hotel rooms above, called the Morton Hotel, the hotel's rooms were recently converted into apartments, and the Overtime Tavern occupies part of the first floor.

Crossing back to the south side of Main Street next to Fairhart's was Hopgood's Arcade Theatre built about 1912. Showing silent movies, the theatre attracted patrons from surrounding communities at the weekend shows. Admission for adults was 25 cents, children under 12, 10 cents.

The owner, Thomas Hopgood, was Morton's

FAIRHART'S DRY GOODS AND GROCERY STORE on the right is shown after a 1950's snowstorm. The store was in business from 1913 to 1986 with the same family in the same location.

C. B. SMITH'S HARDWARE STORE was on the northeast corner of Main and Second where Ron's Service Center (Union Station) is now located. Completely destroyed by the 1924 fire, it was not rebuilt.

WINSBERG'S GENERAL MERCHANDISE STORE on the corner of Main and Second was as early business. Constructed with fireproof walls, it was gutted in the big fire. It was rebuilt and became the Lindley Building in 1926

first mayor in 1913. After the fire, all that remained of his theatre was the concrete projection booth. Later on, A. G. Pecchia operated the business for many years.

Next in line was the Masonic Temple, completed in June 1914 of tile and wood, which survived the 1924 fire. However, on Nov. 24, 1951, just after an extensive remodeling, the Temple suffered its own fire that destroyed the Lodge and Post Office. About 1933, the Post Office which had been located in Tower's Store where the Fire Hall is now on the corner of Main and Third Streets was moved to the first floor of the Temple. The Morton Drug Store had previously moved out of the Temple.

The first Morton Drug Store was a small business owned first by George Nicholai, followed by E. J. Vensky. In 1915, Lumir G. Vitous began the Rexall Store on the first floor of the Masonic Temple, which had only minor damage in the big fire. After a time in the Lindley Building, he constructed the Vitous Building in 1938 next to Phelps' store on Second Street.

The brick building housed the drug store for 32 years until it was outgrown and moved to a newer building next to the present Masonic Temple, next door to the location where it began.

After 30 years, Vitous retired and sold the Rexall Store to Harley Wingrove in 1944; later Kermit Reed bought it, then the present owner, Bill Partridge.

Although it is not located around the main intersection, another prominent business was the garage owned by Ed Cooper and his son, Harry. In 1918, Ed purchased the garage and gas station from Pucket and McClain on the southeast corner of Main and First Streets.

The large building had been a livery stable with hay storage upstairs. Cooper added an automobile repair garage and used the former stable to store cars for loggers who lived in camp.

The old wooden building burned (not in the big fire) and was replaced in 1932 with a small brick service station, which still stands, but which has held a law office and other businesses in more recent time.

This admittedly incomplete history covers only the businesses in the immediate vicinity of the main intersection that burned out in the 1924 fire. A complete record of other enterprises in the town would include such as Morton Hospital and Clinic, Winslow's and Hobb's markets, oil distributors, saloons and all the many mills and logging companies in addition to the small shops and individual businesses that have made up an important part of the community. Some attempt has been made to bring part of the early commercial efforts up to date, but much has been necessarily left out. It is hoped that some idea of these earliest enterprises will give an appreciation of the role played by Morton's original merchants.

Chapter 25

MORTON'S DOWNTOWN
RAZED BY 1924 FIRE

The Daily Chronicle — 1982

July 26, 1924 — "With a loss estimated at more than a quarter of a million dollars the entire business section of Morton on the Tacoma and Eastern Railroad, ... is in ashes today as the result of an early morning conflagration."

Fifty-eight years ago, on a Saturday, that paragraph began a news story in The Daily Chronicle describing an awesome fire that started mysteriously in the then Hilts Hotel earlier that day and spread instantaneously through downtown Morton, destroying 19 to 23 business buildings and several other small structures.

The speed and intensity of the fire overwhelmed fire-fighters, burning their water hoses and driving them from the streets as both wood and cement-block walls came crashing down.

Two buildings, the Fairhart and Winsberg general stores, were supposedly fireproof. The hollow tile walls of the eight-year-old Winsberg building did not go down, but the stock inside went quickly. The one-year-old Fairhart building collapsed within 20 minutes of the time the flames burst through its windows, "flinging its supposedly fireproof cement blocks (in the 1924 Chronicle's words) to tumbling masses across the street as if in wanton celebration of having destroyed $50,000 in a few minutes."

Strangely, the only injury recorded in the catastrophe was to Postmaster N. D. Tower, "who hit himself with a hammer while ripping fixtures from a burning building."

Except for a few small buildings railroad employees lived in, the fire did not get into the residential section, partially stopped by the walls of the Winsberg building. In addition, four business buildings on the fringes of the business section did not burn: The Chesser Garage, the Morton Mirror newspaper building, the Masonic Temple, containing the Morton Drug Company, and the post office.

Ironically, the post office was later moved into the Masonic Temple building and both burned in a fire a few years later. Another building, the Morton Garage, just out of reach of the 1924 fire, also burned in a separate fire a few years later.

About 50 persons, the railroad employees and those who lived above business establishments, were left homeless by the fire, but extreme hardships were avoided as they were immediately taken in by other residents.

Apparently, the businessmen and other community leaders handled the situation with equal ease. In declining an offer of assistance from Tacoma city leaders, Morton's Mayor T. J. Polly sent the following message: "Thanks for kindly offer. No casualties. Seems nothing is needed; provisions coming by night. Will notify if help is needed."

Some businessmen had temporary structures up in two or three days and had reopened for business. Rebuilding of permanent buildings began shortly thereafter, and some business establishments were fully completed by fall.

Mrs. Ruby Waste said she had arrived in the community from California a week earlier and was to have started work as a waitress in Rice's Restaurant the day after the fire.

She had to wait only two days for her job, as Rice had a temporary wooden building set up and open for business, with tables made of rough planks laid loosely together.

The fire seemed to bring out the best in the people of Morton, but, as tragedies seem to do, it also brought out the worst in some. Mrs. Waste said she saw many stores being looted even as many persons were risking their lives trying to

THE RUBBLE OF BUSINESS BUILDINGS was all that remained following the devastating fire of 1924. The view looks southwest toward the Main and Second intersection with the Lindley building (then Winsberg's) on the left.

MORTON'S 1924 MAJOR FIRE started in the Hotel Hilts in the early morning hours of July 26. All the buildings surrounding the main business intersection were destroyed.

RECOVERY FROM THE FIRE was quick as exemplified by Rice's Restaurant which set up business in a wooden shack within a few days. Outside help was refused as merchants banded together to rebuild their businesses.

control the blaze.

Mr. and Mrs. Harry Cooper, who had lived in their present home — just out of reach of the blaze — four years at the time, also remembered widespread looting. Guards had to be posted for many nights after the fire, Cooper said, to protect property.

The Cooper's recollections of the fire also included small fires all over town, started by hunks of burning shingles blown by the wind. He and his wife remember dashing around their yard throwing the burning shingles away from their home while spraying the roof with water from a garden hose.

The Coopers said they had their Model T packed up and ready to get out of town, as did many other families.

Mrs. Ethel Thommen had dual memories of the fire. She had just gotten married the day before.

She was a parttime operator at the telephone office, which had just a single switchboard and few customers with telephones. So small was the service, she said, that the operators were "tickled to death to have a call."

The fire quickly took out what few telephone lines there were, she said, but the switchboard was not burned. It was moved into a makeshift shack the next day and service was soon restored.

The town also had its hero, according to the newspaper accounts. He was 14-year-old Ernie Mackie, whose mother worked in the Hilts Hotel. He got his sister out of the hotel and spread the alarm to others in the building and the community.

Of many present Morton residents queried about young Mackie, a few vaguely remember him, but he moved from the community soon after the fire and no one seems to know what became of him.

Almost all traces of the young hero have disappeared over the intervening years, as have most traces of the fire itself.

MORTON'S FIRST CIRCUIT RIDER REV. RULE, and FIRST TEACHER JENNIE KEADY

Rev. Rule, who was in Morton in 1894, was honored fifty years later along with Morton's first school teacher Jennie (Keady) Corey.

The Rev. William J. Rule, nicknamed "Golden Rule" was a Methodist Church circuit rider assigned the east end of Lewis County in 1893. Riding his horse, he went from homesteads to settlements preaching wherever asked and staying where invited.

In 1945, he wrote his account of those years in *Riding the Upper Cowlitz Circuit, Fifty Years Ago, 1893-1896.* Quoting from the section about Morton, he said, "I heard of Morton — not so much about it for there was not so much to hear about. A post office was there, but no public buildings.

"I visited at Bremer and Cinebar, conducted a funeral and held a preaching service in the Shoestring Valley. I think I was the first minister that acted as a pastor in that section of the country. I called at the homes and recall with pleasure the hospitality shown at the Temple household.

"In 1894, the circuit was divided and the territory east of Mossyrock was not in my charge. One day I met some young fellows from Morton. They told me that there was a community hall being built at that place. There had been no minister or preaching since I left. They would like to have me be the first one to hold a service in the new hall. I readily consented. The hall was to be opened with a dance on July 4th, 1895. The next day was Sunday the 5th. I was there that Lord's Day morning on time."

Miss Jennie Keady came in April 1894 to teach three months of school in the Burnap home. She had come from Napavine on horseback, a trip that took almost two days. She came with the mail carrier as far as the Tilden Post Office where Bert Murray met her with two horses. They stayed overnight at George Bremer's home. They traveled through rain and snow the next day and crossed the Tilton River at flood stage. After fording the river, crossing a swamp, and following a narrow trail along the side of Little

REV. WILLIAM J. "GOLDEN" RULE was the first circuit rider to reach Morton and Jennie (Keady) Corey was the first school teacher. They were together fifty years later at a church reunion.

Mountain, they arrived at Lewis S. Reed's home and Post Office where she lived during the school term.

There were thirteen students that first year, which was Jennie Keady's only term here. The pupils were: Anna, Fred, and Ida Mienars, Ella and Anna Bergen, Grace and Gold Temple, Vannie Monk, Clarence Ross, and four Nicols boys.

Chapter 26

FRED NASLUND
MINERAL'S FIRST BORN

The first child born in Mineral, Fred Naslund, grew up ashamed that his family ate carrots because he thought they were only good for pig food. Naslunds had the first farm in Mineral which was on the south end of Mineral Lake where it was swampy and not heavily timbered as was most of the lakeside. With good soil and sub-irrigation from the lake, their garden was outstanding, with huge carrots and potatoes. As a small child, Fred saw his father thin the carrots and throw the small ones into the pig pen, so that he concluded carrots were pig food, and he didn't want anyone to know his family ate them.

Fred's father Nels Naslund came from Sweden where he had known the Ahlstrand brothers, Emil, Herman, and August, who with the Andersons were among the first settlers around Mineral Lake. Naslund moved his family from Tacoma in October 1893 into a log cabin and property he bought from a pioneer who intended to homestead, but who found the land belonged to Northern Pacific Railroad. He bought it for $1.27 an acre.

The Naslund property became the townsite of the community of Mineral after John Donahue bought them out in 1905. Donahue built the large sawmill that turned the settlement into a boom town. Donahue knew the railroad which would provide the first opportunity to get the big timber to market would reach Mineral in 1906. Later the mill became the Mineral Lake Lumber Company.

Naslund was accused of overcharging Donahue by accepting $5,000 for the lakeside property, but the price was set by Donahue. The Naslunds retained part of their place until 1923. Naslund died in 1920, and the mill burned in 1922.

Fred Naslund was born January 31, 1897, and joined the older children, Freda, Mary, and Magnus. Later David was born. When Fred's birth approached, his father was working in the

THE NASLUND HOMESTEAD LOG CABIN in Mineral was one of the first on the lake. In the back was the mother Ingrid and in front were: Dave, Mary, Magnus (Muggins), Fred, and Freda.

arsenic mine up Mineral Creek and was home only on Sundays. The older children tramping through more than a foot of snow, had to go after a midwife to assist in the birth. The neighbor woman found her way in the dark with a lantern which dragged in the snow beside the trail and left a furrow that his father found when he returned home.

In October 1902, Fred started to school in the log building located where the grade school is now. It was built in 1901 of hewed logs and was about 16 by 20 feet. In a copyrighted booklet Fred described the school: "There were home-made desks and benches, a water bucket on the left side of the door with a dipper hanging from a nail, and a wood stove on the right side of the room. The big boys carried wood in from the shed and packed drinking water."

THE MINERAL SCHOOL IN 1909 included Fred Naslund and his brother Dave. The other students were: Christian Fritz, Esther Bemis, Lloyd Carten, Joe Seymour, Merle Naugle, Fritz Meyer, Leslie Naugle, Henry Seymour, Edith Bemis, Ida Ahlstrand, Gerhard Loden, Howard Naugle, Cecil Seymour, and the teacher Miss Jessie Love, who married Rudolf Auvil.

THE MINERAL JUNIOR BASEBALL TEAM of 1912 had nine players, no substitutes and no coach. The back row were: Bert Schabel, Dave Naslund, Fred Naslund, Henry McAlister, and Gunnar Swanson. In front were: Vic Rowe, Henry Meyers, Joe Seymour, and Bill Hill.

The four Naslund children made up one-fourth of the student body. The teacher spoke Swedish, which was very helpful, because the Naslund family spoke only Swedish in their home.

Fred's oldest sister, Freda, had attended the first log school, located on the present cemetery hill where there were only three months of classes. The school children planted a pine tree and some other trees that are still standing.

In 1907 the second log schoolhouse was taken apart by Emil Ahlstrand, who rebuilt it as a rental house, so that the new school could be built on the same location. During that year school was held in Hard's Hall which was the second story of Hard's Store.

The new school was built of sawed lumber and was just half of the future building; the second half was completed in 1912-13.

The Naslund's lived closest to school and could run home for lunch, eat, and still get back to school for some play time.

The school children used unpainted penny pencils with a little "rubber", but the teacher had a painted one with a real eraser. Fred remembers thinking he "would have everything" if he had one like it.

Fred can not remember a time he couldn't swim. His father fenced in a swimming area on the lake with logs and a picket fence. The children called it "the mud hole" and spent much of the summer there.

One time the Naslund's had a fishing "marathon" when in a short time of fishing from their float they caught 360 trout which their mother cleaned, and their father smoked. In addition to the abundant fish, they always raised all the beef and pork they could eat.

Fred's oldest brother Magnus was called "Muggins" most of his life after he had had a fight with a larger boy and won decisively. A storekeeper witnessed the event and afterwards said to Magnus "You really beat the muggins out of him," and the name stuck. Muggins carried mail on horseback from Elbe to the Mineral Post Office for 50 cents a week.

Marie Fritz, who later married Guy Sutherland, started to school at the same time Fred did. She had to walk from her home at Carlson at the

THIS STEAM DONKEY ENGINE provided Fred Naslund's first job in 1912. He was 15 years old and earned $2.50 a day for ten hours work as the "whistle punk."

THE MINERAL LAKE LUMBER COMPANY was built on the former Naslund homestead. The large mill burned in 1922 and it was not rebuilt, a real blow to the little town.

fork in the road of Highway 7 and Mineral Road South. During the winter when the snow was deep, she missed quite a bit of school, and Fred felt he was a lot smarter than Marie was.

However, Marie not only caught up with him but went so far ahead that when he graduated from the eighth grade, she was already teaching school at a time when only six weeks of normal school were required.

Fred's first trip to Mt. Rainier was in 1906 with his father, two brothers, and two neighbors, Henry Swanson and Harold Lindberg. They went by buggy to Elbe, Park Junction, and Longmire although from Ashford on the road

was barely fit for a buggy. They had to leave the buggy at Longmire and pack all their camping equipment on the horse and hike to Paradise Valley. They set up their tent camp by the Paradise River, and the mosquitoes nearly ate them alive.

When Fred was eight years old, his father, his sister Mary, and he went by train to visit relatives in Stanwood and Mt. Vernon. They caught the Tacoma Eastern at Elbe at 2 p.m. and arrived in Tacoma at 6 p.m. The Union Depot had not yet been built, and a wooden building was in use then. Beside the stairway to the old depot were several Indian women selling woven baskets and

HORSEPOWER WAS IMPORTANT at the big mill at Mineral. The crew which included several Japanese men used horses to move heavy cartloads of lumber.

moccasins; they had a small fire and were cooking supper. Fred had his eyes on them and fell down several steps and skinned his knees.

They walked to the Northern Pacific Depot and took the train to Seattle where they stayed overnight, quite an experience for an eight-year-old country boy to ride on two trains and to see two cities in one day.

The next morning they caught the Great Northern to Mt. Vernon and visited several aunts and uncles and many cousins in the area. He learned his father and uncle were named after the place they came from in Sweden: "Nes" for a point and "Lund", a park, as in Point Defiance Park.

The whole trip was a thrill for a wide-eyed boy whose skinned knees didn't hurt until he got home to Mineral.

One year Fred's father went to Alderton to pick hops for some cash income. To reach his home in one day, he started out at 2 a.m. and hiked until midnight with his pack horse loaded with staple groceries. There was a buggy road through Eatonville to Elbe, but there was not much of a road on the Lewis County side where tree roots and stumps made it a rough ride.

Naslund had a dog with him and as dogs will do, it ran circles around the horse, and by the time they reached Elbe the dog was so tired he thought he would have to leave it there.

Later the family went to Elbe weekly for groceries. When they needed horses shod, they hired the blacksmith Levi Engle, who made the iron cross on the spire of the little Elbe Lutheran church which was built by a man named Charles Lutkins.

Elbe was settled by several German families and was named by Lutkins after the German river. A German Lutheran minister came sometimes to preach in the Elbe church. Mineral had several Scandinavian families that enjoyed occasional services by a Swedish Lutheran minister who stayed with the Naslunds on his trips to Mineral. The pastor enjoyed Mrs. Naslund's excellent cooking and the coffee pot that was always on. The church services were held in Naslund's big kitchen and lasted from two to three hours with the children taking it all in as they sat on the stairway.

In September 1912, when Fred was 15 years old and his brother Dave was 13, they would leave right after school on Friday to hike to the north end of Mineral Lake with their fishing poles and a bag of waffles from the extras their mother cooked for them at breakfast time. There was an old cabin to stay in, and they had an old coat of their dad's to sleep in and the waffles and fish to eat.

The boys always managed to stay long enough to miss Sunday School and church. When hunting season opened in October, they would take extra food for a longer stay. During the 1912 season, Dave shot his first deer. Fred said, "In the spring fishing in the lake was real good and if we fished long enough we missed lots of chores around home!"

Fred's first job was as a "whistle punk" in a logging camp at Riverside, Washington, in June 1912. He stayed in the bunkhouse with the loggers where each one had his own blankets, and there was a big stove in the middle that gave them heat and a place to dry rain-soaked clothes. His job was to blow signals on the steam donkey whistle according to instructions from the rigging crew.

The logging crews worked ten hours a day for $2.50 a day and paid $7.00 a week for board, which consisted of good food and lots of it.

During the Fourth of July shut down, Fred went to the race track in Tacoma and watched Louis Chevrolet, Barney Oldfield, and Ralph DePalma, all famous race car drivers, compete at 70 to 90 miles an hour.

When Fred was in his last year of high school in October 1915, he went to work for the Wells Fargo Express Company in Tacoma, helping load and unload express on Milwaukee passenger trains for $55 a month. His boss knew he wasn't 21 years old, but he knew how to harness a horse, and that was more important.

He advanced to an express messenger for $75 a month working from the Seattle area to Hoquiam until he enlisted in the Naval Reserve on June 20, 1917. His only fear was that World War I would be over before he got into uniform. He was sent for training to the location of the Alaska-Yukon-Pacific Exposition of 1909 which Fred attended. The location became part of the University of Washington campus.

Stationed on the U.S.S. Great Northern, Fred and 400 shipmates sailed to San Francisco where they picked up 270 German prisoners-of-war who were being transferred to a camp in South Carolina, a trip that took them through the

Panama Canal. After the Great Northern went to the Brooklyn Navy Yard to be fitted with anti-aircraft and submarine depth guns, he was stationed on the U.S.S. Utah which spent the remainder of the war on the Atlantic Ocean.

While in New York, Fred met Joe Seymour, one of his boyhood friends from Mineral and was asked to be best man at Seymour's upcoming wedding. Seymour returned to Mineral after the war and spent the rest of his life there. Fred also returned, but he spent only a few months working in the big sawmill before returning to the railroad.

Fred took a leave from the company that had become American Railway Express to go to Alaska for three months, but he stayed three and a half years and worked in a gold mine and on a fishing boat.

Returning to Tacoma in 1926, he bought the place where he still lives. When the Depression hit, he and his mother were raising chickens that cost up to $1.55 to raise to egg-laying age when the price went down to 65 cents each and later to 21 cents each. They ate so much chicken and homegrown potatoes and green beans that he "thinks of Herbert Hoover" every time he eats a chicken dinner.

In the spring of 1934, Fred got a job with Olympic Dairy, that became Arden Farms, and drove a delivery truck for 30 years before retirement in 1962.

In the spring of 1944, he was delivering ice cream to Mannings Bakery as a substitute driver, where a lovely lady, Evelyn, was a cashier. Someone had just dropped a jar of honey, and he offered to help clean up the mess. He says Evelyn thought he "was a pretty good guy."

Eventually Fred and Evelyn were married when her daughter was 19 years old. Two years later they had a son. Everyone in the hospital was excited about that baby because he was Fred's first child at the age of 49.

Although Fred has lived in Tacoma for many years, he keeps in contact with Mineral people through the annual Mineral Old-Timers Picnic, and he likes to remind everyone that he was the first child born in Mineral.

Chapter 27

MARIE SUTHERLAND'S EARLY DAY MINERAL

Free land available for homesteading brought the Christian Fritz family to Mineral in 1891. Their daughter Marie Sutherland lived her whole life on the original homestead and in an interview remembered the early days in Mineral.

Christian Fritz, his wife, his four year old son Frederick, and his father and mother came from Germany to the United States in 1891. Christian's brother and sister had migrated to Tacoma earlier. While the Fritz family were staying in a hotel in Tacoma, they met Louis Shuffenhauer who told them about the wonderful country where he was homesteading. His place is located just north and across the highway from the former Mineral Ranger Station. He told them about land being available just for living on it; they could hardly believe it and lost no time in starting for the Mineral area to claim the property.

The Fritz family moved into their log cabin in August of 1891, spreading their bedding on the floor at night and hanging it outside to air during the day. It wasn't long until they built onto the log cabin enlarging it by raising the roof. After they had quite a bit of clearing done, they found out that they were not on homestead land, but were on a section owned by Northern Pacific Railroad, therefore they had to buy their property instead of proving up on it.

Shuffenhauer, the neighbor who told them about the land next to him, built his log house which is still standing. He was a fine carpenter, and the house was beautifully finished with a carved mantle inscribed with the initials L.S. and the date, 1891.

The enlarged log cabin of the Fritzes was also beautifully finished with split cedar paneling throughout. With the use of only the crudest hand tools, Christian and his brother Jacob were artisans in wood. Jake made quite a few pieces of furniture including a table and two large chest-of-drawers. The drawers are fitted together with perfect dovetailed joints and are decorated with wood carving that is beautifully crafted.

Christian, Jr., and Marie were born during the years the family lived in the log cabin. A few years later the father decided that they should have a larger and finer home. He built the house which Marie and her husband Guy Sutherland made their home. They moved into the new house in 1904; the first winter they were never quite warm enough because the old log house was so much easier to heat than the new home that is a large two-story building.

The Fritz home was close to the trail from Elbe to Morton that was later made into a wagon road. It followed somewhat the same route that the Morton-Elbe highway follows today. The Fritz home was large and the family hospitable, resulting in many overnight guests. Anyone traveling through was welcome; often whole families from Randle or anywhere in eastern Lewis County would be fed and put up for the night. Many times the men were driving herds of cattle or pigs or flocks of turkeys from Randle to market in Tacoma. Some nights four or five cold, wet, and hungry men would be crowded around the small cook stove while Mrs. Fritz was trying to get a meal. There always seemed to be enough food for everyone who came along even though the household consisted of the parents, three children, grandparents, cousins, and an uncle.

In the fall season, they would see large groups of Indians going by with all their supplies carried on poles pulled behind their horses on their way to Puyallup to work in the hop harvest.

About 1900, the arsenic mine on Mineral Creek became the first industry in the area to attract outside attention. The equipment had to be hauled in with horses and wagons since it preceded the arrival of the railroad by several years. A corporation sold stock in the mine that was a prosperous venture until 1922 when a new process recovered arsenic as a by-product in smelting which made the mining unprofitable.

Even before the coming of the arsenic mine, there was a trading post on Mineral Creek about three miles from the present town of Mineral. Around it were scattered cabins and tents in the community known as Mineral City. Later the railroad's location near the lake determined the site of the present town of Mineral.

Adam Sachs had a store in Elbe before there were any in Mineral. After the railroad reached Elbe, Sachs built the first sawmill there. Elbe had a large hotel and community hall also. The hotel was constructed of logs; it was two stories high with a number of rooms. The community hall was used for everything from dances to church services until the little Lutheran Church was constructed. Marie Sutherland was christened in the hall by a Lutheran minister from Puyallup. Elbe had the only church services in the area for quite a few years.

The railroad was extended to Mineral and beyond in 1906. Besides the depot in Mineral, Tacoma Eastern Railroad had depots in Carlson about a half mile from the junction of Highway 7 and Mineral Road South and at Watkins, near the later day Millburg. Watkins depot served a coal mine in the hills to the east of the railroad.

The coming of the railroad turned Mineral into a boom town. Soon there were shacks and tents going up all over the place; the shingle mill was started on the lake front, the large sawmill was built, and coal mines opened in many of the surrounding hills.

Marie recalled a neighbor of theirs was Calvin Fox, a homesteader in the Carlson-Mineral area in 1891. The property lies east of the Mineral-Carlson road where Robert Kenny now lives. To join him, Fox's wife rode a horse from Parkland bringing their nine-month-old baby. Their home had a glass addition to their living room for flowers, and every summer they had a yard full of flowers. Mrs. Fox kept a lovely home with

A CREW AT THE ARSENIC MINE up Mineral Creek were employed from about 1900 until 1922 when the mine was no longer profitable. Arsenic and coal were the only commercial minerals found in the Mineral area despite the name.

JACOB FRITZ AND HIS OXEN TEAM were in Mineral in 1907. In the wagon were: Freda, Lillian, Bertha, and Emma, while Tollof Peterson stood by the team. In the background the frame school was under construction.

more decoration than most pioneer homes had. She covered the floors with rag rugs and had curtains at each window. She was one of the very few to have a dresser with a mirror. Marie remembered a holder hanging by the mirror for the long hat pins the ladies of fashion used in those days.

One time Calvin Fox was coming home from Elbe with supplies hanging from the saddle in a flour sack. Something startled the horse, it shied, hitting sharply against a tree. The blow broke a vinegar jug in the sack, which soaked the baking soda resulting in a foaming mass covering man and horse.

Another time Fox had been hunting with Richard Loden, who homesteaded at Flynn. There was a trail between their homesteads as they were accustomed to visiting and hunting together, but a heavy snow had fallen causing Fox to lose his way. Although he found the path again, darkness caught him before he could get home. He found a pitchy piece of wood for a torch, but blobs of snow falling off the trees kept extinguishing his light. Finally he had used his last match, and in the darkness and heavy timber he had no idea how much farther he had to go. He decided to try shouting to try to summon help; fortunately his wife heard him. She hollered and went to meet him, saving him from

what could have been a tragedy on a very cold night within hailing distance of his home.

The first school in Mineral proper was located on what is now Cemetery Hill. A few years later a log school was built on Emil Ahlstrand's property where the present school stands. Marie started to school there when she was seven years old. Her mother had been reluctant to start her earlier because it was a long walk from Carlson to Mineral on cold winter days. However, Herman Ahlstrand was a school director then; he visited the family and convinced Mr. Fritz that his daughter should be enrolled in school.

The log school had three windows on each sidewall. Inside were the benches, stove, pegs over a bench for hanging coats, a water bucket and dipper. There were about fifteen children who ranged in age from six to sixteen who went to school only three or four months a year.

Marie remembered one teacher vividly: Emily Fagerstrom, a "very talented" young lady. She taught the children to sing in four-part harmony and had quartets sing songs like "Sweet and Low" and "Stars in the Summer Night." Her Christmas pageants were works of art complete with costumes and many parts for the children. She even had some kind of powder she burned to give a scene a soft light-blue glow. Everyone for miles around came to her school programs,

THE FIRST LOG SCHOOL IN MINERAL built on Cemetery Hill was obviously long out of use when pictured. The next log school was located at the present school site.

THE OLD MINERAL SCHOOL was built in 1907 on the present location of the Grade School. It included high school, but students had to attend Morton for a year or two to be certified.

walking, riding a horse, or coming by buggy. If they did not have a kerosene lantern, the farmers would carry a candle in a lard bucket turned on its side with a makeshift handle attached.

These recollections of early days in Mineral by Marie Fritz Sutherland give a glimpse of what life was like in the homestead era. Marie and her husband Guy raised their family in the house built by her father in 1904; they had sons Donald, David, and Dick, and daughters Mary Jane and Joanne. Marie was noted for her intelligence and friendliness and for being a hard working neighbor, traits often found in pioneer families.

Chapter 28

EMIL AHLSTRAND
MINERAL HOMESTEADER

One of the very first homesteaders in Mineral, Emil Ahlstrand always liked to say that when he arrived in the United States from Sweden all he could understand were the dogs and chickens.

Born in Sweden on March 30, 1870, he was the youngest in the family of five. When he was 19 years old, he emigrated with his oldest brother August and August's wife Sofia, setting foot in America on the Sunday before Labor Day, 1889. They left their widowed mother and two married sisters: Edith Lindberg, who came to the States in 1909, and Ida Olsson, who remained in Sweden.

The Ahlstrand brothers arrived in Mineral in 1891. The intervening two years were spent in Tacoma where they joined a large settlement of Swedish people who were living in the South M and South K Street districts.

When Emil made his first trips to Mineral, he had to walk in from Elbe because he could not get a horse in by the trail that went under and over the huge windfall logs. Even if he could have ridden a horse to the lake, there would have been nothing to feed the horse, since the whole area was heavily forested.

Emil homesteaded southeast of Mineral on the East Fork of Mineral Creek in Section 12, Township 14 North, Range 5 East. At that time Mineral City was in existence on Mineral Creek (on the Flynn Road); the present townsite on the lake was just a homestead and there was nothing else around the lake.

Frederick Jonas from Chehalis had a trading post in Mineral City and there was a hotel, livery stable, another store, and a saloon. A cluster of cabins and tents were occupied by prospectors and miners who were convinced the hills were full of valuable minerals.

A reputed silver strike in 1892 touched off a rush to prospect up Mineral Creek, where there was supposed to be Contact City. The city existed only in the mind of a minister from Tacoma, who had become unpopular with his congregation and who had "set out for other fields of fortune," Emil said.

The minister, turned prospector, found a shaft where the silver was reported to be found and discovered, instead, a commercially valuable deposit of arsenic. He set out to sell shares, and as Emil remembered it, he sold to "all the old maids and widows in the vicinity." Glowing descriptons of the mine and the town site were advertised far and wide.

THE AHLSTRAND BROTHERS: Emil, Herman, and August were pioneers on Mineral Lake. They were friendly men with close family ties.

One day a young stranger approached Emil to ask where the railroad was located. When told there was none, he came near tears. "Why I paid a dollar a share for my stock!", he said. Emil picked up a current copy of the Tacoma Ledger to show the youth an advertisement of the Mineral Lake Mining and Smelting Company offering shares at 10 cents each.

Both "cities" faded away rapidly as the mineral strikes did not "pan out". Although what remained of Mineral City and Contact City was washed away in the flood of 1902, the arsenic mine operated profitably until the early 1920's when

EMIL AND CHRISTINA (BROWN) AHLSTRAND were from Sweden. She died in 1907 leaving little Oscar and Vera and an infant who also died. Emil never remarried.

arsenic was found to be a byproduct of a manufacturing process where it was produced more economically than it could be mined.

In 1905, the Tacoma Eastern Railroad line out of Tacoma reached the shore of the lake that formerly had been called "Round Top Lake," thus the location of the Mineral townsite was determined while the name of the lake was changed to Mineral Lake.

Emil established his Mineral Creek homestead, "proved up" on it, received his "patent" as homestead deeds were called, then he sold it about 1900. He bought 40 acres in the corner of a section from Mr. Jonas, who had bought it from Northern Pacific Railroad. That tract of land lies on the southwest shore of Mineral Lake with one small corner extending into the lake. His brother August also settled on the west shore of the lake where he built the first post office in Mineral, a tiny building that still stands.

Emil dismantled the log house on his original claim, transported the building material to the new place where he re-erected his home. The log house stood on the west side of the intersection of the road around the lake (Mineral Hill Road) and Mineral Road North.

Some years later, Emil was clearing land that lies in the "Y" across the road from his house when he had an accident with his team of horses.

The clearing of the property, now owned by the Elmer Sparkman's, was halted while Emil's broken leg healed.

Emil's wife Christina Katherine Brown was born in 1879 in Old Tacoma. Her father had come from the islands between Denmark and Sweden. As a young man he went to Liverpool, England, with the intention of shipping out to sea. In the hiring hall, the list of men who had been hired for a certain ship was called. After the call was given several times for a First Mate named Brown and no one answered, Christina's father responded. He went by the name of Brown from then on, for he had already found that his name was almost impossible for English speaking people to pronounce or spell.

One of the ships on which Brown worked put in at Tumwater, Washington. He liked the Puget Sound country so much that he decided that when he left the sea, he would settle there. When he quit shipping, he lived first in Old Tacoma where Christina was born, then later he homesteaded near Mud Lake north of Eatonville on the present Jensen-Christian Road. A few years later Brown sold the farm, then moved to Mineral on the property now known as the Cline place. One of the main reasons he moved to Mineral was to be near his oldest daughter Christina Ahlstrand.

As was true for most of the early settlers, Emil worked on his homestead part of the year and in a Tacoma sawmill during the winter months until he could develop the homestead. There was transportation from Tacoma to Spanaway, but the last 50 miles he had to walk.

One time before the wagon road was built, Emil and his sister-in-law Sofia had business in Tacoma. They arose very early, starting to walk at 3 a.m.; by walking all day they reached the end of the Lake Park streetcar line that evening then paid a nickel for the ride into town. Emil recalled, "It was quite a walk. We had to allow a whole day for it."

When the first election was held in Mineral, probably about 1900, there were 14 votes cast. Emil was chosen to take the ballots to the courthouse in Chehalis. He started out on horseback after the polls were closed and the votes were counted; by riding all night he arrived in Chehalis about eight o'clock in the morning. There were such close contests between three of the candidates for county offices that Mineral's

OSCAR AND VERA AHLSTRAND, Emil's children, are shown in 1905 while the dog Tutton posed on the horse Bab. Vera married Adrian Davis and lived in Randle for many years while Oscar stayed in Mineral until his later years, marrying Vi Williams when in his fifties.

14 votes decided that election.

Within this same period of time, Emil was hired by an attorney, B. W. Coiner from Tacoma, to deliver some important papers to three people in Eastern Lewis County. Emil rode to Morton where he consulted the postmaster George Hopgood about the location of the settlement named Nesika. Postmaster Hopgood was not sure of the location, but thought he could find it in his papers. All his records were kept in a wooden barrel; he dumped the papers out and dug through them until he found the information. Hopgood told Emil how to go over the hills to Riffe where he could cross the Cowlitz River on a ferry, then follow the river upstream several miles to find Nesika.

When Emil located the man to whom he was supposed to deliver the papers, he found the man was very reluctant to talk to him for fear the law was after him. Emil had to explain that the lawyer's document was notice of the inheritance of some property before the man admitted his identity.

From there Emil continued upstream along the Cowlitz River until he came to Kiona Creek where he located an Indian woman, Annie Sam. He served the papers about some legal action to her, then retraced his path to Kosmos where the trail branched away from the river toward Morton.

The third paper was for someone near Fern Gap, but Emil couldn't even locate a house there. Finally he found some men logging with horses and talked to an 80-year-old man, who called his "boy" (who was only about 60) to direct Emil to the party he was looking for. After delivering the last legal paper, Emil returned home, having made the circuit in three days.

Another time Emil and his nephew took the team and wagon to go to Eatonville for winter supplies. The weather was good when they left home, but when they drew near Eatonville the rain started. It rained harder and harder while they bought their goods and started on the homeward trip.

By the time they reached Elbe, the Nisqually River was a raging torrent. About a mile and a half upstream was a place where wagons could usually ford the river, but now the crossing was washed out and the bank was being undercut. The water was much too high to attempt to take the wagon across, but somehow Emil and his nephew managed to ride the horses across and go on home to Mineral. Later they got some men to return with them who managed to pull the wagon across the river with ropes.

Later the first bridge was built across the Nisqually up the river above Elbe near National. The bridge was formed by first falling a large tree across the river then two smaller trees next to it to hold the roadway of split cedar planks. This original bridge was used when the machinery was hauled by horse and wagon to the mine on Mineral Creek where there was a road that followed the west bank of the stream.

The third Ahlstrand brother Herman and his wife Inga, arrived in Mineral six years after Emil and August, about 1897. They had two children,

Hannah and Charles, and were accompanied by Inga's father Jonas Engstrom, and the Ahlstrand's double cousin Johann Carlson.

Carlson built a sawmill west of Mineral near the intersection of Mineral Road South and Highway 7 where a small community was built around the mill and was known as Carlson.

Emil lost his wife Christina in 1907, leaving a son Oscar, not quite four years old, a daughter Vera, two years old, and an infant daughter who died a few weeks later. Vera's Uncle August and Aunt Sofia took her into their home to rear her.

Emil raised Oscar mostly by himself, with the help of Mr. and Mrs. John Schaffer. Later an aunt kept him until Edith, Emil's sister, came from Sweden in 1909. She took Oscar "under her wing" and she saw to it that he was fed and properly dressed, meanwhile he was with his father every night.

The Ahlstrand brothers always had some money-making enterprises under way; Vera said, "They were always buying and selling property." Emil platted the Ahlstrand Addition in Mineral and he sold many lots, besides building houses for rentals.

Emil built a house for himself and his son from lumber that came from dismantling houses in "Jap Town" across the lake. A number of Japanese employees of the Mineral Lake Lumber Company had lived in their own community. After the mill burned down in 1922 and the Orientals moved to other locations to find work, Emil salvaged building materials. Because the Japanese are such short people, the bathroom door and two closet doors in the Sparkman's house are barely six feet high, requiring a tall man to duck his head to go through them.

All three of the Ahlstrand brothers were very friendly men; they loved to be with people and maintained close family ties, seldom letting a day go by without visiting each other. They all loved to tell stories and joke with others.

Emil saw Mineral grow from the first settlers to a prosperous community supported by the big sawmill and the M. R. Smith Shingle Mill. After the mill burned, the town lost businesses and the population gradually declined. When Mineral was at its height, Morton was the smaller town, but gradually Morton grew and overshadowed the little town on the beautiful lake.

EMIL AHLSTRAND'S LOG HOUSE with a fire ladder on the roof was built first up Mineral Creek, then dismantled and relocated behind Rowe and Hill's store. Neighbors, the Reynolds and Naslunds, joined Emil and Oscar on the right.

Chapter 29

MINERAL PIONEERS: THE AHLSTRAND BROTHERS

When the Swedish Ahlstrand brothers came to Mineral in 1891, there were few pioneers in the area. One was Richard Loden who had a place on the Flynn Road several miles northeast of Mineral. Loden had been told there was a lake in the vicinity, and one day he set out to find it. He followed Mineral Creek down toward the area he had been directed to, then went over the gap between the hills until he spotted the lake. As he approached the water, he could hear hammering across the lake; he started hollering to attract the attention of whoever was there. August Ahlstrand heard him calling, went down to the lake, jumped into his dugout canoe, and rowed across the lake.

When the men met, they tried to talk in English, but got little response; they tried a few words in German and still couldn't communicate. Then one of them tried Swedish and that did the trick — two Swedes from different sections of Sweden, but fully able to understand each other. That was the beginning of a long and close friendship between the pioneers: the Richard Lodens and the Ahlstrand families.

The oldest brother August, and his wife Sofia

AUGUST AND SOFIA AHLSTRAND with their nephew Harold Lindberg came from Sweden in 1889. They did not have children of their own, but raised Harold and their niece Vera (Ahlstrand) Davis.

with the youngest Ahlstrand brother Emil emigrated to the United States in 1889 to a Swedish settlement in Tacoma. After two years there, they homesteaded in Mineral during the days when they had to walk from Elbe on a rough trail, packing their supplies on their backs because they could not get a horse through the dense timber.

August, born in 1858, and Sofia, born in 1864, had no children of their own, but they brought a nephew whom they reared with them. They also took Emil's daughter Vera into their home after her mother Christina died when Vera was two years old. Vera's four-year-old brother Oscar was reared by their father Emil with the help of relatives.

August and Sofia bought property on the northwestern shore of Mineral Lake midway along the length of the lake. There was already a cabin located on the property that is now known as the Berglund place, since Sofia's niece, a Mrs. Berglund, inherited it.

There was a good spring at the base of the hill about a quarter of a mile from the cabin. Sofia carried water from the spring making sure she had all the water she needed by late afternoon, because a bear had a habit of taking his daily bath in the spring about four o'clock, leaving it riled and muddy.

The cabin on August's place had two rooms built entirely of hand-split cedar logs, boards and shakes. Through the years rooms were added until a fairly large house resulted. In the kitchen there was a large corner fireplace with a big woodbox beside it. Many times they would start a fire, then run down to the lake to catch some of the abundant trout for supper.

Sofia had a great love for lilacs as there were many of them in her childhood home in Sweden. As soon as possible they planted enough to make a lilac "summer house" in their yard.

HERMAN AHLSTRAND AND HIS WIFE INGABORG had their children Hannah and Charlie before they left Sweden for Mineral.

There is strong evidence that at an earlier time the Hudson Bay Company had trappers around the Mineral Lake because one of the family found a skeleton beside a kettle that had the company name stamped on it. August had the kettle in his home for years, but evidently gave it to someone who wanted it.

The third Ahlstrand brother Herman, and his wife Inga arrived in Mineral about six years after August and Emil. Herman was born in Sweden in 1861 and Inga in 1862. They had two children, Hannah and Charlie, before they left the old country; they lost a baby girl Ida soon after their arrival in the United States.

Because Sweden was suffering from very hard times, a large group came to this country, most of them settling in Tacoma. The group included Inga's father Jonas Engstrom and the Ahlstrand's double cousin Johann Carlson both of whom accompanied Herman to Mineral. Later Carlson had a sawmill west of Mineral near the junction of Mineral Road South and Highway 7. For many years there was a little settlement there that bore his name.

Herman and Inga homesteaded on the western edge of Mineral Lake between Emil's and August's places. He built a house entirely of hand-split cedar, including the doors and window frames. The house stands two houses south of the large log lodge and is still occupied. In 1899, another daughter was born to Inga in that house and was named Ida after the baby they had lost.

The Ahlstrand brothers always had some money-making enterprises under way; they were always buying and selling property. Herman bought a lot or two from Emil and built a store building with a large hall on the second story on the main intersection in Mineral. William "Bill" Hill had his grocery, dry goods, and feed store there for many years while the hall was used through the years for the Royal Neigbors Lodge meetings and for many parties. The building burned several years ago; it was the only store left in Mineral after Wheeler's and Pye's stores burned down in one disastrous fire some years before that.

During Mineral's prosperous years, Herman had a sawmill and a laundry. In later years, Herman worked for Dr. A. W. Bridge at the Ohanapecosh Hot Springs. He hired Emil to help build the hotel building and several log cabins when the Hot Springs were very popular with people who came to "take the waters" for their health. Many people reported good results from soaking in the hot mineral water.

August had boats for rent on the lake in the early days for 25 cents a day. He and his cousin Johann Carlson owned a launch that they used on the lake. They had a contract to tow rafts of logs from logging camps on Hartman Hill at the northern end of the lake to the Mineral Lake Lumber Mill. Emil's daughter, Vera Davis of Randle, remembers riding on the launch when she was a small child.

August and Emil always had houses to rent, and Vera recalls coming home from school for her lunch to find it in the oven because August and Sofia were papering, cleaning, or painting one of their rental houses. She always felt that it was a special treat when she found a baked sweet potato ready to eat.

August built the first post office in Mineral, a tiny 8 by 8 foot cedar building across the road from his cabin. For several years he had to walk to Elbe for the mail until a trail was built that allowed him to go by horseback. After the Tacoma Eastern Railroad reached Mineral in 1906, the mail came by train. August was postmaster until 1908 when the post office was moved to one of the stores on the main street in Mineral. The Mineral Lake Lions Club maintains the historic little post office.

Herman's father-in-law Jonas Engstrom died in 1902, becoming the first one buried in the Mineral cemetery. Of course, there was no undertaker nor minister in the area, but doing

THE SMALLEST POST OFFICE in the United States was built by August Ahlstrand in Mineral. His nephew Harold Lindberg is on the left.

their best Herman made a casket of split-cedar and August said a few words at the graveside.

August and Sofia were very devout people, dedicated Lutherans; there was always a Bible or hymn book in sight in their home. They entertained many Swedish speaking missionaries who stayed in their home and spoke at community meetings, some of which were held in the Presbyterian Church which is still in use in Mineral.

August was very strongly opposed to drinking and worked diligently to help pass the Volsted Act (Prohibition); many times he paid for outside speakers himself to help promote the cause.

August's and Sofia's nephew (their foster son)

Harold Lindberg worked in the woods as a young man. Tragically, he died of consumption (tuberculosis) shortly before his thirtieth birthday.

Vera recalls that the Ahlstrands always had yeast starter on hand before yeast was available in a store; they willingly shared it with their neighbors. They were glad each summer when the new potatoes were ready for harvest because the potato water made a better starter.

The Swedish people made their own bread, but very little of it was white; they thought the only good bread was rye. They also made their own hardtack from a yeast dough. It was rolled thin on a board, then carefully slid into a clean oven directly on the bottom of the oven. It was a real art to slide the thin dough off the board and into the oven without wrinkling it.

The winter food supply was enriched with sauerkraut, pickled beets, and eggs preserved in water glass; also they enjoyed salt herring that came in barrels from Seattle. These foods were in addition to all their homegrown dried fruits and salted meats.

Some of their staples were ordered from Montgomery Ward in Chicago and came by freight train right to the depot in Mineral, thus eliminating a long, hard trip to the nearest store; many times it saved money, too. They ordered things like flour, sugar, rice, pepper, and cinnamon. "Maybe five pounds of cinnamon did last for years, but it was cheaper that way!" Vera recalled.

THIS HOUSE ON MINERAL LAKE was August and Sofia Ahlstrand's. The tent for nephew Harold Lindberg was supposed to be an outdoor cure for tuberculosis.

Vera remembers going to the train depot to see August off on a trip back to his homeland in 1909. While he was gone during the summer, Sofia set up a tent in the yard near a faucet where they had piped water from the spring, moved her cookstove into the tent, and thereby saved herself the usual housekeeping tasks while August was gone. She had good reason for this — she had to take over all the work of the farm; there were cows to milk, hay and oats to cut with a hand scythe, and a garden to tend.

Vera walked a mile to the grade school, located where the present school is. She went home for lunch; she did not want to carry her lunch because the only place to eat was the dusty basement where the other children were playing while she tried to eat. Frequently she walked the two miles round trip back to town in the afternoon when the train came in with the mail.

When Vera was in grade school, Mineral had grown to a prosperous town; she remembers that there were thirty-two children living around the lake.

Although Emil and Christina had always spoken English in their home, August and Herman's families spoke only Swedish. The result was that Vera could barely speak English when she started to school.

One of Vera's most pleasant memories is of the times she was sent down to the boat dock to fish for crawdads (crayfish) with a soup bone tied to a string for bait. She not only enjoyed the thought of the delicacy they would soon eat (the tails and claws), but she loved the solitude of the lake shore with the beautiful view of Mt. Rainier across the lake.

When the big sawmill was operating, Sofia sold milk, butter, eggs, and chickens to the superintendent and mill workers. She also sold these products to the Mineral Lake Lodge. At that time there were a number of Jewish families who spent the summer on Mineral Lake; they requested Sofia make unsalted butter for them.

The Ahlstrand brothers were very friendly and loved to be with other people. They maintained close family ties rarely letting a day go by without visiting one another. Herman was the most talkative, but they were all good story tellers. All three enjoyed doing things for people. If someone lost his household goods in a fire, the Ahlstrands were among the first to respond with everything they could spare.

August's home was always open to visitors who were well fed and bedded down, and their horses were taken care of, too.

All the brothers were noted for their honesty and generosity and as pioneers they were a good foundation on which to establish the community of Mineral.

Chapter 30

THE LODENS
AMONG EARLIEST IN FLYNN

When Richard Loden settled northeast of Mineral in the district known as Flynn, there were only two other men already located in the vicinity. Joseph J. Bolinger, who arrived just a few months before Loden, was homesteading just north of the Mineral Creek Bridge, as was Guernsey Hardy.

Loden was from Sweden, where the name was written with an accent mark over the "e" and was pronounced "Lodin." He had worked on a big farm in Sweden as a timekeeper. In 1885 he received a letter from an ex-captain living in Lake Park (known now as Spanaway) suggesting the young Loden immigrate. The letters came from Washington Territory because Washington did not become a state until 1889. The year before statehood, Loden came here as a young, single man, 22 years old (he was born October 22, 1867).

Loden and a brother-in-law had previously scouted around in Canada and Alaska for property. After several months he arrived in the Flynn area where he went to work for homesteader Guernsey Hardy on his place located about a mile north of Mineral Creek Bridge. He helped Hardy clear the heavily timbered land; then after several months Loden took advantage of the opportunity to buy the homestead. In an area of thick timber, any homestead with several acres of cleared land was attractive.

Six years later in 1894, the Martin Smeby family homesteaded a mile closer to Mineral than Loden. They were from Norway, but they had been in South Dakota for about ten years. Their daughter Magda, born May 5, 1878, was sixteen when they reached Mineral. Within a few years she became the bride of Richard Loden.

The Loden's first child Gerhard was born in 1898, followed by Axel, Ernest, and Selma. Selma was born several years after her mother was terribly injured when she was gored in the abdomen by a cow. Loden put Magda on horseback and started off for Tacoma; they stayed overnight in Eatonville before completing what must have been a nightmarish trip. Her injuries were so severe that she never regained her health with the result that Selma took over most of the household duties at a very young age. By the time she was about twelve years old, she was baking bread and cooking for the family.

Gerhard remembered his father was a hard worker, as was Magda before her accident. He was a big man, probably weighing 210 pounds; she was very skinny, weighing perhaps 110 pounds. Although they seldom left the farm, Richard made two trips to Sweden, in 1911 and 1926, where he visited all the members of his family, for they had all remained in the old country.

Magda's father Martin Smeby was not known by his family name of Hvem, pronounced "Vam" with a long "a", because after he was married he bought a large farm that was a "sort of village" in southern Norway, according to Selma. All the workers on the farm-village took the name of the village, Smeby, as a surname (which made family relationships very confusing). Smeby is pronounced as if the vowel were a long "a".

In the 1880's a depression so severe that the Smeby's eventually had to auction off the farm with almost all their possessions, including four sawmills hit Norway. As a well-to-do family, Mrs. Smeby "never had to do a tap of work in her life", Selma said. She had two girls who did the kitchen work and a governess for the children, who were the future Mrs. Loden and her twin sister. When they arrived in America, one of the few possessions they had was a trunk of handmade linens that was so heavy "the stevedores remarked it must have rocks in it."

From this position of wealth, the family came to a sod house in South Dakota where Mrs.

THE SMEBY'S WERE EARLY SETTLERS in Flynn near their daughter Magda Loden. Pictured are: her brother Helge Smeby, her father and mother Martin and Martha Smeby, and Magda and her husband Richard holding Gerhard.

Smeby as a forty-year-old woman had to learn a whole new style of life. Later they had a frame house where she scrubbed the bare floors then danced on them. Selma said, "That was quite a thing to make the transition and still be happy!"

Some time later after Smeby homesteaded in Mineral, a couple of men contested his claim, saying he had not done enough of the obligation work to "prove up" on his claim, even though he had already built a house there. Son-in-law Loden came to his rescue. After what Gerhard called a "battle royal", the men were sent on their way running with Loden's dog chasing them. Smeby had been at a disadvantage because of his age and lack of familiarity with the English language.

Before they moved into their new frame house, the Richard Lodens first lived in a log house with a fireplace of ordinary river rock, where Gerhard was born. The kitchen had a wood cookstove with a vent above it to heat the upstairs bedrooms where the children slept.

After a shingle mill was built in the neighborhood and the Tacoma-Eastern Railroad came through, there was a flag station there. A name was needed where the train stopped for passengers and freight going north to Tacoma and south to Mineral. Michael Flynn homesteaded across Mineral Creek, accordingly the railroad company call the stop "Flynn". Flynn was one of the earliest settlers, but he sold out and moved to

Tacoma where he bought property. Some time later he was killed when he was struck by a car.

Before there was a neighborhood school, Gerhard and Axel walked to Mineral, a two-and-a-half mile walk on the railroad tracks (considerably longer by county road). In the afternoon they were let out of school early enough to catch the afternoon train on which they had special tickets to Flynn.

When Gerhard was ten or eleven, his father and Mr. Linde, the boss of the shingle mill, decided they needed a school at Flynn because by that time there were several families with children living there. School was held first in a house left vacant by a man who lost his wife and moved away. Later Loden and Linde went to Chehalis to begin the process of forming School District #125. One square acre was donated for a school located on a knoll by the end of the deadend road; then a contract was let to build the school and the teacher's cottage.

The first teacher was a Miss Tibbits from Juneau, Alaska, who taught several years before changing to the Mineral school; later she married a Norwegian. Married women were not allowed to teach. A red-haired Miss Callison was the next teacher and later a local young woman, Marie Fritz, who married Guy Sutherland, taught there.

In their home the Loden children spoke a mixture of Swedish from their father and Norwe-

THE LODEN FAMILY OF MINERAL included father Richard; sons Gerhard, Axel, and Ernest; and mother Magda. Their daughter Selma was born later.

gian from their mother; they didn't learn to speak English until they started to school. It didn't help Gerhard to have learned to read Swedish from school books his father had brought from his home country.

Before there was anything around Mineral Lake except a homestead or two, Mineral City came into being on Mineral Creek, several miles northeast of the lake. A trading post was established by a Mr. Jonas from Chehalis and a hotel of cedar planks was built, which with a scattering of cabins made up Mineral City. The businesses were built on the basis of reports of rich mineral deposits in the hills; in fact, about 1896 a newpaper falsely reported a gold strike in Mineral City.

One mine did thrive when arsenic was found about seven miles up Mineral Creek, southeast of the settlement. Gerhard recalled seeing "Old

ERNIE LODEN AND HIS SISTER SELMA enjoyed the go-cart that Ernie built using log sections for the wheels. Building projects were his lifetime pursuits.

Man" Meyers hauling barrels of arsenic ore to the railroad with his team and wagon. The mine prospered until about 1920 when arsenic was produced cheaply as a by-product of metal smelting.

There was also an iron mine about halfway to the arsenic mine up Mineral Creek, but it never developed into a successful operation. A slightly more successful venture in Flynn, but of limited duration, was the sawmill built by Carl Soderquist, a Mineral storekeeper, and several other Swedish men. The logging was done by Sam Felt on the hill about a mile above the mill where the timber was loaded on railroad cars.

The mill owners had a little old locomotive that sometimes was not powerful enough to hold back loaded flatcars on the steep, crooked track. Sometimes they ran away taking the engine with them. There was a derail designed to prevent the logging train running out on the line where it joined the main Tacoma Eastern line.

Gerhard could see the track from his home, and one time he had an "inside seat" when the locomotive and flatcars came racing down the hill and one car jumped the derail and entered the main line. Fortunately, because the track ran up an incline there, the runaway came to a stop.

The mill had been built in the early 1920's and stood idle for several years until it was purchased by Ralph C. Wheeler, a storekeeper in Mineral, whose father owned a mill in Tacoma. It was said the mill failed to be a good investment because there was not enough timber purchased with it.

Gerhard never worked at any other job than the family farm, and he never married. Axel ran a donkey engine before moving to Eatonville and building a mill on land his father-in-law gave him near Silver Lake. He also worked on Alder Dam when it was under construction.

Ernie logged for 50 years and built many kinds of equipment, including donkey sleds and snowmobiles, and he was a pilot. He married Vada Scalf and had one son. Selma married Charles Sherwood and had a son and two daughters and worked on their blueberry farm in the Algona district; later they planted an apple orchard in Granger.

Gerhard finished the eighth grade in Flynn, graduated from high school in Mineral, and studied a year or so at Washington State College where he took an agricultural course. As a young man, he wanted to get off the farm for a while. During World War I he hoped to be drafted, especially because of the military training he had had at college. However, the draft board would not consider him because he was the oldest son of the family and a farmer; farming was considered essential to the war effort.

Gerhard and his father farmed about sixty acres, cultivating about forty. When they broke new ground, they planted oats for a nurse crop the first year, then planted grass for hay. Their cattle foraged on the rangeland most of the time, but they were fed during the winter on the oat and grass hay. Later they bought a grinder, raised wheat, and ground the grain for cattle and hog feed.

They sold some hogs "on the hoof" and butchered others for people in Mineral. They sold milk by the gallon, later shipping the cream and after the cream was separated they fed hogs and calves on the skim milk. After Richard's death at 75 on February 15, 1942, Gerhard began raising beef cattle. Despite Magda's poor health, she lived until April 30, 1967 when she was 89 years old.

Although an Irishman's name has long been attached to the area called Flynn, the first settlers in the area near Mineral Creek were mostly Scandinavians. The thriving settlement with their own school eventually decreased in number of residents, but it is now seeing revitalization. Many new families are building their homes along the Mineral Creek Road and they are sending their children to Mineral and Morton Schools. Flynn, first settled in the 1880's, is now flourishing in the 1980's.

Chapter 31

THE HALES OF FLYNN
A SETTLEMENT NEAR MINERAL

From a family history written by Verna (Hale) Bevan.

James D. "Gee" and Eliza Jane (Caudill) Hale came to the Flynn district three miles east of Mineral from Kentucky by way of Missouri. They were married on January 9, 1902, making their first home on Wolf Pen Creek about 20 miles from Hazard, Kentucky. Times were so hard there that they could barely make a living planting corn; in 1905 Gee and Eliza, hoping to have a better life, moved to Missouri.

While in Kentucky, their first son was born on January 15, 1903, named Wiley after Gee's oldest brother. Before he was a year old he died from pneumonia on December 6, 1903. Another son Denver was born on August 9, 1904, who lived only four years, passing away in 1908.

In the meantime, Gee's mother Rebecca died, leaving her two youngest children without a mother. Her daughter Una was about 13 years old while Little Noah was about ten. After Gee's father Noah remarried, the two children went to live with Gee and Eliza in Missouri.

During their three years in Missouri, two children were born: Marcus William on April 17, 1906, and Verna Ethel on February 16, 1908. Gee's sister Una married Harvey Morgan from Bradleyville, Missouri, making their home nearby. In October 1908, both families followed Gee's cousin John Sparkman to Washington State. Una was sick most of the way on the train; Eliza had to nurse both her baby and Una's month old child.

After the train arrived in Olympia, both families went to Matlock where John and Jay Sparkman were working in the woods. The men both got jobs and worked all winter. However, Harvey (Una's husband) could not stand the cold, wet weather and soon they went back to Missouri.

After two years, the Hales and Sparkmans moved to the Mineral area where there was a settlement of people they had known in Kentucky. They settled in a little logging area near the Ladd Coal Mine about two miles from Mineral that was known as Lockhart's Spur because Bill Lockhart was foreman on that section of railroad track. Eliza and Elizabeth, John Sparkman's wife, got the job of cooking for the logging crew while Gee went to work hewing railroad ties by hand from small logs.

Bill Lockhart, the section foreman, and his wife Mary had six children: Herman, Rufous, Viola, Bertha, Grace, and Helen. They lived on the other side of a little stream where one day Mary was crossing on a log when she fell in; the incident was the source of much amusement to the other residents.

JAMES D. "GEE" AND ELIZA (CAUDILL) HALE came from Kentucky to Mineral with Verna and Marcus. They settled in the area known as Flynn.

IN 1910, RAILROAD TIES were hewed by hand by J. D. "Gee" Hale near Mineral for which he
received 12 cents each. His wife Eliza and children Marcus and Verna joined him.

It wasn't long before the Hales moved to Park Junction between Elbe and Ashford. There they lived on a farm that was about a half mile toward the Nisqually River from the depot. Verna remembers it was pleasant living there in a two-story log house with a bay window in the living room. For several months Gee continued to work at Lockhart's Spur, getting home only on Sundays after walking both ways. Hale's second daughter Bessie was born February 2, 1912, while they lived there.

At one time a Morgan family lived in a log cabin down by the river. They had a teenage son Howard who loved to sing. Gee knew a lot of religious songs and Kentucky ballads, and Howard had learned some songs that were new then like "Wait 'Til the Sun Shines, Nellie." They spent many enjoyable evenings together.

Some Indians camped on the flat near Hale's home during the summer while they picked and dried wild blackberries and worked some for a neighbor. The Hale children had never seen Indians; therefore, they were a little bit scared of them; it didn't help when one night Marcus had a bad dream. He thought there was an Indian behind the door. He woke the whole family which didn't settle down until Gee checked the door.

The barn was a two story building with the second story on the bank above the flat, so that they could drive a team into the upper floor and go down a ramp to the lower level by the house. Verna wrote about the Easter when the children saw their mother go up the ramp with something in her apron. Soon Eliza called them to hunt Easter eggs in the hay to the delight of the youngsters.

One time Gee found out that President Taft was going to Mt. Rainier on a certain day by automobile when cars were rarely seen. The family went early, waiting for what seemed like hours, when finally a line of cars came by with Taft riding in a Model T car. They were thrilled when he waved at them.

The Hale children loved playing around the old log house. They had a swing in a big maple tree in the front yard and a large quince tree to play under in the backyard. One time they had a pet fawn for a little while that Gee had found in the woods, but without a milk cow they couldn't feed it. Sadly he took it back into the woods and left it.

Another time the family was down by the river when their little black dog Penny fell in the swift Nisqually River. The children were sure he would drown, but he drifted into a pile of brush. Gee worked his way out to where he could reach the dog and rescue it.

Occasionally a peddler would stop by with his wares in a large pack on his back that was like a double suitcase which he opened on the floor. The peddler, known as "Circus Red", carried many household items and even had several expensive watches that he hoped to sell to loggers. He walked the railroad track, stopping at each little settlement along the way and staying overnight anywhere he was welcomed. When he stayed with the Hales one time, he gave Eliza a pretty little cloth about the size of a napkin. Because she thought that it was too pretty to use, she kept it and Verna has it to this day.

Eliza sometimes worked for neighbor Mrs. Levant Hill who had been a schoolteacher before marriage. Because Eliza didn't have a sewing machine and Mrs. Hill was a good seamstress, the

THE FLYNN MODEL T SCHOOL BUS driven by Rufus Lockhart took children to Mineral School in 1918. The children are: Lutie Charles in front, Marcus Hale behind her, Verna Hale in back, Ernie Loden (boy in front), Cora Charles (long hair), Corrine Charles (bobbed hair), behind her is Minnie Charles. On the right is George Meyer.

neighbor lady made Verna's first school clothes.

The Hill brothers, Levant, Morris, and Peter, all owned farms in what was called Succotash Valley where they occupied most of the flat land. Levant had a nice house that he built before his marriage. The kitchen had a sink, but the water was outside by the porch where there was a pipe from a spring on the hill. Mrs. Hill had a big supply of heavy dishes they used every day. She stacked the dirty ones until they were all used up, then she hired someone to wash them, a job Verna got frequently.

One winter Levant Hill, his wife, and a neighbor girl started to Elbe in their sleigh pulled by their team of horses. A big tree fell on them, hitting Levant on the head, seriously injuring him and one of the horses. Mrs. Hill and the girl walked back to Hale's house to get Gee to help get Levant home. She told Gee to bring his gun to put the horse out of its misery. Levant's head wound was sewed up, but when it became infected he had to be taken to Eatonville Hospital. He was left with an ugly scar for life.

Quite often Jay Sparkman and his future brother-in-law Bill Adams walked the track from Mineral to have dinner with the Hales, which was especially appreciated by the two men who were bachelors then.

Sometimes the family would walk the track to Flynn where two nice houses had been left after the mill was abandoned there. Woodrow and Mary Adams' family lived in one with their children: Pearl, Maude, Fred, Roy, Lola, and Ruth. (Willie was born later.) The John and Virgie Charles family occupied the other house with their children: Minnie, Cora, Corrine, and Lutie.

John and Elizabeth Sparkman stayed with the Hales a few days before they left for Kentucky. Because they didn't like the climate here, (too much rain and cold for them), they lived there the rest of their lives.

One time a man rode a motorcycle to Hale's, and he asked them to store it while he went to Camp 12 to work. Verna wrote, "He parked it in the woodshed and Marcus would sit on it and pretend he was really going places."

Mrs. Engle, the primary schoolteacher at Elbe, coaxed Eliza to let Verna go to school although she was only five years old. Marcus and Verna walked to the depot every morning to ride the train to Elbe; then they walked several blocks to the school. They always got there a little late and they had to leave a little early to catch the train home. Verna was terribly frightened by the conductor because he teased her about punching her ears with his ticket puncher.

During that school year, there was a whooping cough epidemic which Marcus and Verna both contracted. After their little sister Bessie caught it, she developed pneumonia. When she became so sick that her parents decided she needed the doctor, Gee walked to Mineral then around the lake to where Dr. Shad lived. The doctor got on his horse and rode around by way of Elbe because the horse could not cross the railroad trestle over the Nisqually River that people crossed on foot all the time. The trestle linked the end of the road at Flynn with Park Junction.

After Dr. Shad examined Bessie, he told them that she must be taken to the hospital in Eatonville. Eliza got a neighbor to take care of Marcus and Verna who were still ill. When Gee

IN 1917, THE STUDENTS OF FLYNN SCHOOL were photographed by the teacher Mrs. Coleman. In the top row are: Minnie Charles and Maude Adams; in the middle are: Mark Hale, Cora Charles, Fred Adams, and Ernie Loden. In front are: Lola Adams, Jay Boyd, Corrine Charles, Verna Hale, and Roy Adams.

got home that night, he found that he had lost his job because he was late getting to work.

Eliza stayed with Bessie in the hospital for a week, but she died on December 10, 1913, less than two years old. Gee hired Roy Longmire from Elbe to go to Eatonville to get Eliza and the baby whom they brought home in a fancy little coffin in the back seat. Longmire took them to their friends Wiley and Daisy Francis where they expected to stay overnight and bury the baby the next day in the Mineral Cemetery. However, that evening Eliza found Verna had pneumonia, too; consequently, they stayed there to be close to the doctor. They gave Verna a bed in the living room where she spent 55 days while the doctor called every day. At Christmas time some children from Sunday School brought gifts for Verna, and a conductor on the train gave her a beautiful doll, her first.

When Verna continued to run a fever, the doctor brought an ice bag for her head. Marcus was sent to the lake to break ice, but when there was none there, he obtained it at Harry Rowe's ice cream parlor.

Because Verna simply wasn't getting better, Dr. Shad advised them to take her to some warmer place. Since Uncle Wiley Hale lived in Garden Grove, California, that was the logical place to go. Their neighbors took up a collection in Mineral and Elbe to pay the train fare, and two baskets of food were sent with them.

They went to Tacoma on the Tacoma Eastern Railroad to the Milwaukee Depot; then they walked to People's Store to buy a coat for Eliza. It was twilight when they came back to the depot and as country people they admired the clusters of lights on the street. In the depot Verna remembers lying on a bench looking up at the chandeliers which she thought couldn't be prettier.

When they got to Roseburg, Oregon, the train stopped to take on water. When Gee was told there would be a half hour layover, he started uptown to buy a pair of pants. As he got nearly there, the train started to move. In panic he ran back, catching the last car. By that time, the train had coasted to the water tower where they stopped for the half hour.

After Uncle Wiley met them in Los Angeles, he took them on an electric car to his home. To welcome them were Aunt Sarah and their five children. They settled in a small house in back; meanwhile, Gee got work in an orange grove

THE FLYNN SCHOOL, built about 1910, was near the end of Mineral Creek Road. A woodshed and teacher's cottage were included. The older Hale children attended school here.

where the old orange trees were being replaced with the seedless variety. He brought home all the oranges they could eat.

Before long Verna was well enough to walk around the block and enjoy playing with her cousins. One day she and Aunt Sarah were walking downtown when Sarah found a little gold ring with "solid gold" stamped on it. She gave it to Verna.

Because Gee couldn't find a better paying job and Eliza didn't like California, they decided to return to Washington. When Gee found that a boat trip was much cheaper than the train, he bought tickets even though Eliza didn't like the idea. They sailed from San Pedro to San Francisco where they boarded another ship. In the city they saw some of the earthquake damage from 1906.

The trip north was rough, but Marcus and Verna had an exciting time, being the only small children aboard. In their cabin they would take turns standing on the bed trying not to flinch when a wave hit the porthole. Many of the adults were seasick on the rough voyage, including Gee who was sick after every meal, but he never

skipped one. When they finally got to Seattle, Gee went into a restaurant and kept eating until he had consumed six eggs.

Back in this area, they rented one end of the abandoned cookhouse in Flynn, settling in early June, then on July 7, 1914, Mabel Alice was born. Eliza picked a bucket of wild blackberries the same day that she sent Gee on foot to get Dr. Shad to come on his saddle horse. Marcus and Verna stayed with neighbors overnight; the next morning they learned that they had a new sister.

After Gee made a down payment on 40 acres of logged-off land, he, Marcus, and Eliza began clearing off a place for a house. They finally got a milk cow, Moll, which Eliza milked by the fence on their property, so that she would be accustomed to being there. The children were excited about having their own cow for the first time.

The Flynn schoolhouse was on a little knoll not far from their home. There was a different teacher every year with not over a dozen pupils. A teacher's cottage was built on the same acre of ground while the outhouses were located in opposite corners of the lot; there was also a woodshed. One teacher gave Marcus a dime a day to keep the fire going. They went to the first five grades there; then they went to Mineral Grade School by car.

One morning Verna wanted to wear the little gold ring Aunt Sarah had found; her mother thought that it was too loose, but Verna insisted. While playing one of the favorite games at school, "Pom Pom Pull-Away", unhappily she lost the ring.

When children misbehaved in school, they were whipped with a switch in front of everyone which Verna said always frightened her very much.

Gee hired a man to build a little house for his family; when Mabel was about three years old, they moved in. There James Robert was born on September 2, 1918. Verna said, "We had lots of good times in that little house and we always knew we were loved. We didn't have many possessions, but we never knew we were poor."

Aunt Una, back in Missouri, lost her husband, leaving her with four children. Gee sent for them and moved them into the small house.

The 1918 influenza epidemic was just starting to infect many people. Aunt Una went to Carlson (a couple of miles out of Mineral) to take care of the sawmilling Carlson family who were all ill; they needed help and she needed the job. Meanwhile, all the Hales were sick, including Eliza, who was too ill to nurse baby Jim. "Everyone thought it was a pity that he had to be fed with a bottle," Verna recalled.

After neighbor Richard Loden milked their cow, he left the milk on the steps to avoid being exposed to the flu. With many people dying, Dr. Shad told others to avoid going to the burials for fear of spreading the illness. Although Aunt Una was exposed continually, she never did get the flu.

About this time, Gee ordered an Edison phonograph that played cylinder records. When it came into the Mineral depot, he and Marcus carried it down the tracks, a shorter route than the road. They played the six records every night, of course, memorized all of them; Uncle Josh's comedy and all the songs.

Another evening entertainment was "Ring on a String" with everyone joining in except Eliza, who always had darning or sewing to do, but who followed the progress of the game. Because there was no money to buy games, they made a pack of cards they called "Book" from cardboard squares with words and the alphabet on them. The game was played by drawing cards until they had two alike which made a book.

About this time, Gee and his cousin Jay Sparkman joined the Old Regular Baptist Church and were baptized in Round Top Creek. This was a church brought from the hills of Kentucky where the men had grown up. Eliza joined later, as did Jay's wife Mallie.

A big event in the Hale family was when Gee bought a secondhand Model T Ford car in 1918. They went places on Sundays, mostly to Baptist churches in Glenoma, Riffe, and Ajlune. They also went to different towns for baseball games where they knew all the players who were mostly local men.

On September 2, 1919, the Hales made their first trip to Mt. Rainier with the Hills of Mineral who took their son Bill and Pearl Rowe, who later were married. They ate their picnic lunch near Nisqually Glacier where at that time cars would get in line to wait for a group of cars to come down from Narada Falls on the one lane road; then those waiting could go up to Paradise Valley.

After Marie Norma was born April 11, 1922, the need for a larger house prompted the Hales to begin planning to build. They cleared a spot and hired Haze Pellett to build a house that they moved into just before Anna Lee was born on September 11, 1924. With six children they really needed the extra space.

Gee and Eliza reared their six children who survived childhood. When the youngest one graduated from high school, Gee retired to do some "serious farming" as Verna called it. They bought more cows and sold milk. The family felt he never enjoyed farming as much as working in a logging camp, but at least he could work at his own pace. Verna remembers watching Gee hoeing the garden when the donkey whistle blew, seeing him leaning on his hoe handle and looking sad.

After a full life, Gee died at 83 years of age; Eliza lived to 97.

Always good neighbors, the Hales were highly respected in their community and they raised a family of fine citizens. The home place has been divided among the children; today most of them have either permanent or summer homes on the property, and they have remained a close family.

Chapter 32

JAY SPARKMAN
FROM KENTUCKY TO MINERAL

An early resident of Mineral, Wiley J. Sparkman was always known as "Jay." Born November 28, 1881, on Wolf Pen Creek, Knott County, Kentucky, Jay arrived in Mineral in 1910. His childhood was spent in the primitive and often harsh Appalachian Mountains where they had to raise almost everything they ate and wore.

Besides the years in Mineral, this story covers three generations in Kentucky in order to give a glimpse of the kind of life our early settlers left behind when they moved to Washington State.

Jay's father Elijah was a blacksmith and carpenter while farming his 200 acres of steep hillsides and narrow valleys, called hollows, pronounced "hollers" by the natives. They plowed the steep slopes, planted corn behind the plow; then later they plowed between the rows to cultivate the corn which provided a staple in their diet, cornmeal. They raised hogs, geese, and sheep and sometimes ducks, cattle, and turkeys.

They raised sheep for the wool. The whole family had to help wash the wool and pick out burrs; often each one had to clean a handful before bedtime. The wool was then carded before it could be spun into yarn on a spinning wheel. The yarn was used on the loom Elijah built for his wife to weave the heavy cloth that made good, durable pants.

Elijah also made all their shoes from leather made by removing the hair from hides with lye, then tanning it. Lacking shoe nails, he whittled pegs from dogwood to hold the shoes together; the results covered their feet, but were almost too stiff to walk in.

His father did not always have time to make shoes for his three boys until after "the frost had set in." One very cold morning Jay was walking barefoot the three miles to school when his grandfather happened along on a horse. His grandfather took him up and he never forgot how grateful he was to press his cold feet against the warm horse.

All household chores were done by hand in those days. for instance, Jay's mother, Mary "Polly" (Amburgey) Sparkman, had to do the washing by laying the clothes on a block and beating them with a paddle, using soap she had made by boiling the fat of hogs with the lye from wood ashes.

Polly died in 1886 when she was only 30 years old, leaving three small boys: Noah six, Jay five, and John two years old. Jay could remember his mother from only a few incidents, such as the time his father was putting shakes on his grandfather's house. He told his mother that he was going to play under the bank of the creek. Instead, he started off to see his father; he almost got there when his mother caught up with him and spanked him.

Another time, he accidentally hit his brother Noah in the head when they were throwing rocks. His mother, thinking he had done it purposely, was very angry while he was very upset to think his mother would believe it was intentional.

Jay could remember only one severe whipping from his father which was for fighting with his brother John over a bow and arrows. Later he had better equipment for hunting when he earned enough for his first gun, a muzzle loader, by raising turkeys.

In his blacksmith shop Elijah made all kinds of tools, such as one to make tongue-and-groove lumber of poplar. It was a big event when he finally got an old crosscut saw after years of hewing everything with an axe. There was no such thing as a sawmill then; logs were sawed into lumber by hand. Elijah would square a poplar log with an axe; then place it where one man could work above and another below to saw it into one-inch boards.

THE COOKHOUSE AT LOCKHART SPUR one mile from the highway on Ladd Road was run by Eliza Hale and Elizabeth Sparkman (Mrs. John) who were in the doorway with little Verna Hale. J. D. "Gee" Hale is on the steps with Marcus. The crew from the left were: Bill Lockhart, Anice Lester, "Sticker"; behind him was Herman Lockhart, then Johnny Sargent, Will Clayton, and Howard Morgan. On right of the door were: Jim Morrey, Math Clayton with a dog, Wiley Francis and son Gomer, John Sparkman, unidentified, and Jay Sparkman.

Elijah was also a coffin maker. To form the old traditional shape that curved from wide at the head to narrow at the foot, he would cut part way through a board, then soak it in hot water until he could bend it. To finish the coffin he lined it with black cloth.

After Polly died, Elijah's sister Artie cooked for the family for a few months although she was just a child. One time she served a piece of pork without singeing the hair off it; however, Elijah made the boys eat it and not say anything to hurt Artie's feelings.

It wasn't long until Elijah married Matilda "Tildy" (Smith) Hale who was a young widow with two boys and two girls of her own. Jay always said that Tildy treated him and his brothers as if she was their birth mother. Tildy was a good cook even during the time she had to cook over the fireplace, but preparing meals was much easier when they acquired a cook stove.

Once when Jay and his brothers were small their grandfather Wiley J. Amburgey, who was a drinker, had to sleep with them. He told them to jab him if he bothered them, so naturally the boys found plenty of excuses to poke him.

Jay's other grandfather John Sparkman visited their home when the boys were young. He was a small man of Dutch and Irish extraction who was a Civil War veteran on the Confederate side. One of his war stories was about running to a tree during a battle when he said he could have caught a "sifter full of bullets." They also heard stories about the toughness of this grandfather, such as when a log rolled over him he told the men carrying him to be careful because his leg was broken. Another time he caught his hand in

a cane mill, and he calmly gave his son instructions how to release it.

Elijah was a religious man who would not work on Sundays. He didn't have much education, but he could read the Bible with a desire to learn more about it. One Sunday morning his brother Ora was doing practice shooting with a pistol as people went by on the way to church. When Elijah told him to quit, Ora became angry, left home, and never came back.

On his death bed Elijah could not speak, but he was able to motion that he wanted his whole family to join him in heaven. He was only 44 years old when he died on April 25, 1900, of yellow jaundice that he caught from Jay's cousin,

MINERAL'S BIG TREE on Mineral Creek Road was a landmark for many years; the diameter of the tree was about 14 feet. Sunday afternoon hikes to see it were popular; this group included Vic Rowe, the boy in the middle.

JAY SPARKMAN'S HOME was originally a log house built by Martin Smeby. Sparkman had it remodeled with a large addition to make the present farmhouse on Mineral Road North.

James D. "Gee" Hale. He got out of bed too soon, had a relapse, and never recovered.

In 1901, Jay went to live with his Uncle Silas Francis; then the next year he went to work for his Uncle John Amburgey (called John Borax) for 50 cents a day and board. Next he went to Uncle Bob and Aunt Cindy Amburgey's where he was fed, clothed, and treated like one of the family.

About this time, Jay enrolled in a special school in Hindman that had been founded by two women who wanted to give an opportunity for more education to the mountain children. Seeing his potential, they made arrangements for him to go to Berea College, a famous work-study school in Kentucky. He enjoyed the schooling and was doing well until he had eye trouble which eventually caused him to drop out.

He went back to live with Uncle Bob Amburgey; then he got a job surveying in the hill country where division of property was made along the tops of the ridges. He didn't see any future in that job and was not interested when Uncle Bob offered to get him a bank job if he would stay there.

Jay's brother John was already in Washington State. He wrote about the availability of work with better pay; thus in 1907 Jay decided to "pick up stakes and move west." He came by way of Missouri to escort John's wife Elizabeth to Black Lake south of Olympia where John was working in the woods.

He logged for a while; then in 1908 Jay worked for a Frenchman building a "skid road" used to drag logs out of the forest until hard times hit and wages were cut. Hearing of work in Montana, he spent the summer helping run a planer mill in Hamilton, a town located in the Bitterroot Mountains out of Missoula. The hillsides were covered with old pine trees that made excellent "bee trees", and the valley was full of alfalfa which made good honey. One busy day Jay found five bee trees, one of which held at

JAY AND MALLIE (ADAMS) SPARKMAN lived all their married lives in Mineral. Both from Kentucky, they married March 28, 1918 and they reared five sons.

least 200 pounds of honey comb, besides shooting 20 squirrels; both skills he learned in Kentucky. Much later in life he enjoyed having several hives of bees whose stings bothered him very little.

In 1909 he joined his brother John and his cousin James D. "Gee" Hale logging near Shelton. He tended the cable-winding spool on a donkey engine until it was replaced with a drum operated with a lever. While working there for the Simpson Logging Company, the first overhead skidder in this part of the country was brought in and "it really speeded things up when it worked," Jay said. A little over a year later, Gee found out about good jobs around Mineral making railroad ties from small trees, and they all moved there.

Gee made ties while Jay found a job with Carlson Lumber company in 1910, then logged for McFadden on a school section of timber at Flynn back of Gee's farm. In the spring of 1912 he went to work on another school section at Park Junction near Elbe where he was put to work "chunking" on a donkey engine. He had to work with a Japanese man whom he disliked, feeling independent he quit.

In Mineral he was hired to work for the big Mineral Lake Lumber Company for $2.00 a day, later raised to $2.50. Some time after this he was going to quit the mill, but stayed on when the boss offered him $2.75 a day and a better job. Jay worked with a number of Japanese there.

One day he was working on the "slip" where they pulled logs up into the mill when a steam engine governor failed. The sawyer ran out shouting for him to run. They barely got outside on the slip when the racing engine exploded. A large piece of metal tore through the roof; it hit the sawyer and killed him instantly.

After 36 years of bachelorhood, Jay married Mallie Adams, ten years his junior, on March 28, 1918. Mallie came to Mineral the year before with her mother Malissa Adams to join several brothers and a sister. They were all from Knott County, Kentucky; they were acquainted when they were younger. Jay and Mallie took the train to Tacoma; they were married there and returned to set up housekeeping in a house Jay owned. Their first son Elmer Jay was born June 24, 1919, followed by Ernest Adams on December 18, 1920.

Later they bought a farm on the Flynn Road east of Mineral, moving there about 1925 where they lived the rest of their lives. They added to the original log house and remodeled it; the only evidence now of the thick log walls are the unusually wide windowsills. Paul Brutus was added to the family on February 11, 1923.

The family was excited when they got their first car, a 1926 Chevrolet. They no longer had to rely on others to get to church or to town.

The Sparkmans lost a baby boy at birth in 1930; then Willard Dale was born February 18, 1932, and Richard Ivan on August 29, 1935. After having six sons, Mallie always joked that "all my girls were boys."

Mallie kept an immaculate house and was an excellent mother. Even when the boys were small, it was her job to milk their cows; Jay never learned how to milk. She canned hundreds of quarts of fruit every year. She was an outstanding cook; frequently on Sunday she cooked a huge meal for church people who came home with them. She could make several mouth-watering pies in record time. For many years she washed clothes in a hand-powered washing machine with the boys' help; it wasn't until 1932 that she had an electric wringer washer.

After about eight years at the sawmill, Jay changed to the M. R. Smith Shingle Company also located on Mineral Lake where he worked about six years at $4.00 a day until the cedar dust gave him asthma causing him to quit. In 1928, he worked for West Fork Logging Company constructing a railroad up Mineral Creek that was crossed by an extremely high A-frame bridge built on cedar pilings.

After being out of work for a while, a friend made out an application for Jay for the State Highway Department. He got the job in 1932 when the road between Mineral and Morton was not much more than a narrow, winding trail through the timber. He worked on the highways from Elbe to Morton to Fern Gap, down Bear Canyon, and to the top of Riffe Hill. Until the road was improved between Elbe and Morton, much of the work was grading the old road and trying to keep it passable. The winters were a bad time when he often had to help chop or handsaw trees that fell across the road. Once he was returning from Glenoma with a load of hogs when his truck got stuck in the mud in new road construction on the Divide between Mineral and Morton. When some of the hogs escaped, he had to round them up as well as get the truck pulled out of the mud.

His reputation for being observant and sharp-eyed was well established among the men he worked with on the highway. Many times as they drove along the road, Jay would say to the driver, "Hold up, there!" and he would jump out to pick up a lost tool on the roadside, adding to his large collection of hammers, wrenches, pliers, screwdrivers, chains, etc. After 18 1/2 years on the State Highway, mandatory retirement at 70 years of age forced him out of the job in 1951.

He continued to farm throughout the years, supplying milk to the big West Fork Hotel on Mineral Lake and raising hogs on the garbage, much of which was good food wastefully thrown out. Black bears were a nuisance quite often, coming in at night to tip over the feed barrels.

To eliminate the problem, Jay and his son Elmer stayed up one night until after the moon went down when a large bear arrived and Jay shot it. However, in the morning the barrels were tipped over as usual; therefore, they decided the shot had missed. That night the bear hunter's vigil was repeated and this time the bear ran only a short distance. Several days later they found the carcass of the first bear where it had dropped after running across the creek and the railroad track.

Joining the Mineral Old Regular Baptist Church in 1925 and being made a deacon the next year, Jay spent many active years in church work. He was always an enthusiastic supporter of good schools and took an active part in the Democratic Party. Although serious about his stand, his sharp wit was often shown as he loved to tease and be teased about politics. After his oldest son married an active Republican and they had a child, Jay said one day that the youngster couldn't be a Democrat or a Republican, but would have to be a "straddle-pole!"

Although Jay had a severe stroke several years after retiring, he remained active with a keen, alert mind. He kept up on current events through his lifelong habit of thoroughly reading the newspaper. Mallie passed away in August, 1970, at age 79; Jay died in April, 1973, when he was 91 years old.

Always noted for complete honesty and for being a hard worker, Jay was never rich in material things, but he earned a fortune in respect and a wealth of friends.

Chapter 33

WILLIE BEVAN and LADD COAL MINE

An almost forgotten small community and large coal mine existed near Mineral, Washington, in the first quarter of this century. Ladd is remembered by Willie Bevan, whose father worked in the coal mines. The mines were located three miles west of Mineral; today access to the site is by Forest Road 74 that goes by the Pleasant Valley Christian Camp on Highway 7.

The path leading the Bevan family to eastern Lewis County began with Willie's parents' birth in South Wales. His father, Bill, was a coal miner in that corner of Britain until their immigration to the United States in 1905, drawn here by encouragement from relatives.

The Bevans settled first in Iowa with work in a coal mine; then they moved to Colorado for more mining, where Willie was born in 1907. Arriving in Black Diamond, Washington, after receiving letters from an aunt and an uncle, who was coal mining there, Bill heard of the new mine at Ladd and decided to move there in 1909.

The Ladd mine was developed mainly to provide coal for the locomotives in 1904 by William Ladd and John Bagley, partners in building the Tacoma Eastern Railroad. The soft bituminous coal burned well in steam engines and in steamships. Large shipments went to the Tacoma Skinner and Eddy Shipyard which had an interest in the mine in later years.

After the railroad reached Mineral in 1905, a branch line was constructed to Ladd which branched off just south of Mineral. It replaced the original puncheon road to Ladd. The Tacoma Eastern line carried many passengers, besides the 100 tons of coal a day that were shipped out of the Ladd mines at their height of production. For some time the passenger train from Tacoma stayed overnight in Ladd, left in the morning for Morton, then returned to Mineral and went on to Tacoma.

The Ladd community consisted of a store and housing for married men with families, married men whose families were elsewhere (many in

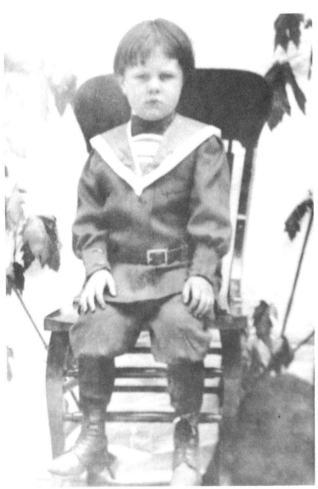

WILLIE BEVAN was five years old in 1912. His parents, who were from Wales, moved to Mineral in 1909 where Willie spent the rest of his life.

their country of origin), and single men. The families lived in two-story houses, while the other men lived in a two-story bunkhouse and ate their meals in a cookhouse which Willie managed to visit once a day for a treat of a cookie or doughnut. The buildings were modern for that time, having running cold and hot water and heat from a steam boiler which was in the midst of the settlement.

There were a few Japanese workers and families that lived separately at Ladd; because the men refused to go underground, they worked around the coal bunkers and cut mine timbers.

Ladd acquired a Post Office in Charles Winsberg's store in 1907 when Winsberg became Postmaster. After Winsberg moved to Morton in 1910, the superintendent of East Creek Mine, D. W. Watkins, became Postmaster and served until the Post Office was discontinued in 1914 during a lull in the mining. After this, Willie, whose family had moved from Ladd to Mineral, delivered the mail from Mineral by walking the three miles up the railroad track after school. For this job he received fifteen cents a day.

"The only hazard walking the tracks to Ladd came not from wild animals, but from a 'bunch of razorback hogs' that the pioneer Joseph Bollinger raised in the swamp," Willie said. "The hogs were often on the railroad tracks and many times 'put a run on the kids,'" as Willie remarked, "They were pretty ornery."

One time after he and Helmer Larson had been to Ladd and had spent too much time looking around there, it was dark when they got back to Bollingers. The boys were running down the track when they stumbled onto the sleeping hogs; pandemonium reigned as boys and hogs ran over each other. It was a tossup who was the most frightened.

The Bevan family were living at Ladd when Willie's sister, Blodwin, was born in 1910. When she reached school age, they moved to Mineral. Willie had been walking to the Mineral School every day since he had started to school at eight years of age. He said that when the snow got deep you simply didn't go to school. Although his parents could speak English which they learned in school in South Wales, they spoke Welsh in the home, and Willie had to learn a new language after starting to school.

The Bevans also lived for a time on the Divide between Mineral and Morton where there was a small coal mine from which it was a four mile walk to school for Willie. A rancher on the Divide, Ben Smith, had a nephew going to school also. Smith had two horses that were half wild that he would sometimes let the boys ride, but Willie joked, "There were a couple of days we spent more time trying to catch those horses than we spent in school." All they had to ride with was a halter and a blanket — "It was kind of a chore to stay aboard!" he said.

On the way to school the boys met the Suter "kids": Bertha, Tuff, and Frank, who lived on the ranch at the end of what is now Roundtop Creek Road; they would walk the remainder of the way to Mineral School together.

When Willie walked from either Ladd or the Divide, he walked the railroad tracks because the road from the Divide was old puncheon and very muddy, while the tracks were clean. "You couldn't hardly walk the road," Willie said. On the way home Mrs. Fritz, Marie Sutherland's mother, waited for him with a cookie or apple, cautioning him each day to go straight home.

However, the caution did not deter him from stopping at the Carlson Mill to "see how that was going." Then there was logging going on above Carlson where Walt Dunlap was running a donkey engine beside the railroad, and Willie had to stop and watch awhile.

One time as Willie headed for home, it started to get dark too early, and he got scared and broke into a run. It got darker and darker, but he had the shiny rails to run between. "It was a scary situation," he emphasized, "I figured I'd spent too much time doing my visiting!" Soon he met his father coming down the tracks to explain to him that an eclipse was occurring.

While Bevan, Sr., was superintendent at the Ladd coal mine, Willie often went with his father into the mines on Sunday evenings to test for methane gas. Big fans at the entrance to the mines constantly pulled in fresh air while drawing the gas out, but the methane would be concentrated in the upper corners of the rooms in the mine. Air shafts slanting down at 45 degrees provided the fresh air.

Bevan used a German Wolf Lamp that originally burned whale oil to test for the deadly gas. When he held the lamp up in possible pockets of gas, the flame would burn above the wick, the higher the flame the greater the concentration of the explosive gas.

After the tests, Bevan made a notation on a blackboard which indicated the number of places in the mine where there was gas and which were safe. The air flow could be controlled with canvas curtains to clear the dangerous places of methane. There were big doors at the entry that were opened to admit the small locomotive that hauled the coal out of the mine, then the doors were closed behind it so that the big fans could work like a huge vacuum cleaner.

Each miner picked up a head lamp at the

beginning of his ten-hour shift. The lamps were constructed so that they could not be opened underground because of the gas; however, many mine disasters and lives were lost by miners outwitting the system. The lamps were designed to be opened only with magnets that drew out two points before the base could be unscrewed.

To illustrate the danger, in 1899 in Carbonado, a mine explosion killed thirty men. Upon investigation, an opened lamp was found along with a pipe and tobacco pouch. Somehow, a miner had opened his lamp with tragic results.

Coal mining at Ladd was discontinued because mining there was no longer profitable partly because fuel oil had become the main source of power for trains and ships, and because of two disastrous events.

The first dramatic event occurred after weeks of heavy rain and snowfall caused a landslide that dammed East Creek on January 2, 1919. When the natural dam broke, it swept through the little settlement knocking the buildings off their foundations and causing the deaths of three persons.

The second misfortune happened in October of the same year when the small locomotive became derailed inside the mine. After getting the engine back on the track, they fired up the engine and a spark lodged in the overhead cedar planking, and it caused a roaring fire. There was no loss of life, but mining was essentially over at Ladd.

Willie Bevan still lives on Mineral Lake. He married Verna Hale, a Mineral girl, in 1929, and they had three children: Marjorie, David, and Kathleen. Willie worked at a variety of jobs, including the Forest Service and logging camps, and managed the M. R. Smith Shingle Company

WILLIE AND VERNA (HALE) BEVAN married in 1929 and had three children. In back are: Marjorie and David. Verna and Willie are in front with Kathleen.

for 25 years; he concluded his working years in the parts department of St. Regis Logging Company. He retired in 1972.

The mines at Ladd, which once produced 100 tons of washed coal a day, and the settlement are almost forgotten, but they are remembered now as an archaeology site registered with the State of Washington and by Mineral old-timer, Willie Bevan.

Chapter 34

ROWE AND HILL — MINERAL STORE

When the last of the old stores in Mineral burned in 1975, a lot of history went up with it. The Rowe and Hill grocery store was built about 1910 by Mineral pioneer Herman Ahlstrand, who with his brothers homesteaded around Mineral Lake. After the store was built, Ahlstrand rented it to another Swedish immigrant Carl Soderquist, who came to this country as a young man as the Ahlstrands did.

Soderquist operated the store as the "People's Store" until about 1919 when he sold it to go into a small sawmill business at the district known as Flynn, several miles northeast of Mineral. It was sold to the Pacific Cooperative League, which turned out to be a racket. Many shares in the store were sold to local people for $100 a share; the investors lost all their money. The remainder of the stock was sold at a sheriff's sale. Harry Rowe and William "Bill" Hill bought the stock and the store and reopened it in 1921.

Rowe and Hill were the father and the husband respectively of Pearl Rowe Hill, who lived all her life in Mineral. The two men operated the store as a partnership until Rowe's death in 1933, when Hill took over as the sole owner and continued in the business until he retired in 1964, according to Pearl.

Hill's retirement came as the result of a costly fire in 1964 that wiped out two of the three stores in Mineral, both Pye's and Wheeler's stores. Welles Wheeler, who operated the store his father Ralph had established in the early days of Mineral, was not ready to retire when he lost his business; therefore, he offered to buy Hill's store. Wheeler moved up the street to Rowe and Hill's establishment where he operated the only market remaining in Mineral until he retired and sold out to Robert Spencer about 1973. Pye's store had been established very early by L. I. Walrath, who sold out to Ford Phelps, then later to Fred Pye.

Pearl Rowe Hill worked with her husband in the business off and on through the years. The

VIC ROWE lived all his life in this existing home. He was the son of Harry Rowe of the Rowe and Hill Store; his sister Pearl married Hill.

only employees were Emil and Deb Bickford, brothers who worked there at different times.

The original store was quite a contrast to the super markets of today. Before the first remodeling, the shelves were built up to the ceiling, and they were reached either by stepladder or by a pole designed to lift items off the high shelves. One hazard was the occasional bump on the head from an item falling as the grocer attempted to get it down, Pearl said with a smile.

The store was lighted with gasoline lights, and it was heated by a big wood stove that was a gathering place for men of the community.

Because most transportation to Mineral was by railroad, all but local produce arrived by train, which also carried the salesmen. With two passenger trains each day, even perishable products came that way. Bread came in big wooden trunks from Tacoma every day.

Home delivery was common then. Soderquist delivered by horse and wagon at first, then later he bought a Model T Ford truck. When Rowe and Hill took over the store, a truck came with it.

The store handled livestock feed that was kept in a back room along with a barrel of coal oil (kerosene) which everyone used to light their homes because there was no electricity in Mineral until the early 1930's. Also there was a barrel of

FRONT STREET IN MINERAL has always been the main street in this town that flourished in the early 1900's. R. C. Wheeler and his mother are standing on the wooden sidewalk.

vinegar which was used to fill gallon jugs the customers brought in.

Dry products such as beans, peas, rice, and coffee were dispensed with a scoop from bins under the counter, then it was weighed and packaged for each customer. Sugar came in 100-pound gunny sacks lined with white cloth bags. Coffee was ground in a coffee grinder as it was sold. Cheese was cut from big "wheels" with a cheese cutter that was round with a revolving blade. Chewing tobacco was sold in pieces cut with a tobacco cutter.

Milk was purchased from local farmers, and it was sold in quart glass bottles. Potatoes and eggs were also bought from local farmers. Butter, milk, and eggs were kept in an icebox cooled with blocks of ice delivered by the train.

Cube sugar sold in little wooden barrels was a favorite of the many Swedish customers even though it was expensive at three pounds for 25

cents. Crackers, some cookies, and pickles came in wooden barrel tubs. For many years cookies were sold from large glass containers before they were packaged as they are now. Candy was sold from glass apothecary jars, most of it was penny candy. Since the candy sold for several big pieces for a penny, children took a long time to decide how to spend their one little coin. The only candy bars were large Hershey bars which cost five cents.

Bacon was sold by the slab with most customers buying a chunk of it, but a few wanted it sliced, which was done with a big knife; there were no meat slicers in those early days. They carried no meats because there was a butcher shop next door in a small building that had been moved in and attached to the store building. In much later years the butcher shop became a store room for Hill's paints.

In the photograph of the interior of the store,

HORSE AND BUGGY were the means of travel on Mineral's main street when R. C. Wheeler was a young man.

R. C. WHEELER'S STORE was operated by his father before him. One of three stores in Mineral, it burned along with Pye's store in 1964.

THE INTERIOR OF ROWE AND HILL'S STORE in Mineral remained essentially the same from 1910 until it burned in 1975. Gathered one morning were: Walt Dunlap, Bert Schabel, owner Bill Hill and J. D. "Gee" Hale.

balls of string can be seen suspended from the ceiling because most items were sacked and wrapped with string.

For many years, the grocer waited on the customer as she read off her list with the grocer doing all the walking to assemble the order in contrast to today's supermarket style of shopping. Hill had customers who made out their own charge slips with complete honesty. For many years everyone charged their groceries and paid once a month.

During the Depression and during strikes, the grocery business was really bad. They could not have stayed in business without a core of dependable people who could be depended on to pay their bills.

The second story of the building was a lodge hall that was used through the years by the Yeomen, Women of Woodcraft, Modern Woodmen, Shingle Weavers Union, and finally by the Royal Neighbors. The hall was large which made it ideal for parties given for the young people of the community.

The old way of conducting a grocery business passed into history when Rowe and Hill's General Store burned on September 23, 1975. Mineral was left with one business, a tavern, until Dick and Leslie Dunlap opened a small grocery in May, 1985.

After a number of years Mineral's population diminished, now the little community is growing with new families making their homes there, so that now they can support a store again.

ROWE AND HILL GENERAL MERCHANDISE in Mineral was in business from 1910 until it burned in 1975. The picture is a painting by Ted Sherrad, who married Marie Hale, a local girl.

Chapter 35

LADD, A COAL MINE and a COMMUNITY

Research and first draft by Patricia Coon

The coal mine and small community of Ladd, Washington, were typical of short-lived mining towns that sprang up rapidly and died just as rapidly. Located in the hills and forest three miles west of Mineral, the mine was worked only from 1906 to 1919.

The outcropping of coal was found in 1904 on East Creek by Edward Hoem, son of the Pleasant Valley homesteader Ole Hoem. The location is in eastern Lewis County, Range 4 East of the Willamette Meridian, Township 14 North, Sections 12 and 13. Access to the site today is by Forest Road 74 off Highway 7 by the Pleasant Valley Christian Camp.

East Creek arises from two spring-fed streams in a narrow valley below Hodgin's Ridge and flows north through Pleasant Valley to empty into Alder lake. When the area was being explored, it was natural to follow the creek upstream where the outcropping of coal was very visible.

The word of the coal discovery spread rapidly; prospective miners hurried to stake claims. The most prominent of these claim stakers were Bagley and Ladd, who formed a partnership not to develop the coal mine since coal had not yet been found when their business relationship began, but because they could see there was money to be made by shipping logs from the heavily forested region in the foothills of Mt. Rainier.

In 1900, four years before the coal strike, private entrepreneur John Bagley, a developer of railways, decided to complete a railroad that had been started south of Tacoma seven years earlier, according to Pearl Engle in her book, "History of Tacoma Eastern Area."

A Portland banker William Ladd learned of Bagley's project and wanted in on the deal; consequently he persuaded Bagley to form a partnership in what would surely be a profitable undertaking. Through the partnership they arranged financing, and Tacoma Eastern Railroad (T. E.) came into being. When the T. E. reached Mineral in 1905, a branch line was constructed to Sections 12 and 13, connecting the claims of Bagley and Ladd, allowing the mining to begin in 1906.

The rich bituminous coal was abundant at the 1600 foot elevation extending to 1830 feet at some of the outcroppings of coal. When burned, the soft coal produced moderate heat for furnace use while supplying fuel for steamships and locomotives in the region.

The first mine to open at Ladd, as it was called, was the William Ladd Coal Company and John Bagley Account. Managed by Bagley, it employed 27 men with 20 working underground and seven above ground. The first year 15,000 tons of coal was produced. The William Ladd Coal Company operated from 1906 to 1909 having dug 33,697 tons of coal for the company.

In 1906, the East Creek Coal Company began operations under President Bagley who employed 22 men, all of whom worked above ground on the outcroppings of coal, processing the coal and cutting mine timbers and other necessary tasks. Bagley's company operated from 1906 to 1916 and during those years the mine produced 247,004 tons of coal.

Bagley and Ladd had invested originally $3,000, a substantial amount early in the century. They had built a coal washing system and large covered bunkers. Washing and sorting was done with the use of shaker racks, similar to those used to sort apples. The shaker mechanism was powered by one of the large steam engines fed by the abundant coal. Electricity for some of the above ground equipment and for the community of Ladd was generated by a water-powered turbine in East Creek.

At the peak of mining there was up to a mile of underground gangways and rooms with air shafts and tunnels throughout the mountainside. Rails were constructed deep into the tunnels to accommodate the miniature steam locomotive that hauled the coal to the surface, a job more often done with mules in other mines. A snow shed was built over the above ground rails extending from the entrance of the mine to the coal bunkers where the washed and sorted coal was stored until it was hauled away by the T. E.

The method used to mine the coal inside the mountain was that of room and pillar with rooms being 25 feet wide and pillars 30 to 35 feet in width. Several gangways were driven inside the slope and rooms opened to seams of coal. The crosscuts within the mine were divided into blocks about 35 feet square. There were times the miners dug until they ran into rifts and had to build gangways over or around these faults or abandon the passageway entirely.

Each mine had two openings, the larger one was used for hauling out the coal, the smaller one provided fresh air for the miners. The entrance to the mine was closed off with doors that were kept shut during work hours while a large fan drew air into the mine and drew out the deadly methane gas. Checks were made regularly for the gas with a special lamp; then when gas showed up, canvas curtains redirected the flow of fresh air to make the room safe.

The miners at Ladd worked a ten hour shift six days a week. Before they entered the mine at the beginning of their shift, they would go to the lamp room to get their head lamp. The miners used a check system to assure no one would be left in the mine. Using a pair of tags similar to those used in the military, the miners would wear one around their neck and leave another on a numbered board. If there was only one tag in the lamp room at the end of a shift, they knew which man was still in the mine and someone would head in after him. If all the tags were present on the board, all the shift was out.

The early coal mine owners did not provide protective gear of any kind for the miner. One sure way of identifying a coal miner was the blue marks on his face. Whenever a piece of coal fell on the man and broke the skin, a permanent blue mark was left similar to that of a dark bruise.

Many of the injuries within the mine were caused by carelessness in regard to the methane gas, which they called "black dank." Because methane is highly explosive, many of the accident reports placed the blame on attempts to relight carbide lamps. In one case a man struck a match to light his pipe and he was killed by the explosion. Despite the little regard for safety in those days, only three men were killed at Ladd and 26 injured, with most injuries involving facial and hand burns.

The men handling the black powder carried enough into the mine each day to blast loose the coal. They drilled a series of holes in the large face of the coal, then filled the holes with black powder and inserted a highly explosive cap. Positive and negative wires were attached to the cap and strung out to a safe distance to be fastened to a battery that had a plunger that was pushed when it was clear to detonate the powder. The caps exploded intermittently to loosen the largest and most desired chunks of coal.

Black powder was used instead of a faster burning explosive which tended to pulverize the coal. The supply was kept in a powder magazine constructed of concrete, which still stands today although it is cracked and doorless. A wooden door instead of metal was used to prevent a spark that could ignite the black powder.

For their long hours in the mine the miners were paid $3.80 in 1910, while a "shot lighter" (as he was called) received $3.95 a day. Engineers got $3.40, but those working above ground as screeners earned only $2.10 if he was an adult and only $1.60 if a boy was employed. By 1919, however, miners were receiving $5.80 a day.

The miners depended on each other a great deal when working inside the mine and most were trained in First Aid. The State Mine Inspector reported in 1919 that a Mine Rescue and First Aid training station was at the University of Washington. The foreman in charge visited the mining camps of the state to train all who desired it. Starting in 1916 contests were held with the crews competing in Mine Rescue and First Aid. It is not known if the Ladd miners competed.

The mining crews represented many countries of origin from which they brought their mining experience. They came from Poland, Czechoslovakia, Italy, Wales and even Japan.

During the last years of coal mining at Ladd,

THE LADD COAL MINE and little community west of Mineral flourished for a few years as the rich coal veins were mined. The miners and their families lived in the two-story houses.

most of the miners in the country struck for higher wages; then strike-breakers made up of immigrants in desperate need of work were brought in. However, the Ladd mines did not take part in the conflict, but it remained open during that time. It was usual, though, for the crews to have fast turnover as miners came and went from mine to mine.

Tacoma Eastern R. R. proved to be a profitable addition to the enterprises of John Bagley and William Ladd, although after a few years the Chicago, Milwaukee and St. Paul Railroad controlled ownership of T. E. through outstanding stock. Bagley remained Vice-president, and General Manager of T. E. and the local name was retained.

In 1909, Milwaukee R. R. (as the main railroad was called) reached the Puget Sound area; by that time T. E. had built 92 miles of track. Also that year The Tacoma Ledger reported Milwaukee officers were elected to the executive personnel and board of directors of the T. E. East Creek Mine provided coal for the two locomotives that ran on the T. E. line and also supplied a substantial amount of fuel for Milwaukee. The Ledger, in an editorial of that day, said that because of Bagley's direction of the system, it was known for hauling more cut timber, considering its length, than any other railroad in the world.

In 1913, Bagley sold the T. E. to A. J. Earling, President of the Milwaukee line; again the local

THE 1919 FLOOD devastated the Ladd settlement which was never rebuilt. A mother and two children perished in the flood. After a fire in the mine, production came to an end.

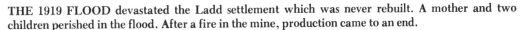

name was continued.

Bagley's son, Albert "Bert", was an engineer on T. E. and hauled on those tracks for several years.

For the three years after 1914, East Creek Mine produced only a third of its normal tonnage. A few men kept the mine open, maintaining it, but it was not fully operational. However, in 1917, a 14 foot vein of rich coal was located, but Bagley, rather than going back into full production, sold out to the Great Northern Railroad for $180,000. While they operated as the Phoenix Coal Company, miners who had left began moving back to Ladd, and a new bunkhouse was constructed in 1918.

Although it appeared the mines would prosper, coal mining at Ladd was discontinued due to two disastrous events and an unpredictable circumstance. The latter was the fact that coal mining at Ladd was no longer profitable, due in part because fuel oil became the main source of power for trains and ships.

The first dramatic event occurred during the winter of 1918-1919 when there were many weeks of heavy rain and snow. On January 2, 1919, a huge landslide occurred on one fork of East Creek when "the whole mountain slid and dammed up the stream," according to Willie Bevan who had lived at Ladd while his father Bill worked in the mines.

The slide happened during the night with the only warning being the failure of the electric light system. Before there was time to investigate why the water power turbine fed by the creek had failed, the natural dam broke, sending hundreds of tons of water, dirt, and debris sweeping down the canyon. The buildings at Ladd were located at the mouth of the canyon so that they received the full force of the flood.

The shop, cookhouse, bunkhouse and the row of two-story houses all were knocked off their foundations while the bunkers and sheds were destroyed, leaving broken timbers and sheet metal roofing strewn all over the site. "It made a mess of the whole thing," Bevan said.

Tragedy struck, too, when a family of four were awakened by the sound of the flood roaring down on them. Thinking it was an earthquake, a miner and his wife grabbed their two children and rushed out the door of their home, encountering the raging water. Before they had a chance to seek higher ground, debris struck the father, knocking the child he held from his arms and sweeping away the mother and both children to their deaths. Two of the bodies were later found downstream in Pleasant Valley.

The mine opened up after the flood, but the little community was not rebuilt; after that, most of the miners walked the three miles of track from Mineral each day.

A second misfortune occurred in October of the same year (1919) when the minature locomotive that carried the coal from the mine to the bunkers was derailed inside the mine. With the use of large crowbars, the miners were able to pry the engine back on the rails, but not before the steam pressure had dropped too low for the engine to be moved. While they were firing up the engine, unbeknown to the men, sparks got up in the overhead cedar puncheon, called lagging, that prevented debris falling on the miners. After the load of coal was dumped, the locomotive started back into the mine where it was met by a wall of flame. The big doors were quickly closed, but that left miners working deeper in the mine, who would not smell the smoke due to the ventilation system. Bill Bevan, Sr., foreman, climbed Hodgins Ridge where the exit of the air shaft was located. He climbed down the 45 degree angled tunnel and led the miners to safety. Willie, who supplied much information about Ladd, remarked, "I'm about the only one in the country who knows where the tunnel is."

In an effort to smother the fire all openings to that part of the mine were sealed off and mining discontinued. Four months later, plans were made to try to extinguish the fire with sprays of water, but as far as can be learned nothing was done so that mining came to an end in Ladd in October, 1919.

The lumber that was left from the houses in Ladd was hauled out to Mineral by the Sokol family in the 1930's. They constructed a large farm house for their family, which unfortunately burned just months after its completion.

Ladd as a coal mine, Ladd as a community, and Ladd as a post office flourished for a few short years. Now the site is overgrown with thick forest and underbrush, living only in memory of a few people and found in dusty records, its niche in history finished.

Chapter 36

The HUGH FAMILY from SWITZERLAND to the "END of the WORLD"

The headlines screamed "BABY HUGH LOST AT SEA" in the newspaper in Basel, Switzerland, the hometown of the Hugh family. The paper explained that the youngest member of the eight children out of fourteen who were migrating to the United States with their mother had fallen overboard in the Atlantic Ocean and drowned. However, the news story was incorrect; that youngest Hugh is alive and well in Morton; she is Martha Hugh Clevenger.

No one knows how the false report reached their hometown, but the incident occurred when the family could not locate three-year-old Martha on the ship. The whole family suffered from severe sea-sickness and found partial relief by lying flat on the floor on their stomachs. This particular day Martha crawled under a bunk to try to find some relief from the illness, and when the mother and children could not find her, they assumed she had fallen overboard.

On the trip across the United States on the train, Bob nearly gave his mother heart failure when he made a habit of getting off the train at every stop. "He had to go and see things, you know. And the train was going to leave him," Martha explained. But the conductor or "whoever it was that looked after the family" would always see to it that Bob was back on the train before each departure, "He was the only one that stayed in trouble."

Before the father came to this area ahead of part of the family, he was led to believe everyone here had a gold mine and was wealthy. And when he came through Mineral, he saw the name of the town and was sure there were a lot of mines. "When we came here there was no gold mine," Martha said emphatically.

Mrs. Hugh was sure she had come to the end of the world when she arrived in Morton. It was in 1911 that the mother and eight of the children

THE HUGH FAMILY OF KOSMOS came from Switzerland. Before they left, a portrait of the family of fourteen children included in back: Elsa, Paul, Gottfried, father Gottfried, Ernest, and Carl. In the middle: Hans, mother Elizabeth, Bob, Herman, and Frieda. In front: Mathilde, Margaret, Max, Martha, and Gertrude.

arrived here to join the father Gottfried and three sons who had come earlier to Kosmos. One older brother Paul came first then Hans and Herman; about a year later the father came.

After traveling all the way from Europe, the family got off the train at the Morton Depot on an August day and found no one in sight at first. That was when Mrs. Hugh declared that they had reached the end of the world. The oldest girl Elsa tried to tell her this wasn't the end of the world, there isn't any end of the world, but her mother wasn't convinced.

She sent the two oldest girls, Elsa and Mathilde, up the little hill to what is now the town of Morton to look for a telephone. They got up to where the Coast to Coast Store is now and saw a sign that read "Telephone" and being unable to speak English they sounded it out as "Tell-e-fonee." They called an aunt and uncle in Kosmos, who expected them, but no one knew when they would arrive.

Still at the depot, Mrs. Hugh paced back and forth and kept wondering "What time is it? What time is it?" Arriving about that time, "Peddler Mike" kept trying to communicate and finally sensed what was troubling her and pulled out his watch to show her it was six o'clock.

The family started out walking to meet the relatives on the old road that paralleled the railroad tracks. When they arrived near the Knittle homestead, Mrs. Hugh was shocked to see the railroad came to an end. Being accustomed to railroad tracks going to Germany, France, and Italy, but never ending, she said, "See, I knew it, this IS the end of the world!"

Eventually the family were met by the father and a cousin in a team and wagon. They all "piled in the wagon" and headed toward their new home. The roads were different then and did not follow the routes they do now. Originally the road went through pioneer Fred Edlund's place on the south side of Davis Lake Valley, then over Kosmos Hill and to Uncle John Uden's extensive property. The children's first impression was that the place was full of Holstein cows, a situation the children thought was just wonderful. "All those cows!" Martha exclaimed, remembering the sight from her childhood.

Peddler Mike, a Syrian whom they had met at the train depot, went through the country with a huge pack made of patent leather on his back. "He came to our house later, ever so many times," Martha recalled, "He carried underwear, jewelry, perfume, towels, and 'just anything'." The peddler took the lid that came way down over the pack, turned it over and laid out everything to show the isolated housewife. A whole department store brought to the door was a real treat!

"So, we left the big city, beautiful city, and settled in Kosmos where there was nothing. Just plain nothing!," Martha said, shaking her head. There was a school and store down on the banks of the Cowlitz River, about a half mile below the later community of Kosmos, across the bridge and to the left. The store was owned by Charlie and Mabel Hopkinson, and the school was just to the north of it. Living in the area were a few hardy souls scattered around what would later be Kosmos, a small community that fell victim to Tacoma City Light's Mossyrock Dam and Riffe Lake that inundates the area today.

The next morning after their arrival Mrs. Hugh and the children awakened at their uncle Remp Uden's homestead, and the mother got up and put on her best black taffeta dress and carefully combed her hair. She went downstairs and said to her sister, "I want to see the city, Kosmos." Aunt Mary said, "Oh, goodness! We are not in a city. This is farmland, this is country." The newly arrived immigrant was very disappointed and again felt she was at the end of the world.

Originally the family name was "Hug", pronounced with a "long U"; after arriving here they found the name mispronounced so frequently that they changed their name to "Hugh", at the suggestion of the grandfather of Eva (Clarken) Bristol, who was going with Paul, one of the boys.

Gottfried, the father, was a cabinetmaker in the old country, but he became a farmer and a parttime roadworker. Where graders are used today, scrapers were used then, horsedrawn and shaped somewhat like the top part of a wheelbarrow. They would fill the scraper with rock or dirt then dump it where it was needed.

The family settled on 40 acres located back of the early pioneer, their uncle Remp Uden, across Rainey Creek at the foot of Dog Mountain. The property belonged to a railroad, but as many early settlers did, they squatted on it, and the parents spent the remainder of their lives there. "In Switzerland there was no such thing as never seeing a house — we were in a city," Martha said, comparing the sparsely settled Kosmos area. Here the children had to walk to school, rain, mud or whatever.

When the Hughs arrived they found besides the Hopkinsons, their grandparents the J. A. Ulsh's; the Uden families, Remp and John; John Clarken, and, of course, the three brothers who had preceded them. The mother's brother John Senn was also a pioneer settler. There was a post office in Fisher's store named Kosmos, then later another one up the valley called Glenoma.

The family spoke German, and the Hugh children who had been in school through the fourth grade had some knowledge of French, but that was no help here.

In the little school house in Kosmos, the children learned English from the teacher Ray Gleason and later were taught by Mary Nicholson and their brother-in-law Sebastion DeGross, who married Elsa. The schools then started beginners in March, then when they entered first grade in September, they had a head start, preceding our government sponsored Head Start program by many years. Martha noted that this was possible in a one-room school house. Mr. Gleason taught Mathilde, Frieda, Bob, Gertrude, and Margaret in the first years here; Martha was too young for school.

The Hugh children had one advantage; many words are the same or similar in German and English. One day Bob was sitting on the porch and Mr. Gleason came along. He was always quizzing the children with, "What is this, what is that?," then they had to answer in English. He held up his finger for Bob and asked what it was and Bob answered, "Finger," which is the same in both languages. He repeated the questions for arm and elbow and got the answers, "Arm" and "Ellbogen." The teacher was pleased that Bob could do so well.

While the Hugh children were going to the little school, a larger school was being built in Glenoma where they continued their education.

The first winter the Hugh family were often hungry because they arrived in August, too late to raise a garden. Mrs. Hugh said, "This is the last winter we are going to spend without enough to eat!" From then on she grew a large garden and preserved much food. In those days there was not much canning; instead foods were salted down.

They learned a method of preserving green beans from an article in the Washington Farmer magazine that sister Frieda subscribed to. They cooked the beans until they were done, put them in jars with a couple of tablespoons of vinegar and salt which was supposed to "keep the ptomaine from forming." When they opened the jars that winter they weren't good, but they were beans, Martha said. Pork was salted down, but "nobody killed a cow; they had no way of taking care of it." Some pork was "corned" like corned beef.

With so many children, the Hugh family always had a lot of fun and were known as a singing family with much musical talent. Although they had no piano in Switzerland or over here, much singing was enjoyed to guitar accompaniment.

One time in Kosmos, Paul and Herman were walking down the road and were feeling blue and lonely. Herman suggested the best thing to do for the blues is to sing, and Paul agreed that was the thing to do, so they began singing and yodeling. "That was something nobody heard here. They didn't know what to think of it," Martha remembered.

Martha met her future husband Jim Clevenger at Kosmos when the little school house and Hopkinson's store were there. It was in the evening after school was out. She came across the bridge and was walking up a little hill when she met a young man pulling a little wagon with a sack of flour in it. Martha thought, "Gee, that's the tallest boy I ever saw!" At this point Jim didn't like any of the girls because they teased him all the time, but because of their age difference Martha hadn't teased him. They saw each other at dances and parties and ran into each other frequently and eventually married.

About once a month there would be a dance in Kosmos, Glenoma, or Morton. Home parties were very popular and were attended by all the neighbors of which there were not too many. At the home parties there was sometimes an organ or piano; Jim played the violin, and Henry Clevenger played the banjo. After they were married, Martha would "second" on the piano, and her brother Paul played an accordian, an old Italian button kind that had no keyboard.

After the Glenoma school house was built, the small schools around there were consolidated, leaving the Kosmos school building empty, so

A CIRCUS BY THE HUGH FAMILY was performed on the Fourth of July during World War I. Crowds came from all over the area to see the tumbling acts.

that it was used for dances. Sometimes the only music was Paul playing the violin, but everyone had a marvelous time. They would take their supper there; they would make coffee, and "They'd have a great time down there," Martha assured.

There were always picnics on the 4th of July. One outstanding one was promoted by Paul, during the first World War. Gertrude, Margaret, and Martha, and some girls from Glenoma designed dresses of crepe paper and created a dance. The location was Uden's farm where people gathered. They even came from Morton on busses that ran every hour. There was an orchestra with Margaret Sifkey on the piano, John Sword on the drums, and Walter Hopgood playing the saxophone. The boys built a dance floor where waltzing and quadrilles (now called square dances) were enjoyed. Pete Stiltner and Charlie Thommen, Frieda's husband, called the quadrilles.

Over the years one by one of the family was married, and they established homes of their own. The three oldest brothers in Switzerland, Gottfried, Carl, and Ernest, planned to emigrate, too, but never did. The sisters married. Besides those already mentioned there were Mathilde and Herschel Wilson, Gertrude and Bill Little, Margaret and Dewey Wilson. The boys Hans, Herman, Max, and Paul married; Bob remained single.

When the Depression hit and banks went broke, for quite a while Martha and Jim Clevenger seldom had a whole dollar to their name. One thing they couldn't afford was yardage for clothing, even though it was ex-

tremely inexpensive at that time. Martha, along with everyone else, made clothing out of fifty-pound flour sacks, which were a good quality cotton fabric. Sugar sacks were of lighter material and were used, too. The flour sacks were soaked in cold water, then boiled to try to get the inked labels out. It didn't always work.

Later the brand names were printed on paper and wrapped around the sacks, an improvement greatly appreciated by those who didn't like branded underclothes. The sacks were used for many things, including pillow cases, night clothes, aprons, and curtains.

Sperry Flour sacks were noted for having permanent ink. This leads to the classic story that everyone is sure really happened. The story tells of a woman who was at a dance, maybe in Morton, Kosmos, or wherever, when she fell down on the floor, her dress flew up, and there was Sperry Flour printed across her underpants.

This article has given the reader a glimpse into the lives of one family of early settlers in Kosmos. The pioneers from East Coast states had many hardships, but those from other countries who could not communicate in English were at a much greater disadvantage. The Hugh family traveled across Europe, across the Atlantic Ocean, and then by train across the width of the United States with eleven children (on two separate trips), settled on undeveloped land in a very small community, made a home, all the while learning a new language. That is difficulty, but the Hugh family conquered successfully and became good citizens in their adopted country.

Chapter 37

EVELYN "EVA" BRISTOL OF KOSMOS

Evelyn "Eva" Bristol's childhood was spent on a homestead farm. She was only a toddler when her parents moved to Kosmos from Renton where she was born October 2, 1896. Her father John Joseph "Joe" Clarken was born November 3, 1864, on Prince Edward Island in Canada; as a young man he came to Washington where he had a sawmill in Auburn. After he homesteaded in Kosmos, he married the daughter of his neighbor on the next farm, Margarite "Maggie" Ulsh. She was the daughter of James Albert and Sarah Jane Ulsh, pioneer settlers and sometime sawmill owners.

When Eva was only five years old, her mother died in childbirth; the baby lived only a few days. There were no hospitals in Eastern Lewis County; therefore, Eva's mother was taken to Chehalis, but in those days there was little that could be done for her.

After their mother's death, Eva and her sister Jessie went to live with their grandparents, the Ulsh's, who reared the girls on their 160 acre homestead.

The Ulsh's came from Ohio, but before homesteading in Kosmos, Ulsh had worked in a gold mine in Colorado. Besides Maggie, they had only

JOE AND MAGGIE (ULSH) CLARKEN were married in 1894. He was an early settler in Kosmos and her parents homesteaded there. Note her elaborate outfit for their wedding.

one other child, Albert, who was a gold miner in Alaska.

Jessie, Eva's sister, married Charles Little. They lived in Kosmos until the town site became part of Riffe Lake; then they moved to Centralia. Jessie taught school in Morton, both before and after marriage.

After Maggie's death Clarken followed the gold rush to Alaska. He stayed there about ten years, returning in 1909. Next he went back to Nova Scotia where he married Edith Pollard. They went to Dabob Bay on Hood's Canal where he worked in a mill for several years before returning to the Kosmos homestead. He cleared land, raised dairy cows and sheep, and later worked for Kosmos Timber Company. After retirement he raised stock.

By his second marriage, Clarken had four daughters: Myrtle Smith of Oregon, Ruby Sargeant of Idaho, Viola Bowen of Randle, and Elva Wright of Morton.

When Eva spoke of the "horse and buggy days," she meant just that, as she said, "The faithful old horse was their only means of transportation and it tilled the soil, logged the trees that became lumber to build their homes, carried the mail and many other things."

With Chehalis, their nearest shopping center, fifty miles away, the early settlers depended on wagon trains that originated in Randle to travel together to help their neighbors along the way, especially when a wagon was stuck in the muddy road.

They had cattle and sheep to take to market as well as droves of turkeys that limited their day's journey to the length of daylight because when it became dusk in the evening, the turkeys went to roost in the trees, therefore ending their travel until daylight. Obviously the trip took several days.

The Cowlitz River was crossed by ferry at Nesika where a Mr. Justice winched a flat boat that held two wagons across the river. Nesika was downriver from Kosmos, several miles above Riffe; both locations are now under Riffe Lake.

The "good old days" to Eva included such chores as hauling water from a creek, spring, or river for all needs, including water for washing clothes on the old "Irish washboard." Every day the coal oil (kerosene) lamps had to be filled, the glass chimneys carefully washed, and the wicks trimmed for light during the evening hours. Everyone raised large gardens, preserved most of the food by canning, and stored root vegetables in sawdust-filled pits. Sauerkraut made from cabbage, a specialty of Grandad Ulsh's, was put up by the 30 gallon barrel; it was his favorite dish.

Below Kosmos there was a log schoolhouse where Eva was the only student for a while, but as more homesteaders came, it grew to five students, and eventually by her eighth grade there were all of twelve students. The teacher was Marjorie Smith from Randle. Eva remembered the recesses when the girls made hats of big maple leaves.

One school day she and Jessie heard a "terrible" noise; quickly they dashed outside to see what it was. Coming down the wagon road was the first automobile they had ever seen, the first car in the valley; it belonged to Reemp Uden. Being country girls, they had to see what kind of track it made.

The Clarken girls walked about a mile and a

JESSIE AND EVELYN "EVA" CLARKEN (in back) were reared by their grandparents Joe and Maggie Ulsh after their mother died. Beside them is their uncle Albert Ulsh in this 1914 picture.

half to school on the often muddy road. They had to wear boots and carry their shoes in a bag to change into at school. The road was so filled with mud holes that they often had to detour out through the brush to get around the big puddles.

Church on Sunday was held in the log schoolhouse with a Rev. Maley coming from Morton. Often he was invited to their house for a chicken dinner after church or to another home where the neighbors gathered for the usual chicken dinner concluding with homemade ice cream made with thick cream from their milk cows.

For entertainment the settlers had spelling bees, debates, quilting bees, summer picnics, and lots of music and square dancing. Much of the music was provided by the talented Hugh family from Switzerland. Eva married Paul from that family when she was 19 years old in 1915. Paul could play almost any instrument and he had a good tenor voice. They had four children: Paul, Jr., Marjorie, Walter, and Gordon (nicknamed "Jug"). After Paul died in 1924, Eva cared for her children alone until 1928 when she married Leo Bristol. They had one child, Eldon, known as "Tony." Because Eva and Leo had a large chicken ranch when the children were growing up, there were jobs for each of them. In 1933 they went into business with a grocery store, butcher shop, and dance hall. At intermission during the dances, Eva often cooked a huge chicken dinner complete with homemade pies to serve as many as 45 people. When Kosmos Timber Company was founded, she ran a

EVA CLARKEN AND HER FIRST HUSBAND PAUL HUGH were married in 1915. Their first children were Paul, Jr. and Margie (now Goodwin). Later Walter and Gordon "Jug" were born.

boarding house for the loggers until the company built a cookhouse and bunkhouses.

When the Kosmos Garden Club was organized in 1941, Eva was a charter member. She was the second president; her sister Jessie was the first. Eva held all the offices through the years of her faithful work for the club, and she was a charter member of the Lewis County Garden Club. She studied to be a qualified judge of flowers and arrangements.

Always active in the flower shows, she helped the Kosmos Garden Club put on a novel show one year with the theme "A Wedding." All the arrangements carried out the theme which surprisingly actually featured a real wedding.

The Morton Grange and Senior Center were also included in Eva's active life. She had been in Grange for over 50 years. One year she was named "Senior Citizen of the Year" for her outstanding volunteer service to the Center.

Eva shared a little history of the post office in the region. When she was a child, the only post office was Fulton, located up river from Nesika. The mail was carried by horseback with extra horses needed for Christmas mail. In 1905 it was moved upriver where it was located down in the gulch near the mouth of Rainey Creek with Mr. and Mrs. Charles Hopkinson as postmasters. The name was changed to Kosmos, the visionary name meaning "the Universe." Near the same location Hopkinson also had the first sawmill in the valley; Ulsh had the second.

In 1912 the post office was moved up near the highway across from the schoolhouse; later the highway ran through the former location of the grocery store and post office. About 1918-20 it was moved to Kosmos corner where the Strubys ran the post office and store which were later run by Frank Bogel and J. A. Ulsh.

The last move was across the highway to the Kosmos Cafe, where Mr. and Mrs. Kenneth Barret ran the post office for seven years. At that time the community of Kosmos had the post office, a cafe, three garages, a tavern, and Kosmos Timber Company. After Tacoma City Light bought all the land in the lower part of the valley and covered it with water behind Mossyrock Dam, Eva said "Kosmos was only memories."

MAGGIE ULSH'S STORE in Kosmos carried general merchandise. On the left is the Post Office in this 1924 photo.

Chapter 38

JIM CLEVENGER, KOSMOS SAWYER

When Jim Clevenger, formerly of Kosmos and later of Morton, was a young man, he participated in some of the most intriguing experiences in the early days of timber harvest in Eastern Lewis County. The shingle bolt drives down the rivers from the homesteads of the early settlers to the shingle mills often provided an important cash income for the farmers. Clevenger worked on drives from as far up the Cowlitz River as the Muddy Fork and down the Cispus River into the Cowlitz and then to the mouth of Rainey Creek where Broadbent and Francis of Morton had a shingle mill.

The homesteaders cut their old growth cedar into blocks measuring four feet, six inches long (some 22 to 25 to a cord). Several men would go together to build a small dam on a creek, forming a pond into which they dumped their shingle bolts. At high water they released the water allowing the bolts to be swept down to the river ready for the drive to the mill. Each man's bolts were identified with brands stamped into the wood.

The shingle bolt drivers took over from there and kept the blocks moving down river, using long pike poles to pull or push the bolts back into the river channel when they hung up on rocks and gravel bars, a job that often lasted as long as a month.

The men had to wade the rivers all day long often shoulder deep. They survived the frigid water by wearing heavy wool underwear and socks. They slept in tents that were erected near the river each night then moved down river as the crew progressed toward the mill. A couple of people went along as cooks (Bill and Gertrude Little cooked on one drive Clevenger was on). They provided hot meals in the morning and evening at the camps; at noon they filled a large kettle with beans or stew to be heated on a campfire for the cold and hungry men.

A rowboat was used on the drives to retrieve the bolts that were hung up on gravel bars or rocks that were in water that was too deep or too rough for the wading men to reach. On one trip Clevenger and Bill Little (who would later become the highly respected game warden) were the boatmen. Two men were needed so that one could guide the boat while the other used the pike pole to dislodge the bolts. On Clevenger's last trip on Goat Creek when they entered the Goat Creek Rapids, the boat went out of control with Little on the oars. The boat was rapidly approaching a rock; Little reversed oars and Clevenger said, "Darned if he didn't break an oar; he was stout as a horse." The current turned the boat sideways which tipped it up at such a steep angle that the five gallon can that contained the noon meal upset. "That scared me, because we were getting down to some rough water and I knew that river. I made up my mind right there it was the last drive I was going on. I don't know why a half dozen of us weren't drowned, but we never lost a man," Clevenger recalled.

He said his brother-in-law Max Hugh did almost drown. Clevenger continued, "If we hadn't gone after him, he wouldn't have lived as long as he did. He was wading right at the mouth of the Cispus River and it was such a pull in that river, an awful suction. They had to go in and get him. The Cispus ran into the Cowlitz there; Hugh was out in the middle of the river. He didn't understand the river too well and where the rivers meet it gets rough." Hugh saw he was going toward the big hole where so many have fished. Little hollered at him to get back out of there; he was getting into deep water. "It's 30 or 40 feet deep there," Clevenger asserted. Hugh tried to go back, but couldn't make it by himself. Little and several others had to go out to save him from a dangerous situation.

There were shingle bolt drives on the Tilton River in earliest years; Clevenger's father Charlie and Harry Cooper's father Ed were on some of them when all the cedar was taken down river to mills at Kelso. Later Broadbent and Francis had a shingle mill at the mouth of Lake Creek in the southwest edge of Morton; this was earlier than their last mill at the mouth of Rainey Creek, east of Glenoma. They dammed Lake Creek which had a lot more water then than it does now so that it made a sizeable mill pond. Shingle bolts were taken down Lake Creek and Highland Creek to the mill.

Old-timers constantly comment on how much larger creeks were in this area when heavy timber covered the hills and valleys. Now one can almost straddle Rainey Creek at low water. "I remember when I was a little fellow you couldn't wade it except at certain places; when we left there you wouldn't get your ankles wet in dry weather," Clevenger commented.

Clevenger was born in West Virginia to Charles and Reedy (Stiltner) Clevenger, their eldest son born January 1, 1899. They already had three girls in a family that grew to eleven children. When Jim was two years old in 1902, the family came West and lived first where the Rainey Valley Cemetery is now. On the first piece of property, they built a log house; on the next place they built a house of rough sawed lumber used as board-and-battens on the two story dwelling.

In 1912 the father "got Oregon fever" when he heard about the homesteads in the Corvallis area, far back in the woods. They were 20 miles from the nearest railroad, fifteen miles from the nearest settlement from where they had to "pack our grub in" for five miles on their backs. His mother Reedy said they should get out of there because the children were growing up without schooling. They stayed in Corvallis long enough for the hop harvest, then back to this area where they lived briefly on the Crumb place on Highland Creek. After a year in Cinebar, they bought a place in Kosmos where they lived when Jim became old enough to go out to work.

Clevenger's first job was at the Ladd Logging camp out of Mineral for Murray's West Fork Logging Company. After that he worked at numerous places, mainly as a railroad-tie mill sawyer. He joined the Modern Woodmen of America in 1918. His last mill work was for Walt Core in Randle where he started in 1929; he worked there occasionally during the Depression and afterwards for a total of 14 or 15 years. However, Clevenger said that during the "Hard Times" the tie mill seldom got orders even when they did get orders; the work often lasted only a few days which provided the only income for the month.

Besides sawing timbers, he also set rachets on the carriage in mills, also he worked for the State Highways for a time. The list of mills he worked for will stir memories for old-timers — Edgar Tiller on Kiona Creek, Ed Studhalter and Gold Temple, Siler, Jack Reed and Steve McMahan, Homer Johnson on the Silva place on Rainey Creek, Miles Tower, young Miles Tower, Broadbent and Francis, and Van Lou, the Dutchman.

"It seemed like those little outfits, they had a habit of going broke. They'd work as long as they could work a man, then they were broke, they claimed," Clevenger related. He was sawing for Van Lou when he married Martha Hugh, the youngest member of the family from Switzerland who migrated here in 1911. Shortly after they married in December, the mill owner went broke, and he lost his December wages. "Maybe you think we didn't have a time," the couple recalled.

The Clevengers are convinced our "kids" have it easy compared to the way they started out. "I don't know if they would survive. Cook on a wood stove. And rub, wash clothes on the board, carry the water. When we got married, he put the well right under the back porch, and it had a handpump. My, I had water, almost in the house!", Martha exclaimed.

The Clevengers bought some acreage, timber land, near where his father had purchased four different parcels of land from Northern Pacific Railroad. After his parents got too old to farm,

THE OLD GLENOMA SCHOOL was completed in 1912 replacing a smaller school across the road which consolidated four log schools in District 209. This building burned in 1932 and it was replaced with the present brick schoolhouse.

he bought their property, bringing his acreage to 110 acres on which they had dairy cattle and they sold milk.

When the Depression hit, they were buying their first 40 acres. Clevenger said, "I owed for it naturally. I didn't know where the money was coming from. So, finally I went down to the bank and told him, you know how the times are. I said I just cannot make payments. Well, he said, you'll pay the interest on the money, won't you? I said I would try. All right. That was the deal."

His last job was with U. S. Plywood at the mouth of Rainey Creek, a job from which he was forced to retire when his legs got so bad that he had to have extensive surgery on the veins.

Clevenger spoke of the large timber that grew in Eastern Lewis County. In the flats at Kosmos there was a huge tree that was over 12 feet through. It was felled by the Davis Brothers, Floyd and Conrad from Riffe. They had to make sidecuts in order for their saws to reach through, even though they were above the thick butt on spring boards. They cut it into 8 foot sections for veneer, but didn't get a block out of it that could be used, because it was a mass of pitch seams going in all directions. In an effort to get some good out of the tree, the Davis Brothers loaded it on a flatbed truck (there were no logging trucks then). The log was so heavy there was danger of tipping the truck over on the highway when they came to a curve with a lot of "super", forcing them to back up probably a half mile to go a different way. They finally got it to a mill in Morton where they dumped it in the pond. "It was so heavy it went right to the bottom. They had a heck of a time getting it out," Clevenger concluded.

Chapter 39

GUS THOMMEN
A LONG TIME KOSMOS RESIDENT

When August "Gus" Thommen was growing up in Kosmos, an exciting event was the arrival of the first automobile in the community. The year was 1908, the car was an International, two cylinders, air cooled, and built like a spring wagon. Thommen's stepfather Reemp Uden bought it in Tacoma; then a salesman drove it up the wagon road through Bear Canyon.

The new auto scared Uden's horses; consequently, they had to shut off the motor when they got near the team. It wasn't long until Uden left all the driving to 15-year-old Gus and his brother Charles, while he went back to using his fancy leather buggy complete with leather-covered fenders. The buggy must have been the Cadillac of its day for it had cost the substantial price of $250. The boys drove the car to Randle and Chehalis occasionally.

Thommen was born in Yonkers, New York, on March 29, 1893, where his brother and sister were also born. Their parents were from Switzerland, having come to the United States as a young couple. When Gus was only two years old, his father died.

His mother's brother John Sands lived on the creek named after him. Sands Creek came to be called Kosmos, a community inundated at the head of Riffe Lake. Sands sent for his sister to join him in the pioneer settlement; she came across country by horse and wagon with her three small children.

When Thommen was a child, the only settlers in Kosmos were John and Reemp Uden, Louie Lindberg, a bachelor Steffon, and James A. Ulsh. After a few years, in 1898, Thommen's mother married Reemp Uden and her sister married Reemp's brother John Uden.

The family lived on Sands Creek for three or four years, then they lived a year at John Uden's until a house was built on Reemp's farm. The children walked to a log school house where for about three years there were only four students. The log school house was replaced with a nicer building of sawed lumber near where the highway bridge later crossed Sands Creek just west of Kosmos. Thommen finished school there.

Thommen remembered skipping school one day when there was a barn raising, a big event in

GLENOMA'S FIRST SCHOOL "BUS" was a horse and wagon driven by Harrison Christian. Teacher Anna Uden (later Fisher) rode the white horse on the right.

those days when all the neighbors got together to put up the frame of a new building. The women cooked a huge meal for the workers, so that along with accomplishing a lot of work, it was a fine social occasion.

When Thommen was six or seven years old, his stepfather took the boys to Chehalis to see the Ringling Brothers Circus. They were there to see the circus wagons unloaded off the train onto the puncheon streets where they sank into the mud; then the elephants were used to push them out. They saw the big tent being put up and watched with amazement as the large tent stakes were driven by six men who hit the stakes in perfect rhythm.

After finishing school, Thommen started farming and hauling logs and lumber. In 1915, he bought a Denby truck, then in 1924 he traded for a Garford two-and-a-half ton truck; in 1927 he got another Garford.

In the meantime, he married Beulah Rea, when he was 25 years old.

He hauled shingles out of the Francis and Broadbent Mill on the Cowlitz River above Kosmos for seven years, before and after his Army service in World War I. He hauled to the railroad in Morton where the railroad-tie docks later were built along the tracks east of town.

Francis and Broadbent had a "fin boom" in the Cowlitz with boards sticking out from the boom to hold it out in the river. The "fin boom" shunted shingle bolts from up-river to the banks of the river by the mill. There was another log boom stretched across the river on large cables connected to a smaller cable on a winch that controled the boom.

One time a flood took out the boom and they lost a large quantity of shingle bolts; that was a substantial loss for the owners.

In those days everyone who had cedar on their property cut shingle bolts to sell which was one of their few sources of income. The price was $2 a cord while shingles sawed at a mill were selling for $2.50 a thousand board feet or $3 for number-one-clear, the best grade. However, Uden's house was roofed with hand-split cedar shakes smoothed with a draw knife as were most of the homes of the day.

Farm produce from cream to hogs was hauled by team and wagon to Glenavon at the end of the railroad on the Divide between Morton and Mineral before the tracks reached Morton in 1910. Thommen continued to farm while trucking, raising milk cows, and later raising beef cattle and chickens.

Thommen remembered when Morton had trees and stumps in the streets. George Linz had a big blacksmith shop on the southwest corner of Main and Third Streets, where Uden had his horses shod. The original owner of the property that is now the main business district was Robert Herselman, who lived in a small white house where the P. U. D. parking lot is now on Main and First Streets.

In 1936, Kosmos Timber Company (which was later purchased by Champion) was started and Thommen worked for them for nineteen years. Also in 1936 he married Ethel Coston Mills, a widow with a son Robert, who took the Thommen surname. Gus and Ethel had a son, Clyde.

Thommen retired as logging foreman at Kosmos Timber in 1959; then he and Ethel moved to Morton in 1960, where he enjoyed carpentry and fly-fishing and raising flowers and vegetables. They celebrated their 35th wedding anniversary a short time before Gus' death on May 20, 1971, at 78 years of age.

Chapter 40

THE RIFFE FAMILY
and VERNIE (RIFFE) SCHOONOVER

Floyd Riffe, whose last name was attached to a post office, a community, and finally to the lake formed by Mossyrock Dam, came to the area east of Mossyrock before the turn of the century.

Riffe was born and raised in western West Virginia and as a young married man moved to eastern West Virginia; his wife Armeda Blankenship was from Virginia. When they moved, they already had four children, one of whom was Vernie Riffe Schoonover, the interviewee for this article, born in Jettsville, Green Briar County, on April 3, 1886.

In the mid-1890's, Riffe wrote to several railroad companies to get the best fare to Western Washington for a group of members of the Primitive Baptist Church, who wanted to migrate west. By that time Riffe and his family were living in White Sulphur Springs. The springs were believed to have healing properties, and many came to "take the waters", including a minister's two little daughters who stayed with the Riffes, but sadly their health did not improve.

After the Riffe family arrived by train in Chehalis, they went by horse and buggy to their new place where they found a dilapidated house to live in until they could build their own. Vernie's 12-year-old sister asked her Dad why after having come through much beautiful country he would bring them to a place where there was nothing but Indians and fir trees.

Eighteen of the families that came west together settled in Verndale, later named Glenoma. Riffe conducted church for them once a month.

Homesteaders had already taken up the land, but they were able to buy an abandoned 40 acre place. To start their new life they had to buy cattle, hogs, horses, and lumber for a house. Soon Riffe started an orchard by setting out 50 fruit trees.

As more settlers arrived, they felt the need of a post office closer than Mossyrock on the west and Baugh, two and a half miles to the east. Baugh was discontinued after Riffe established the post office that he named after himself. Riffe's building had a large fireplace where neighbors would gather and visit.

Vernie emphasized the spirit of neighborliness that prevailed in those days. She said, "Much love and friendship was displayed in those days and many a helping hand was extended to us."

The Riffe family and their church group had not been here very long before people from back East began to come here "like bees to the hive", coming from Virginia, Kentucky, and West Virginia. Soon there was a "pretty good Eastern settlement from Mossyrock to Verndale," Vernie stated.

THE SWINGING BRIDGE AT RIFFE allowed pioneers to cross the Cowlitz River on foot many years before a highway bridge was built.

THIS TYPE OF FERRY was most often used when needed to get to the other side of the river.

THE HIGHWAY BRIDGE AT RIFFE was completed in 1918. Flags decorate the bridge at the dedication ceremony.

Their first Fourth of July celebration in the Riffe community was held in the middle of the main road with games, songs, speeches, and ball games. At other times there were programs at the school and church, with ministers coming from Oakville and Oregon. There were few Primitive Baptists in Washington, but "quite a good many in Oregon."

Floyd Riffe loved to hunt, and he kept the family supplied with all kinds of meat: bear, deer, cougar, raccoon, all kinds of birds, and elk, although elk were scarce.

In addition to the spring and fall trips to Chehalis for bulk supplies, smaller items were purchased at a little store in Mossyrock.

The earliest settlers in southwest Washington all remembered the famous "Dark Day" of 1902. Vernie was staying with her sister Rosa and her husband I. F. Coleman while the young couple was awaiting the birth of their first child. Vernie had picked hops the day before; the next morning when she awakened, it was completely dark. She went for water and could hear a strange "oohing" sound. Everyone was frightened; many thought it was the end of the world. It stayed dark until after noon when they could finally extinguish the kerosene lamps.

Riffe's son-in-law Coleman, had left before

normal daybreak to carry the mail from Mossy-rock to Fulton (later Kosmos) and Verndale. When the sun didn't come up, he was afraid Mt. Rainier had erupted; he returned home, picked up his wife and Vernie, and started for Riffe's residence. Before they got there, they found out the "Dark Day" was caused by the hugh Yacolt Burn, an enormous forest fire that devastated much of the forest between the area north of Mt. St. Helens and the Columbia River.

The Riffe children went to school about a mile uphill, and like all pioneer children they had to wade mud much of the year. Their father made shoes for the family, but they were so big and heavy that the children hated to wear them. Vernie was teased about her big feet. Once when a young minister was visiting, he tried to make her feel better by saying, "That's all right, you've got big feet and all hell can't upset you!"

As the community grew, John Cook built a grist mill on Sulphur Creek a mile and a half west of Riffe, where he ground wheat and corn. Vernie remembered what good biscuits and corn bread they made with their own flour and corn meal.

Riffe found a good spring up on the hill above his property, dug it out, and built a V-shaped trough to bring the water down for a dependable year-around supply. One time Vernie's sister Elizabeth "Lizzie" was following her father as he plowed while she used a hoe to turn the sod when she had a heat stroke. Her little brother had the presence of mind to run to the trough to get water to throw in her face and revive her.

One time Vernie and Lizzie had an experience that was common for early settlers. They were going after the milk cows one evening when they thought that they heard a woman screaming. They hurried home because Lizzie thought it might be a cougar. They told their father, who tracked the big cat with his hunting dogs, but he didn't get it.

While clearing land, Vernie and Lizzie sawed logs with a crosscut saw. With their father's help, the girls carried them to the burning pile. This was in spite of their mother's warnings to not lift heavy loads.

Riffe was often making "deals" on property prompting one visitor, who felt he knew Vernie's father, to say "Brother Riffe will never be satisfied until he gets all the land joining his!" Riffe's first land deal here was with Harvey Blankenship for property known as the Winfield place near the Nesika Post Office; Riffe offered to trade his property for Blankenship's, and the transaction was completed.

The trade was made the year Vernie was to graduate from the eighth grade. In order to complete her schooling, she stayed on the Riffe property to take care of the post office until the end of the term. Vernie and three others comprised the graduating class. Vernie wanted to go on to high school, but the nearest one was in Chehalis, and it just couldn't be managed.

Col. B. W. Coiner, a "big wheel" from Tacoma, owned property adjoining Riffe's land near Nesika. There was a big house built of small logs that Mrs. Coiner did not like living in because she was accustomed to nice homes in town. It didn't help that the moss chinking between the logs was falling out. She was so unhappy that Coiner offered the property to Riffe for $7,000. He could make the deal because by that time Riffe had some money with which to buy it.

Vernie married Orson Schoonover, a son of the family that bought the Swofford place in Swofford Valley where there was also a post office. Vernie and Orson were married on February 3, 1906, when she was almost twenty years old. They had three children: Ruby, Clyde, and Lotus, who died at 13 years of age.

When Orson's brother Oliver died, he left two boys, Elmer about 14 and Del about 11. Vernie took them in as her own. Then Vernie's brother Charlie Riffe lost his wife Lovie (Jordan) Riffe when their daughter Beula was only six weeks old, one more child for Vernie and Orson to rear. Beula married George Cooper, son of Harry and Katherine (Studhalter) Cooper, who were children of early settlers in Bremer.

Although the site of the little town of Riffe lies in the depths of Riffe Lake, it took a concerted effort of local citizens to have the name changed from Davisson Lake, which honored a Tacoma man, to the name of a pioneer family who not only built up this region, but who influenced a number of Easterners to settle here.

Chapter 41

THE GREAT COWLITZ FLOOD OF 1896:
The Shoemacher Tragedy

In November 1896, a heavy snowfall followed by a Chinook wind with warm rain caused a devastating flood on the Cowlitz River. The John Shoemacher family lived near the Nesika Bridge, and as the waters rose, Mrs. Shoemacher, a sister of Dick Stelloh in Mossyrock, wanted them to leave their home, but her German husband being reluctant to leave his stock, refused.

Mrs. Shoemacher's fears became a reality when the flood waters surrounded their home. Shoemacher hastily built a raft and loaded his wife, a 16-year-old daughter Martha, and their four young sons on it.

With a rope attached to the raft, the father got off the raft onto a large stump, but before he could secure the raft, a log hit the rope and jerked it out of his hands. He watched helplessly as the swift current took his family from him.

A Mrs. Teets, who lived across the river, saw the family with the mother's arms around the four little boys while the girl tried to get the raft to shore. She watched with horror as a large uprooted tree fell across the raft drowning the whole family in the raging river.

Shoemacher was rescued three days later when his calls for help were heard. Thomas I. Blankenship and Frank McMahan came to his aid in a boat, and they found him in good shape except for frostbitten feet and hunger.

The mother's body was found buried in the sand just above the Mayfield Bridge; the daughter was found lodged in a log jam a quarter mile west of Riffe. One of the boys was found and was buried with his mother and sister in Swofford Cemetery; three of the boys' bodies never were found.

Shoemacher continued to farm for several years and eventually married again and left this part of the state.

The Cowlitz River did not claim multiple lives again in this part of the country until the Bergen ferry accident in 1915.

Chapter 42

Lewis County Advocate - June 4, 1915

Wagon Plunged Into River; 5 Drown

Residents of Morton Lost Lives Saturday When Backing of Horses Pushed the Riffe Ferry Out From the Shore

———————————— Two Escape Drowning ————————————

Stream Running High and Swift and Those Who Battled With Current Had Little Chance for Lives; One Horse Drowned — Three of Victims Were Children of Frank Bergen

MORTON, May 29 - Plunged into the swollen waters of the Cowlitz river at Riffe on Saturday, when a team of horses which was being driven onto the ferry became frightened and backed off, Mrs. Robert Herselman, Miss Anna Bergen, and the three small children of Frank Bergen were drowned, and Ella Bergen and Bart Bergen the only other occupants of the wagon were saved. All of the victim's were residents of Morton, and were on their way to attend mass at the Catholic Church in Harmony, a small town ten miles west of Morton.

Searching parties from Chehalis, Morton, Harmony, Riffe, and other small towns in the immediate vicinity were formed and immediately made a minute search along the bank of the Cowlitz for the bodies of the drowned. Others in boats breasted the swift stream eagerly searching for any traces of the unfortunate quintet. The fact that the recent rains have brought the stream to a point higher than it has been in years, causes the authorities in charge of the searches to believe that there is little hope of the Cowlitz giving up its dead for many days.

Eye-witnesses say that the fatality occured when the team of horses, driven by Bergen, instead of continuing onto the ferry stopped dead still when the front wheels were aboard, and then in a moment of fright, started to back. This caused the ferry to start out into the stream with only the horses and the front portion of the wagon on board. William Rose, the ferryman,

shouted a warning to the driver. Action was impossible and with a lunge, the wagon's rear was swept from the ferry landing into the water.

With the horses still aboard the ferry and the body of the wagon plunging about in the stream, the unfortunate occupants were swept out into the stream. The resistant force of the bulky vehicle beating against the Cowlitz' raging tide, suddenly taxed the super-human efforts of the ferry hands and the horses to retain their position, and with a mighty tug, the river brought the struggling animals into it's swollen bed and carried the entire party swiftly down stream. One of the horses was later rescued half a mile below the ferry where he was cut loose from the buggy.

Struggling in each other's arms both trying to steer a course towards shore, the Misses Anna and Ella Bergen battled bravely for five minutes with the swift current. Finding herself greatly weakened, both by the chill of the water and the terrible ordeal through which she had just passed in the wagon, Miss Ella Bergen broke away from her sister and struggled towards the shore. Abandoned and helpless, Anna Bergen sank beneath the surface of the Cowlitz. Bart Bergen reached shore in safety a few minutes after his sister Ella was saved.

The other victims were not seen to drown, although many persons attracted by the cries of the unfortunates and the men on the ferry, scurried to the river and stationed themselves along the shore, hoping to be able to render aid.

The victims were all well known in Morton. Word of the tragedy was sent to all the towns along the river, cautioning the inhabitants to be on the lookout for the bodies.

Several Days Later Bodies Not Recovered

Though the search for the bodies of the five persons drowned in the Cowlitz river at Riffe Saturday afternoon, when a wagon backed off the ferry into the stream was prosecuted steadily from that time none of the bodies had been recovered up to yesterday. With the river running high, there is every chance that the bodies were carried long distances downstream and in the water, which has been made muddy by the heavy rains it is impossible to see any object a few inches under the surface. Residents of Riffe and Morton, relatives and friends of those who lost their lives, are staying with the search, however, in the hope that the corpses may be found.

Much comment has been aroused over the manner in the way Riffe ferry is equipped. Many people who have ridden on the ferry declare that for many months it has been absolutely unsafe. Criticism is heard of the practice of the ferryman holding the boat against the bank with his hands while persons and teams were embarking, rather than having a chain or rope for tying the boat and make use of it. When the accident occurred Saturday two men were trying to hold the ferry to the bank with their hands while the team was being driven aboard. When the horses became frightened at the swirling water and the driver gave a tug at the lines, the team started to back with the result that the ferry was pulled out of the grasp of the men holding it, and the wagon and team went into the river.

The ferry is conducted by Lewis County, and William Rose is the ferryman. Mr. Rose says that he was not given time to tie the ferry Saturday before the wagon was driven aboard and that he would have tied the boat securely had he been allowed sufficient time.

The ferry boat has been in service for many years and has for a long time had the appearance of unsafety say people who have had occasion to use the boat. Some declare that they were afraid to drive teams aboard the boat because the craft looked as though it would not sustain the weight of a heavy wagon. Some of these reports were afloat before the Saturday accident and now they are in circulation more than ever.

INDEX